THE COMPLETE OLD ENGLISH SHEEPDOG

Ch. Sir Lancelot of Barvan ("Dudley") winning Best in Show all-breeds at the 1975 holding of America's most prestigious dog event, the Westminster Kennel Club show at Madison Square Garden, New York City. The judge, at left, was Harry T. Peters, Jr., and the trophy was presented by club president William Rockefeller. Sir Lancelot, three years old at time of the win, is owned by Ronald and Barbara Vanword, of Newmarket, Ontario, Canada, and handled by Malcolm Fellows. He thus became but the second Old English Sheepdog to win this high honor, the first having been Mrs. Tyler Morse's Ch. Slumber, back in 1914.—Photo, *Gilbert.*

THE COMPLETE
OLD ENGLISH
SHEEPDOG

by
JOHN MANDEVILLE

First Edition-Seventh Printing
1982

HOWELL BOOK HOUSE INC.
230 Park Avenue
New York, N.Y. 10169

Ch. Norval Pride King and Ch. Lillibrad Lindy Lou, C.D.X., sire and dam of BIS winner Ch. Lillibrad Prince Charming and Lillibrad's Sammy's Shadow—canine star of the Walt Disney movie "The Shaggy Dog." Owned by Lillian Lovejoy.

Copyright © 1976, Howell Book House Inc.
Library of Congress Catalog Card No. 75-30418
ISBN 0-87605-219-7 Printed in U.S.A.

To my wife,

"Mickey,"

whose contributions have been as invaluable toward the writing of this book as they have been for my everyday living.

As early as 1935, Mrs. Serena Van Rensselaer was melding her artistic talent and her great love of the Old English Sheepdog to produce such irresistible drawings as this of "Smiles of Milenick" and "Downderry Dauntless."

Contents

Preface

THIS BOOK is the result of a series of letters exchanged in the fall of 1969 between myself and the then president of the Old English Sheepdog Club of America, Dr. Oren Bush. Dr. Bush offered me, and the club's Board of Directors approved, the job of getting out a club handbook. While circumstances have postponed its printing until now, an explanation of how I went about preparing the book, and an acknowledgment of the fine cooperation I received, remains in order.

It was apparent that the first goal would be to achieve a book that would be of interest and use to the complete novice and the most accomplished veteran alike. To assure stylistic integrity it was decided to compile information from as many sources as possible, and then systematically integrate it into a uniform text. This was done in three ways: research into available published and unpublished written sources, personal interviews, and written contact with as many experienced Old English fanciers as possible. Hand in hand with this third means of gathering information was the express purpose of compiling a book that represented as wide a cross-section of opinion as possible and was based, as much as possible, on the expert knowledge of experienced Sheepdog people.

Most of this information was gathered through an exchange of letters between myself and a "committee" of the Old English Sheepdog Club of America. A tentative outline of the book together with a letter asking for comments, suggestions, and information was sent to virtually every person who had been a member of the Old English Sheepdog Club of America for more than fifteen years, owners of registered kennels, officers and former officers of the OESCA, owners of Best in Show winning OES, and a number of others. Included in this list were: Mr. and Mrs. Robert Abrams, Jr., Mr. and Mrs. James

E. Anderson, Mr. and Mrs. Louis Baer, Mr. and Mrs. Pat Baker, Mrs. Herbert E. Bennett, Mrs. Mona Berkowitz, Dr. and Mrs. Oren Bush, Mr. and Mrs. Lawrence Conklin, Miss Rosalind Crafts, George Demko, Joan Demko, Mr. and Mrs. H. S. Dunning, Mr. and Mrs. Paul Elliot, Mr. and Mrs. Ivan Forbes, Dr. Louise T. Forest, Dr. and Mrs. Erly P. Gallo, Mrs. Clifford Gheen, Mrs. E. Herbert Gilg, Mr. Stan Goldberg, Mr. Alfred Goldman, Mr. Barry Goodman, Mr. and Mrs. John P. Herlihy, Mr. and Mrs. Horace G. Hill, Mr. Roy Isakson, Mr. and Mrs. Earl Jacobson, Miss Vickie Johnson, Dr. and Mrs. Hugh Jordan, Mr. and Mrs. Barry Kohler, Dr. and Mrs. Robert Lamb, Mr. and Mrs. James Leeper, Mr. and Mrs. Louis Loeb, Mrs. B. H. Lovejoy, Mr. and Mrs. J. F. McCabe, Mr. and Mrs. James T. McTernan, Mrs. Cora Marshall, Mr. and Mrs. James Mattern, Mr. and Mrs. Willard Miller, Mr. and Mrs. George Mink, Mrs. Maud Mowell, Mr. and Mrs. John E. Murphy, Mr. and Mrs. Leon J. Nilsen, Mr. Howard B. Payne, Ann W. Penn, Mr. and Mrs. Gordon Perlmutter, Mrs. Harriet Poreda, Mrs. Morris Raker, Mr. Edward P. Renner, Mr. and Mrs. F. E. Rich, Mr. and Mrs. Joseph Saunders, Mr. Harvey E. Schmid, Mr. and Mrs. Leon Shrank, Mr. and Mrs. Eugene Singer, Mr. and Mrs. Marvin Smith, Mrs. Roberta Solomon, Mrs. Jane Swanson, Mr. and Mrs. Hendrik Van Rensselaer, Mr. and Mrs. Alonzo P. Walton, Anne A. Weisse, Mr. and Mrs. Virgil Williams, and Miss Mildred L. Winkels.

More than 80 letters were sent to licensed judges of the breed asking for their opinions on the standard, and how they use it in their judging, as well as for information on the great show dogs they have judged over the years. Additionally the *Bulletin* of the OESCA was used for six months to request the membership of the club at large to contribute information and to express opinions on what they wanted included in the book.

As invaluable as the correspondence and published materials have been in putting the book together, their significance is at least equalled by personal conversations I have had with Bobtail fanciers across the United States.

Jane Saunders, then corresponding secretary of the OESCA, was an incredible help in gathering materials and getting the project off the ground in its early stages.

To Serena Van Rensselaer and Louise Lopino I am indebted for the drawings that so intriguingly capture the spirit of the breed and add sprightliness to the pages of this book.

To my wife I owe perhaps the greatest debt of all. She compiled most of the historical statistics, including a listing of *every* Bobtail to ever become an American champion.

I received an invaluable education in the thinking of many dog people in every section of the country during the preparation of this book, and can only conclude that despite the laments heard so frequently about overpopularity, the Old English Sheepdog has among its followers in the United States a hard core of dedicated, intelligent, serious breeders, who will surely continue to produce the sturdy characters the breed has always known.

—JOHN MANDEVILLE

Author John Mandeville, son Henry, and three Old English enjoy a romp in the snow. Mr. Mandeville is presently assistant to the president of the American Kennel Club.

Ch. Fezziwig Raggedy Andy.

Character of the
Old English Sheepdog

W. GRAHAM ROBERTSON has best expressed
one man's conception of the character of the Old English Sheepdog
in the concluding chapter to his memoirs of late Victorian and Ed-
wardian England, *Life Was Worth Living:*

> Those who have never been privileged to enjoy the affection and
> intimate acquaintance of an Old English Bob Tail Sheep Dog will not
> understand this chapter. How should they? Nearly all dogs are charm-
> ing and lovable, but the Bob Tail as a companion is unique: his store
> of friendship is so inexhaustible, his sympathetic understanding so
> profound, his love, if you are lucky enough to gain it, so limitless that
> he seems to belong to a race apart. He possesses all the canine virtues,
> but adds to them others which I hesitate to call human because they
> are seldom to be met with in humanity. I have known four Bob Tail
> Sheep Dogs intimately and, if only for that reason, I have not lived
> in vain.

High praise, and justly deserved in the opinion of all those who
have lived with and loved the remarkable breed, Old English Sheepdog. Robertson was no mere Victorian gentleman who took the
trouble, for want of anything better to do, to record his memoirs.
He was an artist and early photographer of importance as well as
friend and confidant of virtually every significant literary, artistic,
and theatrical person in England from the 1880s through the First
World War. The first 323 pages of his book detail friendships with
Sarah Bernhardt, James McNeill Whistler, Oscar Wilde, and Henry
James among many others. But the last chapter of the book is re-

served for his "Most Notable Acquaintances," the Old English Sheepdogs Bob, Portly, Ben and Richard. Any contemporary Old English devotee will tell you that this is as it should be.

If you do not mind a dog that is big and hairy, the Old English Sheepdog is the breed for you. Provided, of course, you are willing to tolerate a beast who is determined to be the center of attention at all times, who will never concede for a moment that he is not the master and you the companion, and who is stubborn to the point of exasperation. Old English Sheepdogs are all this and much more. They are loud, robust, active creatures. They would as soon sleep in your bed as not. They can be tremendous slobs, turning the time-consuming grooming job into a disheveled mess with one drink or a quick romp through bushes and flowers. They are also loyal and devoted without being excessively protective. They are amazingly adaptable, capable of living in heat or cold, mountain or desert, city apartment or farm with equal facility. They are homebodies, not in the least given to wandering. They are astute, showing remarkable intuitive appreciation of the fragilities of children and the elderly. They are not fighters, but will when the necessity arises defend home against intruders and themselves from other dogs.

The Old English Sheepdog is placid and even-tempered, but when aroused he can be ferocious. P. Hamilton Goodsell, president of the Old English Sheepdog Club of America for nearly 20 years, tells of being out for a walk in the country with his Ch. Montford Marksman, a neighborhood child and a pair of Sheepdog puppies, when a German Shepherd Dog jumped a brick fence and attacked. Marksman flew to the rescue while Goodsell dragged the child and puppies away. Before Goodsell could intervene in the fight, Marksman had killed the Shepherd and casually returned to his walk.

More recently a member of the Greater New York Old English Sheepdog Club returned home and happened on a burglar, armed with a lead pipe. His Sheepdog overpowered the would-be thief and assailant, and effectively kept him pinned down until the police arrived.

These true stories indicate the breed's deep devotion to his friends. Old English are not, however, true guard dogs. They will almost certainly bark and make a loud disturbance at any unusual noise or goings on, but a stranger is more in danger of drowning in a cascade of licks than being bit, unless he threatens members of a Sheepdog's household. Most people find this the best type of canine companion to have. Old English do not adapt to being trained to attack. Those few that have served in the armed forces in war time were not used for this type of duty, but for rescue work.

By the same token, Old English do not adapt to being chained or confined. They are an outdoor breed but demand human attention and lots of it. The Old English Sheepdog was at one time a herding and guard dog in the western counties of England and Wales, but in the United States few Old English Sheepdogs have ever worked sheep or cattle. The breed is still a robust, active dog. He will work long and hard as family companion and clown.

The Old English Sheepdog is credited with being one of the few breeds of dog with a sense of humor. The breed's intelligence is great, but whether they can talk, as more than one owner has claimed, is a moot point. Old English Sheepdogs are naturally healthy and active dogs. They live long trouble free lives with a minimal amount of regular maintenance.

However much the Old English Sheepdog may seem to be the ideal canine companion, his admirers claim none can compare, there are decided drawbacks to everyone owning this particular fellow. The Old English Sheepdog is simply too much dog for most people. This is above and beyond the fact that Bobtails are too big and too hairy for the majority of dog owners. Sheepdogs are too demanding as individuals for anyone who wants only a "dog." A neglected Old English is a sorry dog. The coat and appearance will of course look terrible and be a possible source of illness and disease on a neglected specimen. But, more importantly, neglect will negatively affect his temperament. Unless you are prepared to cope with a demanding addition to your household, both insofar as keeping him looking his best and attending to his "emotional" health, the Old English Sheepdog is not the breed for you.

You can buy an Old English Sheepdog, and have the papers that prove you are his owner. But in a real and fundamental sense you are never going to own an Old English Sheepdog. If anything, most Sheepdog people will tell you they are owned by their dogs.

A story from Robertson's memoirs may give you an insight into the feeling of Sheepdog people for their dogs. Robertson's first Sheepdog, Bob, was a typical robust, outgoing soul. He lived to be 16 and during his last years was totally blind. In his old age Bob was led about by a less outgoing son, Ben. Ben, too, lived long, but at age 15 he lay dying in Robertson's study. As the end drew near, Robertson was daydreaming and had the vivid impression that Bob was in the room where he had died nearly 12 years before. "Benny had always waited for his blind father, had gone back for him and guided him gently round corners, and I shall always feel that Bob, the strong-hearted, came back in his turn for the timid Benny to help him across the great Barrier." Few breeds of dog demand and inspire the emotional commitment of the Old English Sheepdog.

15

"The Shepherd's Dog", an 1804 painting by P. Reinagle.

The 1770 painting of the Duke of Buccleugh by Thomas Gainsborough.

16

Early History and Development

THE HISTORY of most breeds of purebred dog is murky at best. This is especially so for those dogs valued as workers rather than for their beauty and companionship. The history of some breeds that were the favorites of royalty is well known, and in some instances their pedigrees can be traced back hundreds of years. But working dogs were valued for their ability in the field, not the nobility of their ancestry. Because of this it is almost impossible to trace the ancestry of any working breed back more than a hundred years. This is true of the herding dogs of the British Isles.

There have been herding dogs in England for hundreds, if not thousands of years, but no Old English Sheepdog can accurately trace his ancestry back further than the 1870s. Prior to that time the history of Old English Sheepdogs is at best an educated guess.

All domestic dog breeds are special adaptions of the various wolf types that originally inhabited central Europe and Asia. Old English Sheepdogs probably combine the blood of the fiercer mountain wolf with the earlier domesticated lowland wolf. The mountain wolf is the progenitor of most guard dogs, particularly those with the large mastiff head structure. Herding dogs are descended from the smaller, faster lowland wolf. The Hungarian Komondor more than any other modern breed, represents the combination of the fierce, massive guard dogs with the smaller, faster, more agile herders.

Old English Sheepdogs apparently evolved from almost exclusively herding stock. England had been free of virtually all large predators, except man, for hundreds of years before sheep herding became widespread. Whatever the Bobtail's varied ancestry, it is apparent

17

that by the middle of the eighteenth century, when the wool and textile industry was booming, a number of distinct herding breeds had emerged in England, Wales, and Scotland, and across the English Channel in the Low Countries and France. These breeds were developed from the much older herding and guard dogs of central and eastern Europe. Today's descendants of these eighteenth century workers include—in Europe—the Briard, Bouvier des Flanders, Belgian Malinois, Tervuren and Sheepdog, and in England and Scotland—the Collie, Sheltie, Bearded and Border Collies, and the Old English Sheepdog.

The Bearded Collie is the closest purebred relative of the Bobtail. Old English Sheepdogs at the turn of the century often resembled today's Bearded Collies. Harkaway, one of the most celebrated Sheepdogs of an earlier day and credited with helping to fix correct coat in the breed, was very much like today's Beardie. He was whelped June 8, 1891.

When the first Old English Sheepdog emerged is debatable. It is unlikely to have been as early as some commentators have suggested.

The rather tenuous ancestry of the Old English Sheepdog at the turn of the century in part accounts for Aubrey Hopwood's assertion that the first true Bobtail can be seen in a painting by Gainsborough of the Duke of Buccleugh done in 1770. Hopwood's book, *The Old English Sheep Dog from Puppyhood to Championship* published in 1905, remains one of the best sources of information on the breed, but his reference to the Gainsborough painting is almost absurd. He even claims the dog pictured with the Duke bears close resemblance to contemporary specimens of the breed, but study of the pictures of such early twentieth century greats as Ch. Fairweather or Ch. Shepton Hero shows scant likeness. Hopwood no doubt wanted to impress his readers with the breed's distinguished background, or he suffered from an overly vivid imagination. At the very least he was unfamiliar with the history of the Buccleugh painting. The painting was done by Gainsborough in 1770. It received wide distribution and continuing circulation because it was engraved in mezzotint by John Dixon in 1771, not John Boydell as claimed by Hopwood. Before Hopwood claimed the Duke's dog for Old English fanciers, other commentators had variously identified it as a Russian spaniel, a water spaniel, and a lowland hound among others. Charles Cooke in his book on the Dandie Dinmont terrier in 1885 claimed the Duke's dog for that breed. More recently Bearded Collie devotees have argued the Duke's dog is their own. Obviously, short of discovering a heretofore unknown letter of the Duke's stating exactly

Old English Sheepdogs at turn of the century often resembled today's Bearded Collies. At top is Eng. Ch. Cannamoor Glencanach, Bearded Collie owned by Lawrence M. Levy. Below, Harkaway, a celebrated Old English Sheepdog whelped in 1891.

what type of dog it was he thought so highly of to sit for a formal painting of himself with, we are never going to know the animal's breed.

But common sense eliminates the Old English Sheepdog as a logical possibility. *Burke's Peerage* states the third Duke of Buccleugh and fifth Duke of Queensbury, Henry Scott, was born in 1746, and died in 1812. The Duke was in residence at Bowhill in Selkirk, Scotland in 1770, when the painting was done. The original hangs to this day at Bowhill. Gainsborough was born and raised in Suffolk on the eastern coast of England. Toward the end of the nineteenth century an occasional Old English Sheepdog was seen in Suffolk and Norfolk, but all accounts locate the origins of the Old English Sheepdog in the five southwestern counties of England. It would seem then, because of the Duke's Scottish residence and Gainsborough's eastern county origins, the painting cannot be of even the remotest ancestor of the Old English Sheepdog. The Duke's native Cheviot Hills are the traditional origins of both the Dandie Dinmont and the Bearded Collie. The fanciers of these two breeds can argue among themselves with more confidence that the Buccleugh dog is a predecessor of their breed.

During the nineteenth century a number of drawings and paintings were done that may or may not be direct ancestors of today's Old English Sheepdogs. These drawings and paintings all show a Collie-like dog with a dark, rough coat. Two of the earlier, more likely to be Old English, are an engraving done in 1808 by H. R. Cook of a painting by J. Ward, and an 1835 painting by Sidney Cooper of a dog lying down making it impossible to see the tail, but it is marked and coated like an Old English.

The emergence of the Old English Sheepdog as a distinct breed cannot be dated by the practice of docking tails. Tails have been removed from dogs since antiquity. The practice was brought to England long before the Norman conquest in 1066. Feudal nobles maintained vast estates as hunting preserves. It was thought that by docking tails of the peasants' dogs the animals would not be able to run down small game, depleting the lord's lands of rabbit and depriving the lord of good sport. A dog without a tail was presumed to have lost his rudder for easy, fast maneuvering.

At one time tail docking was also used to designate working dogs. These animals helped the peasants in their daily work and were consequently not taxed. But this appealing explanation is not entirely adequate in dating or explaining the Old English Sheepdog's emergence as a distinct tailless breed. Dog taxes were never common in

20

England. They were in continental Europe. As late as the 1930s dog taxes were a serious detriment to breeders in the majority of European countries, but not in England. The Old English Sheepdog and the Pembroke Welsh Corgi are the only breeds among many well-established workers in England that have emerged with docked tails. Tail docking probably came about by accident, became associated with a particular strain of workers, noted for certain characteristics and abilities, and was thus incorporated into the breed.

Old English Sheepdogs were being exhibited and registered in England and the United States before the breed was definitely and distinctly identified as the Old English Sheepdog. The breed was first shown at a dog show at Islington, England in 1865. Old English were given separate show classification for the first time at Curzon Hall in Birmingham, England in 1873. The first registrations of "Sheepdogs, short-tailed English" with the English Kennel Club were in 1877. Two were registered, both named Bob, numbers 4541 and 4542 belonging respectively to F. Aggriss and the Marquis of Blandford. Aggriss's Bob whelped in 1870, breeder and pedigree unknown, later went to one of the earliest known Old English Sheepdog breeders, R. J. Lloyd-Price of Rhiwlas, Bala, North Wales. The Marquis' Bob, whelped in 1873, also has no known breeder or pedigree.

The English Kennel Club's stud book continued to register the breed as "Sheepdog, short-tailed English" well into the 1890s. At the same time Collies were registered as "Sheepdogs, rough-coated" and "Sheepdogs smooth-coated." The first American stud book registration for the breed was as "Sheepdog, English Old-Fashioned Bob-tailed" in 1886. Prior to the turn of the century in the United States the breed was eligible for competition in Collie classes. This fact was no doubt uncomfortable for many early Collie exhibitors. At the first Collie Club of America specialty show held at the Metropolitan Opera House in New York City on November 29, 30, and December 1, 1899, the Old English Sheepdogs, Sir Charles (owned by R. H. Williams), Gillie (owned by J. W. Morgan), Sir Ethelburg (also owned by Mr. Williams), placed first, second, and third respectively in the Open Dog class. Williams' Dame Elfrida was fourth in Open Bitches at the same show. In fairness to Collie people and the 54 other entries at the show, the judge, Henry Jarrett, was a long time fancier of Old English Sheepdogs. These winnings by Old English Sheepdogs at the Collie Club specialty show underscore the still-emerging identity of the breed as late as 1900.

Only a few years earlier it would have been virtually impossible

21

to distinguish between the various drovers' dogs scattered throughout the southwestern counties of England and northward through Wales to the Scottish border, except for a docked tail here and there. They were small to medium sized dogs, between 17 and 23 inches at the withers and from 40 to 65 pounds in weight. Coats were shaggy, but less like today's Bobtail than the rough Collie. Coloring was widely varied with black, brown, and tan markings still common in the 1890s. The characteristic fall, or heavy face coat, was little more than a fringe at the brow. Soundness, at least as defined by today's show standards, was minimal. Front ends were especially weak. The topline, which as much as any characteristic, came to separate the Old English from other herding breeds, was not clearly defined as sloping *upward* from the withers. Heads were narrow and muzzles tapering. It was only through determined breeding to the standard in the 20 years after it was written by Freeman Lloyd in 1885, that the Old English Sheepdog emerged during the first decade of the twentieth century as a distinctive breed, surprisingly similar to today's specimens.

Old English Sheepdogs in contrast to most breeds that have come from fields and farms as workers to bench shows as purebred, bathed and polished specimens have had the good fortune to have had devoted, long-lived admirers who published many of their experiences and reminiscences. Freeman Lloyd and Henry Arthur Tilley are the most notable of these. Their experience with Sheepdogs began in the 1880s and continued uninterrupted into the mid-1950s. From them it is possible to piece together the development of the breed from last decades of the nineteenth century when the basic stock was acquired by the Tilley brothers and other breeders directly from the farms of western England.

The Old English Sheepdog was far from firmly established in England at that time. This was because the breed as a distinct herding, all-purpose farm animal was not clearly established as different from the numerous drovers' dogs of western England and Wales. Many people felt the breed was in danger of disappearing altogether. Lloyd says the American interest in the Bobtail "helped to appreciate the market value for Old English Sheepdogs in their native country." In the troubled times following the Second World War American interest again played an important role in the breed's continued success in England.

Lloyd's contributions to purebred dogs in general and the Old English Sheepdog in particular have never received proper recognition. He was born and raised in Wales, where he began his career as a buyer, exporter and writer on purebred dogs in the early 1880s. He had a hand in the bringing of many of the first Sheepdogs to the

Freeman Lloyd.

Old English Sheepdogs at a 1904 show.

United States. In this role he came to know and be a close associate of the few Old English Sheepdog breeders of the day, including James Thomas of Great Bookham, Surrey, Herbert and Robert James of Hill Farm, Roose, Pembrokeshire, Wales, E. T. "Ted" Rees from Wales, Dr. John Griffith-Lock of Tenby, Dr. G. C. Edwardes-Ker of Suffolk, D. Parry Thomas of Pontypridd, South Wales, R. J. Lloyd-Price, Mr. J. Perryman, and Mr. W. Nevins among others.

His acquaintance with the breed and these men resulted in his being asked to write a standard for Old English Sheepdogs in 1885. Lloyd describes the process by which he set the standard down on paper in an article in the *American Kennel Gazette* in 1929. Lloyd's draft of the standard was polished by Dr. Edwardes-Ker and has remained to this day the unchanged official standard of the breed in England. The official American standard was adopted directly from the English standard. It too has remained unchanged to the present time, although it is somewhat more detailed in parts than the original English standard.

When Lloyd first became interested in the breed in the early 1880s, there were not many of them to be found. Those about were almost exclusively the property of farmers, whose sole concern was the utility of their dogs as workers. Lloyd says it was common in this period to select the pick of a litter by removing puppies a distance from their dam with the first one getting back to her the pick. A blue or wall eye was also highly valued by the farmers in selecting their stock. It was believed that a dog with a wall or blue eye would never go blind. Not until the standard was adopted in 1885, and the Old English Club of England founded in 1888, was the breed assured of continued support and development.

Lloyd credits Dr. Edwardes-Ker with giving the Bobtail the impetus toward a permanent, if small place, in purebred ranks in England. Registrations in the English Kennel Club's stud books throughout the eighties and nineties were largely the result of Edwardes-Ker's breeding.

The first Old English Sheepdogs in the United States were owned and shown by the Glencho Collie kennels of S. M. Cleaver located in East Bethlehem, Pennsylvania. The Glencho Kennel's Bob, registration number 3163, page seven, *American Kennel Register*, Volume IV, number one, January 1886, was the first Old English Sheepdog registered in the United States. Bob's breeder and whelping data are not known, but his exporter Mr. M. H. Lowe of Wednesbury, England, furnished the pedigree that "Bob's sire and dam can lick all creation driving sheep or cattle." Bob was also the first Sheepdog shown in the United States, at Philadelphia in 1885.

24

Glencho also registered the first Old English bitch, Judith, in the United States. Judith was whelped October 26, 1883 by Bob out of Gipsey, who was by English Ch. Sir Guy out of Dame Dorothy. Judith was bred by Dr. Edwardes-Ker. She was the dam of the first American bred and registered litter of Old English Sheepdogs, sired by Bob and whelped November 11, 1885. The first American bred litter of OES was thus the product of a father-to-daughter breeding. From it came the Glencho Kennel's Dame Hester, the first breeder-exhibited Sheepdog in the United States, and also the first Bobtail to be shown in the Midwest when she took a variety class First at Milwaukee in 1886.

The practice of registering purebred dogs with the American Kennel Club was not widely accepted until almost 1900. Between 1886 and 1898 Old English Sheepdogs trickled into the United States, were shown, and bred, but following the first registrations of the Glencho Kennels in 1886 and 1887, no other Bobtails were registered with the AKC until 1898.

Sheepdogs were given a major impetus in the late 1880s by William Wade, a wealthy industrialist from Pittsburgh. Wade felt that America needed a wide variety of purebred dogs. He frequently acquired different breeds and deposited them, together with instructions on feeding and care and a supply of food, on the doorsteps of friends he thought suited to the particular breed. He introduced the first Russian Wolfhounds and Mastiffs to the United States in this manner. When Wade became interested in the Old English Sheepdog, he hired Freeman Lloyd to write a pamphlet about the breed. Wade had it published by the magazine, *Turf, Field and Farm* in New York City at his expense in 1889. This public relations promotion of the breed helped introduce Bobtails to dog enthusiasts in the New York metropolitian area. From the 1890s until the 1930s, when the center of activity moved to New England, virtually all significant Old English Sheepdog activity in the United States took place within a 30-mile radius of New York City.

The first separate class for Old English Sheepdogs in the United States was at the fourteenth Westminster Kennel Club show held at the American Institute Fair Building in New York City on February 11, 12, 13 and 14, 1890. The judge was Reginald F. Mayhew. S. M. Cleaver owned both entries, the dog Orson and the bitch Queen Vick. Tradition has it the first separate Old English class was at the 1893 Westminster show. No Sheepdogs were shown at Westminster that year, although the dog Hempstead Bob, who was supposedly the first Bobtail shown at Westminster, was exhibited at the American Pet Dog Club show at the Lenox Lyceum in New York City on May 30, 31 and June 1, 2, 1893, probably the basis for the incorrect assumption that Bob was at Westminster that year. From the middle 1890s, Old English Sheepdogs were seen at the various shows in New York, Detroit, Pittsburgh, Chicago, St. Louis, and Boston that comprised the annual spring swing around the East for dog show fanciers.

The Hempstead Farm kennels of Thomas Terry and James Mortimer was the first registered OES kennel in 1896, when the American Kennel Club began registering kennel names. There were three Old English Sheepdog kennels registered with the AKC in 1896: Hempstead Farm, Colonel A. B. Hilton's Woodlawn Park, and Henry Jarrett's Wellesbourne. Terry and Mortimer were associated in livestock and dog breeding at their farm on Long Island. Terry managed the farm and Mortimer acquired their dogs in England and around the United States. James Mortimer was the most important person in establishing purebred dogs as a popular sport at the turn of the century. He was the first great dog show superintendent, all breed-judge, and general expert on all matters having to do with purebred dogs. In the early 1890s, Freeman Lloyd sold several Sheepdogs, out of Edwardes-Ker's breeding, to Mortimer. This formed the basis of the Hempstead Farms' Old English kennel. In addition to Hempstead Bob, they widely exhibited the dogs Herdsman II and Lord Mayor in the middle '90s.

J. Pierpont Morgan bought Herdsman II in 1895. Morgan was only the first of a succession of wealthy Americans that owned, bred, and exhibited Old English Sheepdogs in the early years of the twentieth century. Of the ten wealthiest families in the United States, with fortunes far in excess of 100 million dollars, the Goulds, Harrimans, Guggenheims, and Vanderbilts all owned, showed and bred Bobtails. Most of the other names prominently associated with the breed until the Second World War were independently wealthy, if not in the same class as the Vanderbilts. From P. Hamilton Goodsell, Morris Kinney, William A. Jamison to Mrs. Lewis Roesler Renner, Old English Sheepdog fanciers in the United States were wealthy people who moved in the highest levels of society in New York City, Newport, Southampton, and Tuxedo Park, New York.

The Morgans were principally known for their Collies. Their Cragston Kennel had many of the big winning Collies in the first decade of the twentieth century. Briefly they also had many Old English Sheepdogs who were widely shown. Included in this group was the dog Gillie, Winners at Westminster in 1899, 1900, and 1901.

Other names linked with the breed at the turn of the century period included: Harvey Hill and his bitch Daisy, acquired from the Glencho Collie kennels; and Colonel A. B. Hilton, owner of Woodlawn Park Kennels, who showed his dog Boxer III and his bitch Mayoress of Newport (Boxer was Winners Dog at Westminster in 1895, '96, '97 and '98. Mayoress was second in bitches in 1895 at Westminster and Winners in '96, '97, and '98. Both of these dogs were bought by the Wilford Kennels in the fall of 1896.) F. A. Watson owned and showed Clarissa, Samson, Sir Charles, and Trilby among others in the middle nineties. Trilby was acquired by the Round Plain Kennels of John Caswell and shown along with his other Bobtails, including Bouncing Bob, Lady Grizzle, Sir Grizzle, Lady Buff, Sir Grizzle II, and in 1898 F. A. Watson's Clarissa. In addition, F. Fosheim, the Donnybrook Kennels, F. W. Neuman, John Harvey, G. T. Kallas, R. H. Williams, S. Frazer, and Abraham Fletcher of Cameron, West Virginia with his dog and bitch, Thuxton Bob and Blue Mabel, all owned, bred and showed Sheepdogs before and just after the turn of the century. The Morgan's Gillie and Fletcher's dog and bitch were registered with the American Kennel Club in 1898 and 1899 respectively, the first registrations since the eighties and beginning the complete registration of all Old English with the AKC.

Gillie, Thuxton Bob, and Blue Mabel were all grandchildren of Watch Boy. Watch Boy, his son Young Watch, and their immediate turn of the century descendants Ch. Stylish Boy, Ch. Shepton Hero, and Ch. Brentwood Hero were the most important Sheepdogs on either side of the Atlantic in this early period. There are few Old English Sheepdogs alive today that cannot trace their ancestry back to one or another of these dogs. Ch. Fezziwig Ceiling Zero the great show winner and stud dog of the late '50s and '60s is a direct father-to-son descendant through his sire Farleydene Bartholomew, 15 generations removed from Watch Boy. International Ch. Unnesta Pim, the prolific producer of champion get in the later 1960s is also a direct father-to-son descendant of Watch Boy at the fifteenth generation. The same thing is true of virtually all other major names in American, English, and European Sheepdogs today. Every pedigree that contains one or another of the famous Downderry dogs of the Merriedip kennels of the 1930s can be traced back to these same dogs.

The 1903 Westminster show brought Old English Sheepdogs into prominence in the United States. Freeman Lloyd judged the breed that year. The Tilley brothers, Authur Steeds and Henry Arthur, of Shepton Mallet, England brought over a large Old English entry. Shepton has been one of the most prominent names in the history of Sheepdogs. The Tilleys were among the first Englishmen to seriously begin breeding Bobtails in the eighties. They acquired their first Old English Sheepdog directly from the farms of western England. Over the years Shepton has been associated with more Old

English Sheepdogs than any other kennel. Arthur died in the late twenties, but his younger brother Henry was continuously active until his death in 1955. Henry's daughter Florence has kept the name Shepton current in Sheepdogs into the 1970s, a remarkable record of continued association with the breed.

The Tilleys knew Old English. They also knew the requirements for a working farm dog. They were among the most versatile breeders of all time. They bought and sold dogs of all bloodlines in order to improve their own stock. Virtually every name associated with the breed in England or the United States through the Second World War acquired stock at one time or another from Shepton. The Tilleys wanted a Bobtail capable of working. They bred for soundness and type first and foremost. Henry frequently expressed the opinion that size per se was of secondary importance to type and working ability. He thought there was need in the breed for Bobtails as large as 28 inches at the withers, and as small as 18 inches. In his judging he put up the biggest and the smallest, demanding soundness and type above all.

Among the Bobtails that the Tilleys brought over for the 1903 Westminster show were Merry Party, Bouncing Lass, Stylish Boy, Blue Boy, Boy Blue, Cowboy, Crossroad Caprice, Crossroads Quality, Diana Rough, Dusty Queen, English Betty, and Twinkling Star. Lloyd put Merry Party up in dogs and Bouncing Lass in bitches. Bouncing Lass had reputedly cost more than a thousand dollars as a pup. She was the best traveled Sheepdog of the day, returning to England after her win at Westminster and then coming back in 1904, when she was again Winners Bitch. The Tilleys thought their best Bobtail was Stylish Boy. Lloyd found Merry Party to be his winner, with second going to Stylish Boy. Merry Party was purchased by Mrs. Richard Harding Davis, one of the first prominent turn of the century American fanciers.

Stylish Boy and three bitches were sold to the theatrical producers and entrepreneurs, Charles Frohman and Charles B. Dillingham. Frohman and Dillingham were the first twentieth century Americans to maintain a large kennel principally devoted to Old English Sheepdogs. Between 1900 and 1914 they owned, imported, and showed numerous Old English Sheepdogs. Their kennel, Hidden Brook Farm at White Plains in Westchester County, New York, was managed by Jack Harrison. Harrison was an Englishman, familiar with dogs here and in the British Isles. He ran the kennel and made decisions on who to breed and what new stock to acquire. Many Sheepdog fanciers in the pre-World War II years left all the decisions relating to the dogs to their kennel managers.

More important than their activities as breeders and exhibitors

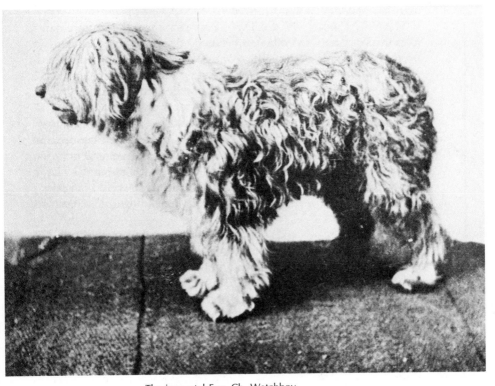

The immortal Eng. Ch. Watchboy.

was the publicity that Frohman and Dillingham brought the breed. They were widely known in the upper levels of society in the New York metropolitan area. They introduced the breed to their friends, many of whom acquired Bobtails. Some of these became prominent early breeders. Most important of this group were James A. Garland, Reginald C. Vanderbilt, and O. C. Harriman. Vanderbilt and Harriman in turn bred dogs that were acquired by the major American breeders that emerged in the World War I period. Morris Kinney, P. Hamilton Goodsell, and Mrs. Wilbur Kirby Hitchcock were the most significant of these. Through the breedings of these three, many contemporary American Old English Sheepdogs can be traced back to the foundation stock of the breed at the turn of the century. Among others, virtually every dog with Amblehurst, Downeylane, Greyfriar, and Lillibrad, as well as to a lesser extent, Double JJ, Shaggybar, Silvershag, and Tamara, in their pedigrees can be traced back to the Sheepdogs bred by these people.

In terms of his impact on the breed Stylish Boy was the most important dog the Tilleys brought with them. Exactly how much Frohman and Dillingham paid for him and three bitches is not known. It was rumored the four dogs cost from $10,000 up. Because of a serious fire in 1904, Frohman and Dillingham gave Stylish Boy to Reginald C. Vanderbilt. Vanderbilt's Sandy Point Farm kennels in Newport, Rhode Island bred and showed many important Sheepdogs until 1912, including the Stylish Boy son Sandy Point Rags, who was widely used at stud. Vanderbilt showed Stylish Boy extensively. He was Winners Dog at Westminster in 1905. In 1906 he became the sixth Old English Sheepdog to complete an official American Kennel Club championship.

Stylish Boy has left an almost incalculable impact on the breed. He was an all-white headed dog, and is credited by Henry Arthur Tilley and Freeman Lloyd with stamping this trait on the breed. His sire, Young Watch, and Young Watch's sire Watch Boy, were not all white-headed, but nearly so, and tended to pass this characteristic onto the breed. They were all sound, typy dogs, widely used at stud.

Stylish Boy, bred by Dotts and Sheperd, whelped September 4, 1898 was out of Larkfield Watch Lass. Watch Lass as well as Young Watch were both sired by Watch Boy. Thus, Stylish Boy had the same dog (Watch Dog) as a grandsire on both the sire and the dam sides of his pedigree. This form of inbreeding has been used by purebred dog breeders since records have been kept, to fix desired characteristics and traits in a breed. Through Stylish Boy and many other offspring, including Sir James, The Czarina, Roseberry, Victor Cavendish, Lord Cedric, Grey Queen, Royal Duke, Lady May, Lady

30

Heartsease, Lady Blue, Watchman, King Kroonah, and others, Watch Boy and Young Watch have had a vast impact on all English Sheepdogs, in England and the United States.

Stylish Boy's career was typical of imported Old English Sheepdog studs in the first 25 years of this century. He came to the United States as an older dog of proven merit in the show ring and at stud. For a variety of reasons, not the least of which was the willingness of American fanciers to spend large sums of money for dogs they wanted, all the important English studs between 1900 and 1925 came to the United States.

Included in this group were Ch. Shepton Hero, Ch. Brentwood Hero, Ch. Night Rider, Ch. Tip Top Weather, and Ch. Montford Marksman. This continued importation of top English producers kept American and English Bobtails similar, both in type and pedigrees and bloodlines.

Championships are only an approximate indication of a dog's worth at any time, but especially was this true before the 1960s when the breed was rare and shows were difficult to get to. However, in the first decade of the twentieth century 15 Old English Sheepdogs finished official American Kennel Club championships. One of these was Stylish Boy; another was his half-brother, out of Young Watch, Ringlow's Sultan. Three were sired by Stylish Boy: Rowsley Conquest, Dolly Gray, and Kenvil Blinkers. Of the remaining ten, six were directly descended from Young Watch or his sire Watch Boy, while a seventh's ancestry is completely unknown. In addition to this champion get, Stylish Boy sired many dogs, both in England and the United States, that played important roles in various breeding programs.

Following the breed's introduction at the 1903 Westminster show the most prominent members of New York society acquired them. The high point of this early social acceptance came at the 1904 Westminster show. Sheepdog entries were made by the Vanderbilts, the Goulds, Morgans, Frohman and Dillingham, the Richard Harding Davises, the George Steadmans, as well as the Tilleys among many others. The social prominence of the owners of the Old English Sheepdogs being shown attracted a huge crowd of the City's upper crust, including a high percentage of the Four Hundred. The social importance of the owners and spectators at the Old English ring prompted the superintendent, James Mortimer, to go into the ring and discreetly advise the judge George Raper to "take plenty of time, the dogs in the ring are the property of some of our leading Americans." Mr. and Mrs. George Steadman's Wilburforce was the Winners Dog. For the second straight year, the Tilleys Bouncing Lass was Winners Bitch.

Nineteen hundred and four was an important year in the history of Sheepdogs in the United States beyond the social prominence the breed attained. In that year the first Bobtails completed official championships, and, more importantly, the Old English Sheepdog Club of America was organized. The first Old English Sheepdog to gain championship status was Mr. and Mrs. William C. Eustis' bitch Lady Stumpie, bred by Dr. Griffith-Lock, by the Mayor of Newport out of the Czarina, whelped June 30, 1896. The second champion was a dog, Potsford Bob, also bred in England by A. Over, owned by Mrs. L. Trowbridge Martin, whelped in November 1897, by Lion out of Judy. Lady Stumpie and Potsford Bob were indicative of a trend in Old English championships in the United States until the 1960s. Few Bobtails completed championships before they were three or four. Puppies were shown, as were youngsters, but few dogs won points until they were fully mature. Until after the Second World War, it was common not to show a dog until it was four or even older. Over the years, several Old English Sheepdogs finished at ten years of age.

The Old English Sheepdog Club of America was organized in 1904 largely through the prompting of Henry Arthur Tilley. The Club was recognized by the American Kennel Club in 1905, the year from which the OESCA dates its founding. It is one of the 25 oldest breed clubs in the United States. The original members were H. W. Berryman, William C. Eustis, Charles A. Griscom, J. K. Warren, James A. Garland, G. M. Sidenberg, Reginald C. Vanderbilt, Richard W. Davis, and Mrs. J. C. Norton. The founders, together with Harry T. Peters, J. W. Morgan, J. P. Welsh, Louis Hood, and C. B. Dillingham carried the club through its first decade. During and after the First World War a new generation of fanciers, chiefly Morris Kinney, P. Hamilton Goodsell, and Mrs. Wilbur Kirby Hitchcock, emerged and in turn carried the club to the Second World War. The Old English Sheepdog Club of America achieved its zenith in its early years between 1921 and 1929. At that time several breeders and exhibitors of great importance were active. The club's first specialty show was held in 1921. Thereafter specialty shows were held yearly, except for 1925 and 1928, until 1931.

Of the early breeders and exhibitors, the most dedicated was James A. Garland of New York City and Newport, Rhode Island. Garland was apparently introduced to Sheepdogs by Frohman and Dillingham and his Newport neighbor, Reginald C. Vanderbilt. He set about acquiring the stock to start an extensive breeding program in 1905 and 1906. Garland hired Arthur Merrill to supervise and manage his North Prudence End kennels in Newport. Merrill was an expert in the care and conditioning of long-coated breeds and well-informed about Bobtails in the United States and England. Garland, unlike most of his contemporary OES fanciers, kept an active hand in the basic decisions having to do with his dogs.

Garland showed four imported Sheepdogs to championships, Captain Rough Weather and Dolly Gray in 1906 and Ringlow's Sultan and King Edward in 1907. All four were direct descendants of Watch Boy. Dolly Gray was thought to be the best Old English Sheepdog bitch in England when Garland bought her. She was sired by Ch. Stylish Boy.

Unfortunately for the breed, Garland died a relatively young man of pneumonia in 1907. His wife attempted to continue the kennel for a year, but gave it up in 1908. Garland's daughter, as Mrs. Winchester Fitch Ingersoll in the late '20s, was briefly active as a Sheepdog breeder under the Shelterfield kennel prefix. However, Shelterfield was most interested in Sealyham Terriers, and was involved with Bobtails for little more than two years.

Beaver Brook Kennels

Garland's sudden death was a major setback to the breed in the United States. His loss was to a certain extent compensated for by the emergence of the most successful Old English Sheepdog kennel of the day, Mrs. Tyler Morse's Beaver Brook Kennels. If it were possible to compare show records then and now it might be that the Morse dogs were the most successful in the history of the breed. They dominated Old English in the United States from 1908 to 1918. Where all-breed competition was offered they dominated that as well. Purebred dogs as a sport have always attracted wealthy, flamboyant personalities. Mrs. Tyler Morse must rank as one of the most interesting personalities ever involved with Old English. As interesting as her personal history is, it is important to remember that she also had the greatest Bobtails of the day.

She was born Allon Fuller, the daughter of George A. Fuller, one of New York City's first great construction magnates. He left her a fortune of two million dollars on his death. At the age of 17, in 1895, she married Harry S. Black. Black was said to have been a comparatively poor man when he married Miss Fuller. Using his wife's money he built a real estate empire that in short order multiplied her already tidy fortune. Somewhere along the line, Mr. and Mrs. Black became disenchanted with one another. They were divorced amid wild rumors and hints of scandal on May 31, 1905. Justice Keogh of the Supreme Court at White Plains, New York, in granting the divorce, ordered the court papers sealed so that details of the separation were not made public. It was made known that Black returned six million dollars to his wife, representing her fortune and the profits he had made on it. Little more than six months after her divorce, on January 17, 1906, Mrs. Black married Tyler Morse.

Morse had been interested in purebred dogs for several years, although never Old English. He had registered the Beaver Brook Kennel prefix with the American Kennel Club in 1903. Mrs. Tyler Morse's interest in dogs was extensive. She was primarily responsible for building the Beaver Brook OES kennel. Mrs. Morse did not entirely disappear from the front pages after her marriage to Tyler. In 1907 she attained further notoriety when she announced the loss of her $40,000 pearl necklace, which it developed she had checked into the safe at the Hotel Savoy and forgotten.

Mrs. Morse was as controversial in death as she had been in life. Unfortunately for Old English Sheepdogs she died a young woman, of pneumonia, on October 10, 1915. Her will added to her intriguing personal history. Her estate, valued at something in excess of six million dollars was entrusted to her ex-husband, Harry Black. He was given a flat payment of $250,000 in lieu of any claim against the estate. Tyler Morse was named executor. He was bequeathed the estate as well as Morse Lodge, the estate at Westbury, Long Island with the stipulation that if he ever remarried, he would forfeit all right to the property. Morse never remarried. When he died in 1933, he willed the kennel, buildings, and grounds to his kennel manager, Arthur Merrill.

Merrill came to the Morses from James Garland's North Prudence End Kennels, following Mrs. Garland's decision to give up the dogs in 1908. Merrill, with Mrs. Morse's backing, was responsible for the success of the Beaver Brook Old English Sheepdogs. The Morses spared no expense in acquiring the best dogs available in England, and in providing Merrill with the facilities, equipment, and help to maintain the dogs. The result was the best conditioned Sheepdogs in the United States or England at any time until the present.

The Morse dogs were widely reputed to have been excessively coated. By the standards of the day they were. But in light of today's standards, they were well-conditioned show specimens. Their great coats were the product of meticulous maintenance.

There is no way to compare the winnings of show dogs before the Second World War with contemporary winners. And the further back one goes, the more difficult it becomes. In the years before, during, and after the First World War, few dog shows offered all-breed competition. There were few shows of any sort. Today it is almost impossible to appreciate the importance of Westminster in this early period.

Eng. Ch. Fairweather, of the great "Weather" line bred by Mrs. Fare Fosse, England, at turn of the century.

Eng. Ch. Roughweather, bred by Mrs. Fosse.

Eng. & Am. Ch. Dolly Gray, rated as best bitch of the breed in England when imported to America by James Garland in early 1900s.

The two top awards in each breed at the time were for Winners Dog and Winners Bitch. Morse Sheepdogs were Winners Bitch at Westminster each year from 1908 to 1918, except 1911, and they owned the Winners Dog in all the same years except 1909, 1911 and 1916. In addition to taking these top spots in the breed, their bitch Ch. Slumber was Best in Show in 1914. In 1915 their Ch. Brentwood Hero was second Best in Show, a win Slumber repeated in 1916.

The Morses imported more than 25 Bobtails from England, including the two top producing studs of the day, Ch. Shepton Hero and his son, Ch. Brentwood Hero. These dogs were "unavailable at any price" on first inquiries by the Morses. However, they both ended up in the Beaver Brook Kennels on Long Island. How much they cost is not known, but Shepton Hero at almost four in 1909, apparently cost $2,500 and Brentwood Hero was only slightly less, although rumors circulated that both dogs cost more than $15,000 apiece.

Shepton Hero was whelped March 24, 1905 by Lord Cedric out of Avalon Lass. He was bred by the Tilleys. (Lord Cedric was sired by Ch. Stylish Boy out of Ch. Bouncing Lass, both of whom were sired by Young Watch. Avalon Lass was a granddaughter of Bouncer on both her sire and dam's side of her pedigree. Bouncer was in turn sired by Stracathro Bouncing Bob, also the sire of Watch Boy.) Shepton Hero was Winners Dog at Westminster in 1910.

Brentwood Hero was whelped April 22, 1908 by Shepton Hero out of Brentwood Country Girl. Like his sire he was a noted winner and producer in England before the Morses bought him. He had a more distinguished show career in the United States than his sire, going Winners Dog at Westminster in 1913, 1915, and in 1918 when nearly ten years old. In 1915, he was second Best in Show at Westminster.

In the spring of 1909 the Morses imported from Martan Palfrey the bitch Nightmare, in whelp by John O'Dreams. John O'Dreams was a grandson of Young Watch through his sire Roseberry, while Nightmare was a granddaughter of Stylish Boy through her sire Handsome Boy. Nightmare's litter of nine was whelped June 25, 1909. The Morses kept the entire litter for their breeding program. This consisted of four dogs—Daylight, Good Morning, Midnight, and Searchlight, and five bitches—Aeroplane, Handsome Girl, Headache, Moonlight and Slumber. This litter became the first of many Sheepdog litters over the years that have contained many dogs of superior quality.

Midnight and Slumber were extensively shown. They completed their championships in 1912. Midnight was Winners Dog at Westminster in 1912, 1914, and 1917. Slumber was Winners Bitch at Westminster in 1912, 1913, 1916, and 1917. She was not entered in the classes in 1914, but her kennelmate Ominous substituted for her and went Winners Bitch.

Eng. and Am. Ch. Shepton Hero.

Eng. and Am. Ch. Bouncing Lass.

Ch. Slumber, foremost Sheepdog of her day, Best in Show at Westminster in 1914. Owned by Mrs. Tyler Morse.

The beautiful sterling OESCA Challenge Bowl, donated by Tyler Morse.

Slumber may have been the greatest show Bobtail of all time. She was apparently only defeated by one other Sheepdog, her kennelmate Ch. Brentwood Hero. When there was all-breed competition, she seldom lost. In 1914 she was the capstone to the Morses' sweep of breed and all-breed honors at Westminster. Her litter brother, Midnight, was Winners Dog. Only Morris Kinney's win of Reserve Dog with Night Rider prevented the Morses from winning the top four spots in the classes. And Night Rider was sired by another Morse dog, Ch. Brentwood Hero. Slumber and her kennelmates were the Best Team, while Midnight and Ominous were Best Brace in Show.

Slumber climaxed the Morses' winning by going Best in Show over 1,721 dogs on February 26th. The judge was Midgley Marsden, the foremost English all-breed judge of the day. Marsden was recognized as one of the most knowledgeable dog men on either side of the Atlantic. His praise of Slumber was lyrical. He stated flatly she was the greatest Old English Sheepdog that had ever lived, and that in his opinion he had never seen a dog of any breed that more closely resembled the standard of breed perfection than did Slumber. She did not rest on her laurels after this exalted win. She was Winners Bitch and Best of Breed at Westminster twice more, in 1916 and 1917. In 1916 she was second Best in Show all-breeds at Westminster.

Her Westminster breed victories in 1916 and 1917 also made her the first OES to win the Old English Sheepdog Club of America's solid silver Challenge Bowl. The Bowl was donated to the club by Tyler Morse. It was then and is today the pinnacle of success for an Old English in the United States. Originally it was offered at Westminster to the Best of Breed winner. The rapid growth and expansion of the OESCA in the 1960s resulted in the Bowl being offered several times a year. The Club then decided to revert to the original policy of offering the Challenge Bowl at one show designated the national specialty of the Old English Sheepdog Club of America for the year. The Challenge Bowl has long been regarded as one of the finest perpetual trophies offered by a breed club in the United States. It could not be duplicated today for less than $2,000. Morse, like many others, was hard hit by the stock market crash of 1929. He was sitting next to Freeman Lloyd during the judging of the 1930 OESCA specialty, when Lloyd commented on the bowl's beauty. Morse replied, "Friend Lloyd, if I were donating it now, it would have to be made of nickel."

Few kennels have dominated a breed as Beaver Brook did from 1910 to 1918. Mrs. Morse's death in 1915 at the age of only 37 cut short the kennel's activity. Beaver Brook produced a number of homebreds, many of whom played significant parts in the breeding programs of others. However the major Beaver Brook contributions to the breed were as exhibitors and popularizers, and as the owners of great imported studs that were widely used by American breeders.

Tyler Morse carried on the showing of Beaver Brook OES for three years after his wife's death. Over the years he served purebred dogs and the Old English Sheepdog Club of America in many capacities. For many years he was a member of the Board of Directors of the American Kennel Club. He was an officer of the OESCA for more than ten years as well as its AKC delegate for many years. He was a widely known and respected judge of Old English Sheepdogs and most other breeds. He was the judge at the second Old English Sheepdog Club of America specialty show in 1922. In 1926 he was one of five judges to select the Best in Show winner at Westminster.

The untimely deaths of James Garland and Mrs. Tyler Morse had lost the breed two of its staunchest supporters, but fortunately there were a number of dedicated if smaller breeders and exhibitors in the period. O. C. Harriman was the most prominent of this group. As a judge Harriman had a continuing impact on purebred dogs. He was licensed as an all-breed judge in 1931, and capped more than 60 years of activity by selecting the Best in Show winner at the 1971 Westminster Kennel Club show.

Kinnelon Kennels

In the years just before and after the First World War a number of American OES fanciers with the means of the Garlands and the Morses emerged. These World War I breeders and exhibitors have had an impact on the breed down to the present.

Morris Kinney was one of the most prominent names associated with purebred dogs in the first 25 years of the twentieth century. In addition to Old English Sheepdogs he had winning Mastiffs and harlequin Great Danes. He was a Director of the American Kennel Club from the First World War until the middle 1920s. He was at various times secretary (1915–1923), AKC delegate vice-president, and president of the Old English Sheepdog Club of America. Until 1934, when he became the first man elected honorary president of the OESCA for life, Kinney was a member of the club's Board of Governors. He was also a judge and collector of dog books. Kinney donated many of his early English Kennel Club Stud Books and other volumes to the American Kennel Club Library.

Kinney maintained his kennels on his 5,000 acre estate, Kinnelon, in Butler, New Jersey, 20 miles northwest of New York City. Kinnelon's OES facilities consisted of five large runs measuring 15 by 70 feet, and 15 smaller runs 6 by 40 feet. Two dogs were kept in the smaller runs, and two or more in the larger ones. Separate yards and facilities were maintained for puppies. The entire kennel was supervised by Rudolph Dallstrom, who together with Kinney made all the decisions concerning the dogs.

Kinney raised his dogs in the English tradition. They were well fed and cared for, but not coddled. His dogs were given an opportunity to be household companions, usually with his kennel man or hired help. He kept one house dog at a time himself. He never kept a stud as a house dog. The dogs were exercised vigorously everyday, usually together or in groups of five to ten. They were kenneled in draft-free, dry, but unheated kennels the year round. Kinney thought carrots were an excellent coat conditioner. His dogs received a pound to a pound and a half of kibble with cooked beef and carrots four days a week. The rest of the week the beef was fed raw. All adult dogs received the same ration once a day.

Morris Kinney was recognized as one of the most successful breeders of his day in both the United States and England. He might have been the greatest breeder of all time, except for his habit of packing up and traveling for extended periods to the far corners of the world. His kennel was as fully stocked as it had ever been, with proven winners and producers as well as promising youngsters, when he decided to disperse the kennel and travel in the fall of 1926. Virtually every dog was sold off, and Kinney left the following spring for a lengthy world tour. During the next five years he was seldom in the United States. Although he was encouraged by many to return and again take up active breeding and exhibiting, he was never again active as either breeder or exhibitor.

Kinney's travels between the early years of the century and the First World War, and again immediately after the war, were of invaluable help to him in acquiring information and background on the breed as well as the stock from which he built his kennel. He was widely known and respected by English breeders of the day, and over the years he traveled much to England to buy new dogs to complement his own bloodline and correct weaknesses. He personally selected and bought most of his imported dogs.

His success as a breeder stemmed from his thorough knowledge of the breed, clear idea of the ideal he wanted to achieve, and readiness to acknowledge weaknesses and faults in his own dogs and go elsewhere to compensate for these deficiencies. He never hesitated to admit that a planned breeding did not work out as he had hoped. He never hesitated to use a stud from another American breeder on one of his bitches if he felt the dog would improve the breed better than any stud of his own. Kinney's single purpose as a breeder was to produce the best quality Old English Sheepdog. Many have claimed to

Ch. Kinnelon Milkmaid,
owned by Morris Kinney.

Ch. Kinnelon Mother Carey, bred and owned by Mr. Kinney.

have, but few have had the open-minded, candid honesty that characterized Kinney's efforts to produce the best possible Old English, irrespective of where he had to go to get what he wanted. Kinney never bred a dog and bitch that had the same fault, however minor. No dog was used for breeding unless it was basically sound and typy as he understood the standard. Kinney did not believe that any breeding system could be successful of itself, but that with care, good dogs bred to good dogs would produce good dogs. He did not inbreed closely. He never had a father-to-daughter or sister-to-brother mating. Not because he opposed such breedings, but because he never felt he had the animals with which to make such a match. He seldom made a complete outcross. His dogs were usually descended from the same animals in the second and third generations of their pedigrees.

Kinney showed his dogs regularly. He had his share of winners, but he was not primarily interested in winnings or show records. Frequently, he did not bother to attend shows at all, although he had his kennel man on hand with a full complement of Kinnelon entries. Between 1914 and 1924, 43 Old English Sheepdogs made AKC championships. Kinney owned nine of them or slightly more than 20% of the total for the years he actively exhibited. Four of his champions, Night Rider, Tip Top Weather, Shepton Spark, and Elusive Tramp were imports, only Elusive Tramp being a bitch. The other five, Kinnelon Kitty Ann, K. Mother Carey, K. Selection, K. Hallowe'en, and K. Tower, as well as many winners for others, were homebreds. Over the years he had a succession of wins at Westminster. When the Old English Sheepdog Club of America began holding its own specialty shows, largely because of Kinney's efforts, his dogs won at them.

Morris Kinney began importing Old English to the United States in the summer of 1912, after one of his many trips to England. His first import was the bitch Falcon Lassie bred by W. Burgoyne by Falcon Valentine out of Arklowe Marguerite, whelped January 1, 1909. This bitch was typical of every Sheepdog Kinney bought in England in the next decade. She was a mature dog, proven as a winner and producer, and in Kinney's opinion best suited for producing the sound, typy dogs he wanted.

In terms of their impact on the breed the most important Bobtails Kinney imported were the dogs Night Rider and Tip Top Weather and the bitches Wangler and Minikin. As Watch Boy and Young Watch had been of fundamental importance to the breed before the turn of the century and Ch. Stylish Boy and Ch. Shepton Hero and Ch. Brentwood Hero had been in the first decade or so of the century, so Ch. Night Rider and Ch. Tip Top Weather were the most significant studs of the World War I period. Night Rider was bred by E. C.

Young, by Ch. Brentwood Hero out of Lady Rider. Through Brentwood Hero he was descended from Stylish Boy and in turn Young Watch and Watch Boy. Lady Rider was a granddaughter of Ch. Captain Rough Weather through her sire Rough Rider. Captain Rough Weather was in turn descended from Watch Boy. Lady Rider's dam, Clatford Nella, was descended from Stracathro Bouncing Bob, Watch Boy's sire. Kinney bought Night Rider because of the quality of his get. In the United States he produced numerous winners for Kinnelon and others. Night Rider's last Kinnelon litter was out of Wangler, whelped August 9, 1919. It included the dog Kinnelon Tower and the bitch Kinnelon Hallowe'en.

Hallowe'en was regarded as the best Old English bitch, and possibly the best Old English Sheepdog, in the United States in the early twenties. She was Best of Breed at Westminster in 1923, and Best of Breed at the OESCA specialty shows in 1923 and 1924. Only three bitches have ever gone Best of Breed at OESCA specialty shows, Hallowe'en is the only one to do so twice.

Kinnelon Tower had an interesting early history. Kinney had decided to give one of the dogs from Wangler's litter to his manager's parents, who operated a large farm in Iowa. As puppies Kinnelon Rider was considered the most promising and Tower was sent to Iowa to learn to work. Three years later Dallstrom visited his parents and was overcome by Tower's potential as a show dog and stud. He brought him back to Kinnelon. Tower excelled in the show ring and at stud. He produced many winners, including the all-breed Best in Show winners Cliffwold Sweet William, Cliffwold Minstrel Boy, and Kinnelon Scally Wag, Tower, Tenacre Grenadier, Montford Marksman, and Beau Brummel were the four leading studs in the 1920s.

Scally Wag had a distinguished career in the show rings and at stud. He was whelped September 7, 1924 out of Minikin. Both Mrs. Wilbur Kirby Hitchcock and P. Hamilton Goodsell considered Scally Wag to be of too great potential for Kinney's own breeding to be sold. However, Kinney sold him to Mrs. Herbert Bennett of Hollywood, California. Mrs. Bennett showed him widely on the West Coast and used him at stud until his death in August 1937. Scally Wag was never defeated by an Old English after Mrs. Bennett acquired him, and seldom by any dog of any breed. He won many Bests in Show in California, including Santa Barbara three times. He was the sire of Mrs. Bennett's homebred Ch. Sunny Boy, many times a Group winner in the thirties and also widely used at stud. Scally Wag and Sunny Boy made many appearances in the movies, including prominently with Jean Harlow in "Bombshell". A number of contemporary West Coast OES can trace their ancestry to this father and son combination of the late twenties and thirties.

Mrs. Herbert Bennett with Ch. Blue Baron, Jr. and his brother White Baron.

Ch. Kinnelon Scally Wag, BIS winner of the '20s, bred by Morris Kinney and owned by Mrs. Bennett.

Jean Harlow, legendary Hollywood figure with two champions owned by Mrs. Bennett.

Ch. Tip Top Weather had a greater impact on the breed than Night Rider. It is possible to trace seven to fifteen generations of direct breeding to him on both sides of the Atlantic. Fezziwig Ceiling Zero's imported sire Farleyedene Bartholomew is the ninth generation of direct father-to-son breeding from Tip Top Weather. He appears many times over in the backgrounds of virtually all Downderry, Pastorale, and Pickhurst breeding. The major post-World War II European kennels, Reeuwijks and Shaggy Wonder, trace most of their stock back to him. The great imported Swedish stud of the late sixties, Unnesta Pim, is descended from Tip Top Weather many times over. Tip Top Weather was bred by one of the greatest early English breeders, Miss McTurk, by Typical Weather out of Clara. Typical Weather's sire was Storm Cloud who was by Rough Weather out of Fairweather, while his dam was sired by Stylish Boy. Clara was descended from the same basic stock to Stracathro Bouncing Bob as well. Kinney bought him when he was almost three years old. He had been widely used at stud in England. One of his English bred sons, Shepton Moonshine, was the most important English stud in the early twenties. In the United States, Tip Top Weather was successful at the shows and at stud. He was Winners Dog at Westminster in 1916, interrupting the otherwise complete dominance of the Morse dogs there between 1912 and 1918. His litter by Shepton Nancy, whelped May 25, 1915, was the first Kinnelon-registered litter of Old English Sheepdogs. He sired many winners and producers with the Kinnelon prefix, including: Kinnelon Bogey, Fascination, Speculation Selection, Kitty Ann, Aviator, Leader, Caboose, Stump, Cocktail, and Mother Carey. Tip Top Weather was the first OES stud to produce more than five champions in the United States.

The First World War caused severe dislocations for dog breeders in both the United States and England. The impact of the war on American breeders was principally to cut off the supply of new and valued imports from England. English breeders were of course severely limited by the prolonged nature of the war and its demand on all available resources and manpower. However, the First World War proved relatively mild in its impact on Bobtails in England as well as the United States, when compared to the crippling effects of World War II. If anything the first World War helped American Old English fanciers at least at the start. England went to war in the summer of 1914. It was nearly three years later, in the spring of 1917, that the United States became involved. During the early years of the war it was relatively easy for Americans, particularly wealthy ones like Kinney, to travel between England and the United States. This was especially true after Germany abandoned submarine warfare for the first time. The demands of the war both on economic resources and food as well as manpower forced many English breeders to curtail or even discontinue altogether their breeding programs. The United States proved a ready market for many English dogs. The severity of the war on the homefront combined with the willingness of such people as Kinney to pay large sums of money, accounts for their being able to obtain dogs that in normal times would have been unavailable at any price. Tip Top Weather was available only because of the war and Kinney's unrefusable offer. He is thought to have cost more than $4,000. With the German resumption of unlimited submarine warfare and American involvement it became impossible for private citizens to travel to England. The importation of dogs from England ceased for two years.

One of the most interesting dog stories that emerges from the First World War concerns a pair of American-bred Old English Sheepdogs, Haig and Pershing. Both dogs were bred by their owner, Mrs. Walter H. Colverd of Sausalito, California, the picturesque bayside community across the Golden Gate bridge from San Francisco. Mrs. Colverd was the first West Coast OES fancier. Her Almonte kennels had most of the "firsts" for Sheepdogs in California, including the first champions, Shepton Lassie and her son John Bull in 1917. Mrs. Colverd's puppy, Prince Chap O'Windsor was the first OES to win a Group in California, as well as the first and virtually only OES puppy ever to win a Group. His victory came at the Del Monte Kennel Club show on June 7 and 8, 1925, when he was just off the train from the East. He went from the six-to-nine-month puppy dog class to first in the Working Group. Unfortunately Chap and 15 of Mrs. Colverd's other Bobtails died in an outbreak of distemper in her kennel in 1926. She rebuilt and was on the way to establishing a major breeding kennel on the West Coast, when she was struck and killed by an automobile on December 27, 1927.

Mrs. Colverd's first OES was named Rags. He was bred by H. Moss of St. Kilda, Victoria, Australia, whelped on January 9, 1912, and was the first Australian bred Bobtail to end up in the United States. Rags was the sire of both Pershing and Haig. Haig was whelped December 28, 1916 out of Shepton Lassie, who was descended from Watchboy and Young Watch on both sides of her pedigree. Pershing was two and a half months younger than Haig. At six months of age Mrs. Colverd sent them to England to be trained and used in the war effort. They were both trained as ambulance dogs. In this work they carried a saddle-pack of emergency medical supplies and stimulants. They were sent into the "no man's land," between

47

the Allied and German entrenchments. They were trained to seek out the bodies of wounded and dead English soldiers. If the victim was conscious he could use the supplies the dogs carried in their backpacks. The dogs were trained to distinguish between a live but unconscious soldier and a dead one. They were taught to snatch a button from a wounded man's uniform. From a dead man they were to take a helmet or cap: if that was gone a shred of uniform, or if the victim had been stripped of his uniform, a stick, stone or even a mouthful of dirt. With the button or other article the dog would return to the ambulance it worked from and guide stretcher bearers back to the victim.

Haig was credited with saving 700 lives in this manner and Pershing with 362. Pershing was wounded three times and Haig twice. Both Haig and Pershing were returned to Mrs. Colverd in California in 1918, in rundown, but otherwise decent shape. In California the dogs made an extended motor tour raising money for the Blue Cross relief effort for animals victimized by the war. They raised tens of thousands of dollars and along the way were initiated into the Elks, Redmen, Pocahontas, Brotherhood of the Methodist Church, Women's Temperance Union, White Ribbon, and the Boy Scouts among other clubs, orders, and associations.

There were almost no other Old English Sheepdogs anywhere on the West Coast until the 1960s. Mrs. W. A. Ward of Diablo, California, acquired stock from Mrs. Colverd and the East in 1919, and was active as a breeder for a few years. Ward-bred dogs, out of Colverd Mary, were sold East to Leo Singer and then to Mrs. Joseph Urban, wife of the internationally famous architect of the 1920s. Mrs. Urban became closely associated with Mrs. Wilbur Kirby Hitchcock, and was active as a breeder and exhibitor throughout the '20s. She was a member of the Board of Governors of the OESCA from the mid-twenties into the mid-thirties. Her bitch, Pepi, by Desyre out of Colverd Mary, produced several champions and other winners and producers in a number of breedings to Mrs. Hitchcock's studs. By Beau Brummel, she produced Diva, Beau, Fritz, Frouzy, Rowdy, Pepita, and Sweet Miss Mary. A 1924 litter by Happy Boy included Sir Joseph and Lady Mary, both of whom Mrs. Urban kept herself. They swept the top places at the 1926 OESCA specialty, with Sir Joseph going Winners Dog and Best of Breed and Lady Mary going Winners Bitch. Pepi was an all-white bitch, having only a dark right ear.

Chris Shuttleworth, the professional handler from Anoakin Kennels in southern California, and later all-breed judge, was another of the few Old English fanciers on the West Coast. He owned and showed to their championships Bushnell True and Bushnell Bobs, both of whom he had acquired from the Bushnell kennels of Bushnell, Illinois. In the spring of 1922, Shuttleworth acquired, apparently on Morris Kinney's recommendation, the prominent English stud Good Morn. Good Morn was bred by Mrs. F. Gatehouse, whelped June 11, 1920, by Raker Boy out of Betsy Day. Betsy Day was one of the most prolific English Bobtail bitches. As early as 1915, she had produced May Morn Weather, who was subsequently imported and widely shown by William A. Jamison. Raker Boy was a grandson of Ch. Brentwood Hero, while Betsy Day was a granddaughter of Ch. Shepton Hero. Shuttleworth offered Good Morn at public stud for $50. Kinnelon Scally Wag and his son Sunny Boy were handled to their victories by Shuttleworth. These few people, together with Mrs. E. F. Sager who owned and showed the imported dog Montford Monitor to Group wins at Stockton and Modesto, California in August and September 1927, and Mrs. J. M. Fitzpatrick of Portland, Oregon who acquired a few of William Jamison's Bobtails, constituted the only Sheepdog people on the West Coast before World War II. In 1932 Hazel Foster Collins of the still active Driftwood Kennels in Washington acquired her first Old English, Blue Boy, by Big Brutus out of Comic, whelped February 28, 1932.

The ending of the First World War was followed by a flurry of activity by American OES fanciers. Kinney was able to make his customary annual trips to England for the first time in two years, and he acquired a number of bitches. William A. Jamison's Willinez Weather kennel, P. Hamilton Goodsell's Tenacre kennel, and Mrs. Wilbur Kirby Hitchcock also came to prominence in this period.

Willinez Weather Kennels

Jamison was a wealthy merchant from northern New Jersey. He maintained an extensive kennel in Holmdel. Jamison's Willinez Weather kennel name, officially granted to him by the American Kennel Club in 1920, was prominently associated with Old English Sheepdogs, Airedales, and Wire Fox Terriers until the middle 1920s. Jamison's personal contact with his dogs was limited. The decisions concerning the dogs and the kennel facility were made by his employees Charles Holmwood, Fred Leighton, and according to Freeman Lloyd, Ada F. Coombs. Coombs was an officer of the OESCA for several years. She was vice-president in 1924. Jamison's contribution to Old English Sheepdogs was quite significant, especially so in light of the fact he was active for less than five years. Ill health and his death in the mid-20s led to the kennel being gradually dispersed, with the Sheepdogs going first.

Aside from the quality of the dogs Jamison imported and bred,

49

their success in the show ring, and the general use of his studs by other breeders, the name Weather in large part accounts for his continued widespread reputation. Weather figured prominently as a name in the Old English Sheepdog world in England and the United States from the turn of the century to the Second World War. The originator of the Weather Kennel prefix and its rightful owner was the celebrated English breeder and exhibitor, Mrs. Fare Fosse. Mrs. Fosse owned, bred, and showed a succession of great dogs from the later 1890s through the 1930s. Her stock figures prominently in the background of all early English and American breeders. All contemporary Old English Sheepdogs can be traced back to one or another of the important dogs she had over the years. Jamison got his first Bobtails from Mrs. Fosse and at the same time borrowed her kennel name, added Willinez and registered it with the AKC. For the most part Jamison's dogs were registered without the Willinez part of his official kennel name. The use of Weather shows up again on this side of the Atlantic in the thirties when the Canadian, Leonard Collins, bred and registered Ideal Weather. Ideal Weather was descended from Mrs. Fosse's dogs, but not entitled to the name either.

Jamison was active as an exhibitor and breeder for little more than five years, between 1918 and 1923. He bred four litters, whelped May 18, 1918, February 16 and 25, 1920, and January 15, 1921. He owned five OES champions, two imports and three of his own breeding. He bought and bred several champions for others. His dogs were actively shown for little more than three years, between Westminster 1920 and Westminster 1923. In that time he dominated the breed. At the 1920 Westminster show four littermates of his breeding. International Weather, Clovelly Weather, Victory Weather, and Lucky's Fair Weather went respectively Winners Dog, Reserve Dog, Winners Bitch, and Reserve Bitch. Only the Reserve Bitch was not actually owned by Jamison. In 1921 at Westminster, Clovelly Weather was again Reserve Dog, while his new import bitch, May Morn Weather was Winners, with Victory Weather, Reserve. In 1922 at the Garden, International Weather was Winners Dog and May Morn was Winners Bitch for the second year in a row. The Reserve Bitch was Morris Kinney's Kinnelon Hallowe'en, one of the few times she was beaten by any Sheepdog. In 1923, International Weather was Winners Dog at Westminster for a third time. Clovelly Weather made one of the last appearances of a Willinez Weather Old English when he went Winners Dog at Westminster in 1925.

Jamison's dogs, International Weather and New Jersey Weather were Winners Dog and Best of Breed at the first two Old English Sheepdog Club of America specialty shows in 1921 and 1922 respectively. The first OESCA specialty shows were held as independent specialties in conjunction with an all-breed show. So that in the morning the dogs would compete at the specialty show, and then in the afternoon at the all-breed show under a different judge. At the 1922 OESCA specialty show held in Tuxedo Park, N.Y. on October 7, New Jersey Weather was Winners Dog and Best of Breed for five points in the morning under Tyler Morse. Later that day at the Tuxedo Kennel Club's show under J. B. Cooper, New Jersey Weather was again Winners Dog and Best of Breed for an additional five points. Under Cooper, Jamison's bitch Victory Weather moved up to Winners for five points, after have gone third in the Open class under Morse at the specialty show.

Few people in any breed have owned animals of such uniform high quality as Jamison. He imported four dogs from England. The first two were brother and sister littermates, New Jersey Weather and Lucky Weather bred by Mrs. Fare Fosse, whelped June 28, 1916 by Weather Optimist out of Phyllis Fair Weather. Weather Optimist was a grandson of Ch. Brentwood Hero, while Phyllis Fair Weather was descended from Watch Boy and Young Watch. Jamison bred Lucky Weather to Morris Kinney's Ch. Tip Top Weather. From this litter came four champions. In 1920, Jamison imported the bitch May Morn Weather, bred by Mrs. G. B. Allen of Manchester, England by Tip Top Weather out of Betsy Day, whelped May 17, 1915. Tip Top Weather was imported by Kinney shortly after he serviced Betsy Day. Betsy Day was sired by Kinney's first great English import, Ch. Night Rider, while her dam, Clatford Psyche, was a daughter of Ch. Shepton Hero.

Jamison imported one other Bobtail, Willinez Weather Bill Sykes, bred by G. F. Wilkinson, whelped June 9, 1919 by Night Raider out of Stourton. Jamison sold Bill Sykes as soon as he arrived in this country, and he became the foundation stud of the first Far Western OES kennel. This was Mr. and Mrs. Russell K. Daughtery's Russber Klimate Kennel located at Colorado Springs, Colorado. They showed and finished Bill Sykes as well as Fairweather Klimate (in 1922), Russber Klimate Bill Sykes (1923) Russber Klimate Peggy (1926), and Russber Klimate Nicholas Nickleby (1927). Nicholas Nickleby was Best in Show at the Nebraska Kennel Club show held at Lincoln, Nebraska on September 9, 10 and 11, 1925. The kennel was sold to Mr. and Mrs. Spencer Penrose in 1926, who continued to employ Daughtery's kennel manager, Thomas Pierrepont. In 1926 and '27, Nicholas Nickleby and Peggy were widely shown in the Great Plains area and had many wins including Best in Shows by Peggy at Denver in April and Nicholas at Pueblo in September.

Lucky Weather's litter by Tip Top Weather contained the four champions International Weather, Clovelly Weather, Victory Weather, and Lucky's Fair Weather, as well as the stud Pennsylvania Weather. International, Clovelly, Pennsylvania and Jamison's imported New Jersey Weather were all widely used at stud. It is to these dogs through the breeding of P. Hamilton Goodsell and Mrs. Wilbur Kirby Hitchcock, and later Thomas W. Barr of Lyndhurst and the still active Amblehurst kennels that the longest line of American-bred dogs can be readily traced. Many contemporary American Old English kennel prefixes including Amblehurst, Double JJ, Downeylane, Greyfriars, Lillibrad, Shaggy-bag, and Tamara, among others can be traced directly back to one or another of these dogs and through them to Young Watch and Watch Boy. Lucky Weather's litter was considered one of the best litters of any breed of purebred dog whelped in the United States at the time. Jamison kept all the dogs in the litter except the bitch Lucky's Fair Weather, who was sold to Ernest P. Andrews. Andrews' Amberley kennels in Detroit, Michigan was one of the first Bobtail kennels in the Middle West. Andrews showed Lucky's Fair Weather extensively, finished her championship and produced many winners and producers out of her by his stud Andy, including John Halifax Gentleman, Amberley Country Girl, Amberley Shepherdess, Lady Halifax, and Lady Peggy.

Tenacre Kennels

Toward the end of the First World War one of the great figures in the history of American Old English Sheepdogs enlarged his activities. This was P. Hamilton Goodsell, who with his son P. Hamilton Goodsell, Jr. registered their kennel, Tenacre, with the American Kennel Club in 1918. Tenacre was Goodsell's estate in White Plains, Westchester County, New York. Goodsell, like his friend Morris Kinney, was a wealthy traveler. Few people have had the experience in Old English Sheepdogs and purebred dogs in general that Goodsell had in more than 50 years of continuous activity. He had Sheepdogs in England beginning in 1892. One of the last Bobtails of his breeding, Tenacre Heather, owned by Mrs. Laura Dohring, was Winners Bitch at the 1944 Old English Sheepdog Club of America specialty show. Goodsell was an officer of the OESCA for more than 20 years between World War I and World War II, during most of those years serving as president. He collected and published OESCA yearbooks annually in the early twenties, and after a ten year hiatus put out another yearbook in 1935. He succeeded Morris Kinney as honorary president of the OESCA for life, until his death in the early fifties. He was a director of the American Kennel Club, eventually becoming its first vice-president, and no doubt would have been the next president if he had not been forced into a semi-retirement as the result of an injury. Throughout the thirties he wrote a nationally syndicated newspaper column on purebred dogs. Goodsell was also a widely respected judge, doing Old English at Westminster in 1923. He was widely sought after as a judge throughout the twenties, when he was no longer exhibiting.

Goodsell was the first major figure in American Old English Sheepdogs that not only bred and owned the dogs, but conditioned and showed them himself. As a handler he won many Bests in Show, as well as Best of Breed at four consecutive OESCA specialty shows with three different dogs. His homebred Ch. Tenacre Grenadier was the first Old English Sheepdog in the United States to be entirely owner-conditioned-and-handled to a Best in Show win, the victory coming in August 1924 at the Southampton Kennel Club all-breed event under judge Theodore Offerman. Goodsell's contributions to the breed as importer, handler, club officer, judge, and writer were tremendous. They might have been greater, except that he was already into his middle years when he became active after World War I, and in 1928, he suffered a severe injury to his face that eventually forced him into semi-retirement in 1930. He was injured when he fell over his 11-year-old household companion Tenacre Blueberry in the dark and struck his face on the edge of a table.

Like virtually all other Old English stock in the United States and England, Goodsell's basic breeding Bobtails were descended from Watch Boy and Young Watch through Stylish Boy, Shepton Hero, and Brentwood Hero. Tenacre's basic breeding stock was assembled during the First World War from O. C. Harriman, the Tyler Morses, and Morris Kinney. The first Bobtails acquired were the bitches Shepton Jessica and her daughter Lady Diana from Harriman. Lady Diana must rate as one of the most remarkable Old English bitches yet produced.

Goodsell like Kinney, Jamison, and Mrs. Wilbur Kirby Hitchcock consistently bred high quality Sheepdogs. His breedings were always matings of dogs and bitches descended from the same general dogs, Brentwood Hero, Shepton Hero and so on, two or three generations removed. More than any other prominent breeder Goodsell went outside his kennel for stud service for his bitches. He kept a few high quality studs, which he used infrequently himself, but were widely used by others. Goodsell felt that a good breeding kennel was built upon systematic breeding of high quality bitches to the best studs available. He felt few studs were of sufficiently high quality to be used at stud, and was more than ready to admit that the best studs for his bitches were usually not his own.

The most important homebred Tenacre Bobtail was the stud

Tenacre Grenadier by Mrs. Hitchcock's Lord Handsome out of Lady Diana. Lord Handsome's dam, Lady Jessica, was a litter sister to Lady Diana. Aside from being the first owner-handled Best in Show winning OES in the United States, Grenadier had a succession of other important wins, including the Working Group at the Eastern Dog Club's show in Boston in 1928, among four times he placed in the Group there. He was also fourth in the Working Group at the only dog show ever sponsored by the American Kennel Club in Philadelphia in 1926. Before his death on June 12, 1931 Grenadier was widely used at stud.

Goodsell was out of the country traveling for 18 months in 1925 and 1926. Much of the time was spent in England visiting various kennels and evaluating the breed there. He was invited to judge the English OES club's specialty show. Goodsell returned to the United States in September 1926, with four Bobtails, the dog Montford Marksman and the bitches Elkington Belle and Lady Elkington for himself and the bitch Lady Grizel of Brushwood for the W. Fitch Ingersolls of the Shelterfield kennels. In a lengthy comparison of the breed in the mother country and the United States in the midtwenties, Goodsell concluded English dogs were better in the "hindquarters, texture of coat, depth of brisket, spring of ribs, soundness and action," while American dogs were better in "head, foreface, bone, conformation and markings, disposition, and eye color." He thought that many of the English dogs were ''unreliable as far as disposition goes, except of course with their owners." Although he also added that the English dogs were used as general purpose farm dogs for the most part, one of their tasks being to keep an eye on the place and suspiciously give any strangers the once over. The four Old English Goodsell brought back were all sired by Ch. Elkington Squire, one of the most noted winners and producers of the twenties in England. He was a grandson of Tip Toes, who was out of Tip Top Weather and hence through him to the Watch Boy-Young Watch dogs. He was also descended from the Watch Boy stock on the dam's side of his pedigree.

From 1927 to 1931, Goodsell's OES were Best of Breed at every OESCA specialty show (there was none held in 1928). Montford Marksman was Best of Breed in 1927 and 1930. At the 1929 OESCA specialty Goodsell's bitch Lady Elkington was Winners Bitch and Best of Breed, at the only show at which she was ever shown. In 1931, the Shelterfield Kennels-bred, Goodsell-owned bitch, Shelterfield Furbelow was Best of Breed. Furbelow was sired by Tenacre Grenadier out of Lady Grizel of Brushwood. In her entire career she lost only twice to other Sheepdogs. At the 1927 OESCA specialty show, before Goodsell acquired her, she was third in her puppy class. Her

Ch. Montford Marksman, outstanding stud of the late '20s,
owned by P. Hamilton Goodsell.

Ch. Happy Boy, 1929 Specialty
winner, bred and owned by Mrs.
Wilbur Hitchcock.

Sir Joseph, Specialty winner owned
by Mrs. Joseph Urban.

Ch. Shelterfield Furbelow, a top
bitch of the '30s, owned by Mr.
Goodsell.

other loss came at the 1936 OESCA specialty show, when at more than nine years of age she was first in Open bitches, and Reserve Winners to Mistress Quickly of Tenacre. This win came two years after she had broken her right hind leg. Goodsell thought she had the finest hindquarters of any Old English he ever saw. She lived to be nearly 15, dying in February 1941. She never produced any pups, although bred several times.

In September 1926, Goodsell had gone into Lincolnshire to the Home Farms of the squires of Elkington to see George F. Wilkinson. Wilkinson, like his father before him, was the shepherd of the Elkington estates. He was also one of the greatest breeders of Old English Sheepdogs in the breed's history. Ch. Elkington Squire was only the latest in a long string of great dogs he had produced. Dogs of his breeding were in every significant Old English breeding program in England and the United States from before the turn of the century until well after his death in 1931. Wilkinson had the two-and-a-half year old dog Montford Marksman on hand as a worker and stud. Goodsell saw in him the qualities he considered necessary in the United States, and persuaded Wilkinson to sell him the dog.

Montford Marksman together with Morris Kinney's Ch. Kinnelon Tower, Mrs. Wilbur Kirby Hitchcock's Ch. Beau Brummel, and Goodsell's Ch. Tenacre Grenadier were the most important American studs in the 1920s. They were all descended from the same early twentieth century greats, but only Marksman was imported. His breeder was O. Cameron, whelped April 29, 1924 by Ch. Elkington Squire out of Lady Bessa.

Goodsell called Marksman, "the greatest Bob I ever knew." When he left the United States he intended to look for a good English stud to service the high quality American-bred bitches being produced. He wrote of his thinking and search at the time, "I considered, and later the club (OESCA) came to agree with me, that we were producing a dog that, by its size, was straying from the type which was in the minds of those who drew up the original standard for the breed. Incidentally, one of those sponsors, Freeman Lloyd agreed with me."

Marksman was 24½ inches at the withers and weighed 70 pounds, dimensions Goodsell considered ideal for the breed. Marksman's speed, agility, and strength were remarkable. In addition to the incident with the German Shepherd mentioned in chapter one, Goodsell liked to tell how Marksman could "keep up with and outlast my boy's Russian Wolfhound, a breed noted for its speed." Marksman was shown a total of nine times in the United States. Six times he was Winners, Best of Winners, and Best of Breed. Included in his wins were two Old English Sheepdog Club of America specialty shows, a Westminster Group third, two other Group placements, and a

Best in Show all-breeds at the Long Island Kennel Club show held at Babylon, New York on September 2, 1929.

Shortly thereafter recurring difficulty, resulting from his fall the year before, forced Goodsell to largely disperse his kennel. He kept six dogs including Marksman, Tenacre Grenadier, Lady Elkington, and Shelterfield Furbelow. He had continued success at the OESCA specialty shows in 1930 and '31, but they were almost the only shows where he exhibited. He also resigned his first vice-presidency of the American Kennel Club, his judging license, and tried to retire from the presidency of the OESCA. He attended an occasional show and bred a rare litter throughout the '30s, but was never again active as a breeder or exhibitor on his earlier scale.

The Hitchcocks

Mrs. Wilbur Kirby Hitchcock of Pleasantville, New York was the third, along with Morris Kinney and P. Hamilton Goodsell, of the triumvirate of great American breeders that emerged from the First World War. Mrs. Hitchcock and her husband had careers in dogs similiar to Kinney and Goodsell. They were successful as exhibitors and breeders. They served the Old English Sheepdog Club of America in a number of capacities for more than twenty years. Mrs. Hitchcock was secretary of the OESCA from 1923 until her sudden death on September 9, 1937. In this capacity she wrote a column on Old English Sheepdogs for the *American Kennel Gazette* virtually every month from 1926 until her death. Wilbur Kirby Hitchcock served the OESCA as treasurer and AKC delegate from the mid-20s until the end of the Second World War. From 1930 until Mrs. Hitchcock's death they maintained the largest Sheepdog kennel ever assembled in the United States, with more than 60 dogs of all ages at their place. The Hitchcocks never registered a kennel name.

Mrs. Hitchcock was an able and respected judge, no doubt because of her bluntly-stated, strongly-held opinions. She was for American-bred Bobtails of correct working size and condition. Mrs. Hitchcock was the most outspoken critic of the tendency toward excessive size in the 1920s. She had no use for a Sheepdog that was more than 25 inches at the shoulder. She considered the top winning all-breed special of her good friend Mrs. Laura Dohring, Ch. Cliffwold Sweet William, faulty in type because he was 26 inches at the withers.

Between 1922 and 1937, Mrs. Hitchcock owned and finished 16 champions, Lord Handsome, My Delight, Blue Bells Lady, Little Boy Blue II, Winchester Boy, Lovely Weather, Beau Brummel, Lassie of the Farm, Lady Eve, Tenacre Lady Luck, Happy Boy, Sweet Miss Mary, Handsome Bobbie, Talisman, True Lady, and Raggedy Ann. None of them were imports. Ten of the 16 were bred by Mrs. Hitchcock. The ten homebred champions together with Lovely Weather, Lassie of the Farm, Tenacre Lady Luck, and Sweet Miss Mary were all sired by Hitchcock-owned-and-bred studs. The only dogs shown to championship by Mrs. Hitchcock that were not either sired by one of her studs or actually bred by her were Blue Bells Lady (whelped September 18, 1914) and Winchester Boy (whelped August 24, 1916), both bred by John Piorkovski, out of Blue Bell III by Ch. Ridgeleigh Hero. The average age of the 16 on completing their championships was six and a half years. Sweet Miss Mary, bred by Mrs. Joseph Urban (out of her Pepi by Beau Brummel) was whelped on May 25, 1921 and finished in August 1931, at ten years and three months. Hitchcock dogs were not shown until their mature merit could be evaluated. This meant dogs were not shown until they were proven sires of quality get. Most bitches as well were proven before being shown. At important shows, such as Westminster and OESCA specialty and supported shows, the Hitchcocks would enter in all classes, frequently 15 to 20 dogs. However, like Kinney and Goodsell, they were interested, at least until the 1930s, in shows as an opportunity to compare their dogs with other breeders', not in winning for its own sake.

While the importance of Mrs. Hitchcock's breeding in terms of its continuing impact on the breed was greatly diminished in the thirties, this is not to say she did not produce quality dogs. In the late spring and early summer of 1937, just three months before she died, Mrs. Hitchcock finished her bitches True Lady and Raggedy Ann, while her special Ch. Handsome Bobbie was holding his own in competition with some of the great Old English of all-time. True to her beliefs about showing, True Lady was nearly seven when she finished in the summer of 1937, having been whelped September 16, 1930. Raggedy Ann by Beau Gallant out of My Pretty Jane, both of whom were sired by Beau Brummel and owned and bred by Mrs. Hitchcock as well, was whelped April 13, 1932. Ann was never entered at a show until Morris and Essex 1937, when she was Winners Bitch for five points. A week later she was Winners Bitch at Greenwich and Longshore for two more five point majors and a championship, all in eight days and three shows.

Mrs. Hitchcock was past forty when she saw her first Old English Sheepdog on Riverside Drive in New York City in 1912. She thought the dog "looked like an overgrown Skye terrier." In the spring of 1913, she bought her first Sheepdog, Frouzy Bobbie, from his breeder Miss Elizabeth Philip of Claverack, New York. Bobbie was whelped November 30, 1912 by Rambling Robert out of Lady Bobbie. Rambling Robert was a direct descendant of Dr. Edwardes-Ker's stock of the 1880s, while Lady Bobbie was a grand-daughter of Watch

Mrs. Wilbur Kirby Hitchcock.

Mrs. Hitchcock's Ch. Beau Brummel.

Ch. Lassie of the Farm, owned by Mrs. Hitchcock.

Boy. In 1914, Mrs. Hitchcock bought the bitch, Lady Jessica, from O. C. Harriman. Jessica was a litter sister to Goodsell's Lady Diana, by Lord Hiddenbrook out of Shepton Jessica and a direct descendant of Stylish Boy, Young Watch, and Watch Boy on both sides of her pedigree. Frouzy Bobbie was bred to Jessica when she was nine months old, and the first of several litters from these two was whelped on November 9, 1914. From this litter came the champion studs Lord Handsome (finished in 1922) and Little Boy Blue II (finished in 1923). The dogs and bitches out of Frouzy Bobbie and Lady Jessica were the foundation of Mrs. Hitchcock's entire breeding program. At her death she was breeding from the great-great-grandchildren of her first two Bobtails, having owned and bred all the generations between herself.

In addition to the two champion sons noted above, Bobbie and Jessica were the grandparents of Mrs. Hitchcock's Chs. Beau Brummel, My Delight, and Lovely Weather, and the great-grandparents of her Chs. Happy Boy, Lady Eve, Lassie of the Farm, and Sweet Miss Mary. Lord Handsome and his two sons My Delight and Beau Brummel out of Blue Bell's Lady whelped August 10, 1918, were important studs in the late teens and twenties. Her most important stud of the later twenties was Happy Boy, whelped December 20, 1922 by Kinnelon Tower out of the Frouzy Bobbie-Lady Jessica granddaughter Dame Cleta. In the thirties her most important stud was Handsome Bobbie, whelped July 10, 1931 by Cliffwold True Knight out of Kinnelon Mona. Handsome Bobbie was a youngster by Mrs. Hitchcock's standards when he finished in the fall of 1933, at slightly more than two years of age. He was the youngest Bobtail Mrs. Hitchcock ever finished.

Over the years Mrs. Hitchcock's studs produced many winners and producers for others, including P. Hamilton Goodsell's Ch. Tenacre Grenadier, and Mrs. Joseph Urban's specialty winning littermates Sir Joseph and Lady Mary. However, in all her years as a breeder, during which time she produced more Old English Sheepdogs than any individual American breeder, she only bred one champion for someone other than herself. This was James T. Miller's Ch. Pickwick, by Master Bob out of Blue Blossom. Pickwick finished in 1937. Miller succeeded P. Hamilton Goodsell as president of the OESCA in 1938.

During her career Mrs. Hitchcock had a succession of wins at Westminster and OESCA specialty shows, as well as at most of the important all-breed events of the day. Beau Brummel was Winners Dog and Best of Breed at Westminster in 1926. Her great winning bitch, Lassie of the Farm, out of Viola by Beau Brummel, whelped July 30, 1922, was Winners Bitch at Westminster in 1926, 1928, and

1929. In 1929 she was also Best of Breed and fourth in the Working group there. Lassie is the only OES bitch to place in the Group at Westminster since the system of awarding four places was adopted in the mid-twenties. Lassie was the winning bitch at the 1927 OESCA specialty show, as well as the winner of the Working Group at that year's Morris and Essex event. Mrs. Hitchcock's first win at an OESCA specialty show was in 1923, when her dog My Delight was Winners. Her Happy Boy was Winners Dog at the 1929 specialty, and in 1936 her Ch. Handsome Bobbie was Winners Dog and Best of Breed.

Cliffwold Kennels

One of the Hitchcocks' closest friends in Sheepdogs was Mrs. Laura Dohring. Mrs. Dohring was one of the most important exhibitors and breeders of Sheepdogs in the twenties, although not on the same scale as Kinney, Goodsell, or Mrs. Hitchcock. She served the OESCA in a variety of capacities in the twenties and thirties, principally as a member of the Board of Governors. From 1942 until 1943, she was the secretary of the OESCA. In the fall of 1929, Mrs. Dohring moved in, dogs and all, with the Hitchcocks in Pleasantville. She continued to live at the Hitchcock place after Mrs. Hitchcock's death in 1937. In 1946 she and Wilbur Kirby Hitchcock married. Mrs. Dohring's kennel was established in 1919, at her home in Edgewater-on-Hudson, New Jersey. She purchased her first dogs from John Drew. Drew was the breeder of Mrs. Dohring's Ch. Donna of Cliffwold, whelped May 8, 1917 by Beaver Brook Conqueror out of Sandy Point Lass. Conqueror was sired by Ch. Brentwood Hero, while Lass was a granddaughter of Ch. Stylish Boy through her sire Sandy Point Rags. Mrs. Dohring was the first great woman handler of Sheepdogs. She was also the best conditioner and groomer of the twenties. Her dogs were flawlessly presented in outstanding condition. Many of the prominent newspaper and magazine columnists of the day felt Mrs. Dohring's Bobtails, particularly Chs. Cliffwold Sweet William and Cliffwold Minstrel Boy, deserved higher Group placings or even Bests in Show on their presentation and perfect conditioning alone. Mrs. Dohring handled Donna to her championship in 1921. In 1925, when nearly eight years old, Donna was Winners Bitch and Best of Breed at Westminster.

Donna produced one of the great litters of any breed during the 1920s by Morris Kinney's Ch. Kinnelon Tower on January 7, 1924. From this litter came Mrs. Dohring's champions Cliffwold Sweet William, Minstrel Boy, and C. Blue-eyed Mary, as well as Sir Jasper of Cliffwold, owned by the famous opera singer, Mrs. Idelle Patterson. Sir Jasper was a multiple Group winner, including the then important shows at Southampton and Storm King, New York on August 6th and 27th, 1927. Blue-eyed Mary, Sweet William, and Minstrel Boy all made important wins with Mrs. Dohring handling. Mary was Winners Bitch at the 1930 OESCA specialty show. Sweet William was Best of Breed and fourth in the Group at Westminster in 1927, while Minstrel Boy was Best of Breed and second in the Group in 1928. Sweet William and Minstrel Boy were both multiple all-breed Best in Show winners. They combined as a brace to win the Working Group at the 1928 Westminster show, although Sweet William was all-white headed and larger than the dark-eared Minstrel Boy.

Sweet William was the largest Old English Sheepdog in the United States, at least in the show rings, in the 1920s. He was 26 inches at the withers and weighed 90 pounds. Sweet William was recognized as a flashy, basically correct Bobtail by the principal authorities of the day including Mrs. Wilbur Kirby Hitchcock, P. Hamilton Goodsell, Morris Kinney, and Freeman Lloyd, but they considered his smaller brother Minstrel Boy to be the better of the two dogs, because Sweet William was faulty in type because of his size. Every breeder of the day, until the post-World War II period, considered overall size an important aspect of correct type. Writing in December 1926, Mrs. Hitchcok said of the two brothers, "(I) believe that Minstrel Boy, on account of his smaller size, is more the desired type of Sheepdog, than his better known brother Sweet William." If it had not been for Sweet William's obvious merits the committee of the OESCA that reviewed the standard in the spring of 1927, would have either recommended a height of 25 inches as a maximum, or made anything over 26 inches disqualifying. While Sweet William was not disqualified by the new height recommendation adopted in the fall of 1927, Mrs. Dohring decided to stop showing him except at Westminster or specialty shows and then only in special classes or as a brace with Minstrel Boy. Minstrel Boy was then widely shown, and did all-breed Group and Best-in Show winning as had Sweet William.

Ch. Cliffwold Sweet William, BIS winner, bred and owned by Mrs. Laura Dohring. At 26″, Sweet William was the largest Old English of the twenties.

Ch. Donna of Cliffwold, foundation dam of Cliffwold Kennels, bred by John Drew.

Ch. Cliffwold Minstrel Boy, BIS winner, bred and owned by Mrs. Dohring.

Mrs. Lewis Renner (in dark dress near center of photo) judging Old English Sheepdogs in England in the 1950s. The dog third from left is Farleydene Bartholomew, who Mrs. Renner put up as a puppy, and who was latter to play so important a part in the development of the Van Rensselaers' Fezziwig Kennels in America.

The Middle Years

AMERICAN interest in purebred dogs began in the late nineteenth century. From the beginning, English experience and procedures served as models for the American fancy. This was true for the Old English Sheepdog as a breed, as well as for most other breeds, and for the world of dog shows. American dog shows originated as copies of English shows. The style and emphasis of American shows gradually changed during the first three decades of the twentieth century, but as a sport, still closely resembled English practice and tradition in the middle-twenties. In the late twenties a series of changes took place in the world of American shows that gradually transformed them, so that by the end of the Second World War the nature of American shows was considerably different from English. The easiest way to characterize these changes is the word professionalization.

Dog shows were always intended to be part spectacle and part sport, as well as being an opportunity for breeders to gather under an impartial eye and have the merits of their breeding evaluated. There have always been sportsmen in the world of dog shows who support winners, and are not actively involved as breeders. However, until the middle 1920s the emphasis of dog shows was overwhelmingly on the breed ring. Few shows offered Best in Show judging. Where Best in Show judging was offered, the method of selection was much different from today's procedures. Best in Show judging was open to any champion of record, although attaining a championship was considerably more difficult than today. The most important wins at a dog show were Winners Dog and Winners Bitch. Champions were shown in the Open classes until the late twenties, and continued to be shown in the Open class although less and less frequently through the thirties. This was similar to English competition for challenge certificates to the present day. A top winning dog or bitch could prevent other deserving dogs from acquiring the necessary wins to finish a championship. This fact, combined with the relatively small number of shows and the difficulty of traveling, makes it impossible to adequately compare show records or numbers of champion get of the breed's greats before the Second World War and today. As late as 1927, Mrs. Laura Dohring offered a fifty dollar cash prize for the Old English dog or bitch winning the most points during the calendar years 1927 and 1928. The winner was Mrs. Wilbur Kirby Hitchcock's Ch. Lassie of the Farm with 29 points. Mrs. Dohring's Ch. Cliffwold Minstrel Boy was runner-up with 21 points.

The variety group classification system as it currently exists did not evolve until the twenties. In the middle-twenties the system of awarding four places in each Group, and from the Group winners selecting a single Best in Show winner developed. The American Kennel Club in publishing official show results was slow to give its unqualified sanction to this new development. The AKC's traditional emphasis was on individual breeds, not the more glamourous, but less important in terms of a breed's welfare, winning of Groups and Best in Shows. Beginning in the mid-twenties the AKC gave official sanction to this new trend in the world of dog shows by publishing results beyond breed winners. At first only the Best in Show winner was listed. This started with the 1925 issues of the *American Kennel Gazette*. In 1927 the *Gazette* began publishing winners in the variety Groups, but not until seven years later, with the listing of the first 1934 all-breed shows, were all Group placings and the Best in Show winner published in the *Gazette*.

Hand in hand with this development was the increased professionalization of presentation and grooming of all-breeds. Dogs that required grooming, from Terriers to Poodles to Old English Sheepdogs, had to be more carefully prepared for the show ring. Beginning in the twenties and throughout the thirties this trend continued. A new type of professional dog man developed along with this trend. There had always been professional handlers. However, for the most part these men were associated with one kennel, and perhaps a few breeds, as kennel manager. Among their responsibilities was showing the dogs. Increasingly handlers emerged who worked for many clients handling a wide variety of breeds. This trend was officially sanctioned by the American Kennel Club with its decision to license handlers, and the formation of a professional handlers' association.

These new trends coupled with other factors had a major impact on Old English Sheepdogs. As one of the hairy breeds, increased emphasis on grooming and presentation, of course, meant that Bobtail fanciers would have to be more careful in preparing their dogs for the ring. Before Mrs. Durham-Waite of the Downderry Kennels in England and Mrs. Lewis Roesler of the Merriedip Kennels in the United States it was extremely uncommon for a Bobtail to be touched with a scissors. Not even the feet were trimmed to make a neater appearance. Initially the greater emphasis on presentation meant OES were made neater for the ring. They were not shaped. Mrs. Roesler played a major role in improving the presentation of OES in the United States, but she was an outspoken critic of trimming the rear, let alone shaping the neck, head, shoulders, and so on.

A second development in OES, dating from the twenties, was the disappearance of fanciers who had familiarity with the breed as workers. This was true on both sides of the Atlantic, but in England the breed remained a general purpose farm dog much longer. In the United States the breed had never actually been used for work, although scattered here and there were instances where Bobtails had earned their keep as something more than companions. American fanciers of the first three decades of the twentieth century were familiar with the requirements for a working dog and with the working OES of England. It was these American fanciers, the last actually aware of the requirements for a working Bobtail through knowledge of farm conditions and the breed's working traits in England, that undertook a thorough investigation of the standard in 1927, with the primary intention of stemming the increase in size. The emphasis on Group and Best in Show judging in the twenties had accelerated the tendency toward breeding larger Bobtails. A big Sheepdog was a flashier, more impressive sight in Group and Best in Show judging.

The decision to review the standard was not lightly undertaken. It was discussed at the Old English Sheepdog Club of America's annual meeting in the fall of 1926, but no definite decision was made. All members were then given the opportunity to express their opinions in response to a letter sent out by the secretary. Mrs. Hitchcock publicly discussed the thinking of the club in her column in the *American Kennel Gazette* in the fall of 1926, and throughout the actual process of review in 1927. The decision to review the standard was officially made in conjunction with a special meeting of the OESCA held at Westminster in February 1927. A committee was appointed to review the standard, take the matter up with the English Club and English breeders, and then make recommendations to the OESCA as a whole at the annual meeting in 1927.

The committee appointed to review the standard was one of the best informed panels ever assembled on both the Old English Sheepdog and purebred dogs in general. Mrs. Wilbur Kirby Hitchcock was appointed chairman, and charged with the responsibility of conducting all correspondence and keeping the membership of the OESCA informed as to the committee's activities and decisions. The other members of the committee were P. Hamilton Goodsell, Morris Kinney, and Walter J. Graham. The committee had nearly 100 years experience in the breed between them. Graham in addition to having had and raised OES for years was an expert on dog behavior and training. He had worked on canine intelligence and trainability, using specifically Old English and their herding instincts and abilities. He later published his ideas in the February 1931 *American Kennel Gazette*. Graham, Kinney, and Goodsell had all served several terms on the Board of Directors of the American Kennel Club and on its various special committees. Goodsell and Graham were both officers of the AKC. All four committee members were licensed judges of the breed.

The committee agreed that for the most part the standard was perfectly acceptable as it read. The standard called for a sound, balanced dog of sufficient bone and substance to work sheep or cattle in a wide variety of terrains and climatic conditions. In later years Mrs. Hitchcock remarked perhaps the committee should have been somewhat more careful in its review, inasmuch as the section on eye color refers to dogs having glaucous colored coats. Glaucous is sea green. Goodsell and Kinney gathered opinions from their numerous contacts among English breeders. Freeman Lloyd, who had written the standard while a young man, was still alive and active. He had long since become a permanent resident of the United States, and his views were sought out. In a long letter to the committee on March 23, 1927, Lloyd traced the development of the breed, who had owned them, and what use they had been put to in the eighties and nineties in England. He said, "I have observed that Bobtails have been getting very big, not to say oversized during the last fifteen years, or perhaps more. I declare that many Bobtails are oversized; and there is no reason for a big Bobtail."

The American Kennel Club in attempting to find a satisfactory way of classifying dogs for shows had divided all breeds into four classes in 1920, large, medium, small and cage-sized. The Old English Sheepdog was officially classified as a medium-sized breed along with the Basset Hound, Bulldog, Chow, and Poodle, among others. The committee found no breeder in England or the United States who felt the breed benefited from being higher than 25 inches and weighing more than 80 pounds. Of all the people contacted, only the versatile Henry Arthur Tilley was willing to permit a Bobtail of more than 26 inches under any circumstances. Tilley said the breed could and should tolerate Sheepdogs as tall as 28 inches and weighing as much as 100 pounds. Tilley also emphasized there was room in the breed for Sheepdogs as small as 18 inches and weighing less than 45 pounds. The OESCA committee did not agree with Tilley. They felt the breed should be taller than 22 inches, but less than 25. Only P. Hamilton Goodsell and Mrs. Wilbur Kirby Hitchcock were willing to admit a bitch as small as 20 inches. In making its recommendations to the OESCA membership the committee was divided at first in what to do. Initially the suggestion was discussed of stating a dog of more than 25 inches was objectionable. This was changed to suggesting any dog over 26 inches be disqualified. Finally the committee decided to recommend the sentence, *"A height of twenty-six inches or over for dogs or bitches to be considered objectionable and not to be encouraged."*

Because the committee felt this sentence was in part too much of a concession to the increase in size that had taken place during the twenties, they recommended it be put in the standard in italics. The committee's recommendations were unanimously adopted by the OESCA at its annual meeting in the fall of 1927. (It was to remain in the standard until October, 1953, when the club elected to remove it. The insertion of the size specification, and its subsequent removal, constitute the only two changes ever made in the standard in this country.)

The Old English Sheepdog Club of America was racked by disagreement among its members in the late twenties. These differences had nothing to do with the standard, but contributed to the isolation of the Hitchcock group and its control of the OESCA, which combined with World War II resulted in the club's virtual disappearance after Mrs. Hitchcock's death. At the annual meeting of the OESCA on October 31, 1929, P. Hamilton Goodsell felt compelled to read a harsh statement about the state of the club, before agreeing to serve another term as president. Goodsell noted, "There has been, for the past year or more, dissension in our club and a lack of co-operation among the exhibitors, several of them seeming to care more about having their individual dogs win at the shows than for the general good of the breed." Following a lengthy commentary on the problem Goodsell hoped, "that in (the) future all members (will) work together in harmony as was the case only a few years ago." It should be noted that the disruption within the Old English Sheepdog Club came at a time when the quality of Sheepdogs was higher than ever. In comparison to the few that were registered each year Bobtails were doing incredible all-breed winning. Difficulties in the OESCA were smoothed over but not righted.

The gradual disappearance of the old-timers that had carried the OESCA through the glory days of the twenties, resulted in a continued erosion of the club. The first OESCA specialty show had been held in 1921. They were held annually thereafter until 1931 except in 1925 and 1928. From 1931 until 1950 the OESCA sponsored specialty shows only three times, 1936, 1939, and 1944. At each show the turnout was good, but the impetus to keep the club functioning was not there. Fortunately, the activity of New England fanciers kept the breed on an even keel throughout the period the OESCA itself was virtually nonexistent.

The depression that so disrupted American life in the 1930s did not have as much impact on the Old English fancy as one might expect. To a large extent, the fact that the breed had never been very popular, but the fanciers that had existed were people of great wealth helped. Old English registrations and importations continued at the same pace throughout the thirties. The impact of the depression in England and the outbreak of war resulted in a sharp upturn in the number of Old English exported to the United States in the late thirties.

At shows Old English enjoyed a fantastic string of successes. At Westminster, Old English placed in or won the group in every year but three from 1927 until 1942. Elsewhere they did as well or better. An Old English Sheepdog, Ch. Ideal Weather, was Best in Show at the second largest show ever held in the western hemisphere, the 1938 Morris and Essex event with 4,850 dogs entered and 4,213 actually competing.

While the numbers of Old English registered annually remained stable in the thirties, and the quality of the breed if anything advanced from its traditional high quality, the nature of the breed's fanciers changed. Three things happened. First, one kennel dominated the breed for a decade as never before. This was Mrs. Lewis Roesler Renner's Merriedip Kennels. Second, a succession of great Canadian-bred dogs won big in the United States and played an important part in the development of the breed. Third, new breeder-exhibitors emerged. It is from this group, including Mrs. Claude Crafts' Rosmoore dogs, Mrs. D. Mather Briggs' Cartref dogs, Mrs. Mildred Lyndley's Lynnhaven dogs, Mrs. Mary Schloss' Mobla dogs and the Alonzo P. Walton, Jr. Royal dogs, that many of today's kennels emerged. These new fanciers also began a new trend among Bobtail devotees. For the first time in the United States the breed passed into the hands of many small breeders and exhibitors. Until the late thirties American Old English had been overwhelmingly concentrated in the hands of a few breeders and exhibitors, who maintained large kennels.

Helen Margery Lewis (later Roesler, then Renner) with Ch. Downderry Voyager and Ch. Downderry Irresistible.

Merriedip Kennels

Mrs. Lewis Roesler Renner was one of the most knowledgeable dog people ever involved in breeding and exhibiting Old English Sheepdogs in the United States. Prior to taking up Bobtails in 1926, the then Mrs. Roesler had bred Pugs, smooth and wire Fox Terriers, Irish Water Spaniels, Welsh Terriers, and Cairn Terriers. In 1932 she began breeding Welsh Corgis. She was active with them for nearly a decade after she abandoned Bobtails altogether in the early fifties. She was licensed to judge four Groups and most other breeds. Mrs. Renner's judging was widely respected in the United States, Canada, and England. She officiated in all three countries on many occasions until ill-health forced her to give up judging in 1962. She served the Old English Sheepdog Club of America as president on numerous occasions, and together with a few other fanciers was principally responsible for the club's rehabilitation in the late-forties and early fifties.

Mrs. Roesler was widely traveled. She knew the principal breeders, bloodlines, and dogs in England in her day. Although she was still breeding and exhibiting Old English on a small scale in the early fifties, her principal contribution to the breed was made between 1931 and Westminster 1942, when her great homebred Ch. Merriedip Master Pantaloons (call-name Rocket, because he was seen as a flyer from the time he was whelped), was first in the Working Group there. Between 1931, when her first OES became a champion and 1941, Mrs. Roesler owned 17 Old English Champions: Downderry Voyager, Downderry Irresistible, Downderry Volunteer, Merriedip Ethel Ann, Snow Bunting of Merriedip, Lucien of Lavenderlea,

71

Ch. Merriedip Ethel Ann, Group winner, owned by Merriedip Kennels.

Ch. Hammerwood Hobbledehoy, a BIS-winning import, owned by Merriedip.

Mrs. Renner handling her Ch. Rosmoore St. John to Best American-Bred in Show at Ladies Kennel Association show (Garden City, NY) in 1942. The judge was Charles P. Scott. In center is Mrs. H. H. Neal, club president.

Mistress Patience of Pastorale, Merriedip Kitty, Mistress Petticoats of Pastorale, Walleyed Snow Bobs O'Merriedip, Merriedip Ethelyn, Merriedip Vindex, Merriedip Master Pantaloons, Hammerwood Hobbledehoy, Merrie Dip of Pastorale, Rosmoore Saint John, and Rosmoore Claudia O'Merriedip. In those same years she imported and sold Mrs. Claude Crafts her first Old English champion, the dog Blueberry Blaise, as well as providing Mrs. Crafts with the bitch, Merriedip Trouble, from which she in turn bred her first champion, the bitch Naughty Marietta. Merriedip also bred Mrs. D. Mather Brigg's first champion, the bitch Merriedip Silverdale, finished in 1938, and Mrs. Alonzo P. Walton, Jr.'s first champion, the bitch Mistress Merrie O'Merriedip, also finished in 1938. Dr. George A. Wiseman of Chicago purchased two Bobtails from Merriedip, the bitch Ch. Merriedip Tag-A-Long finished in 1939, and the dog Ch. Merriedip Bob-A-Long finished in 1941, both of whom were all-breed Best in Show winners.

Of the first 17 Merriedip champions, 11 were imports, nine from England and Snow Bunting of Merriedip and Walleyed Snow Bobs O'Merriedip from Canada, four were homebreds, and two Rosmoore dogs were bred by Mrs. Crafts out of Merriedip studs. Seven of them were Best in Show winners. Voyager, Irresistible, Volunteer, Master Pantaloons, Hobbledehoy, Merrie Dip of Pastorale, and Rosmoore Saint John, and an eighth, her first imported dog Downderry Vanquisher, who never completed his championship was also a Best in Show winner. Five others, Snow Bunting, Ethel Ann, Lucien, Mistress Petticoats, and Vindex were Group winners. Merriedip Tiny Tre, by Downderry Irresistible out of Shelia of Ways Green, whelped July 14, 1931, at 14 months was also a Group winner. Tre made the front pages of virtually every paper in the country when Mrs. Roesler gave him to Mrs. Franklin Delano Roosevelt at the White House in 1933. Tre was not the first Bobtail to take up residence at the White House. Miss Helen W. Bones, address the White House, Washington, D.C. registered in October 1914 the dog Hamish of Bewley (by Bob of Bewley out of Venus, whelped August 29, 1914), bred by Mrs. Edward Parker Davis.

Much of the credit for the success of the Merriedip dogs in the show ring must be given to Mrs. Roesler's kennel manager and handler, George McKercher. Mrs. Roesler maintained her kennel at her summer home in Great Barrington, Massachusetts. She registered the Merriedip kennel prefix with the AKC in 1930.

Mrs. Roesler became interested in Old English Sheepdogs in the middle twenties. In 1926 on a trip to England she began looking for dogs. In the next 15 years she returned to England as frequently as possible. On every trip she traveled widely, going from kennel to kennel searching for high quality dogs to use in her breeding program. She was interested in top quality show dogs and potential breeding stock. Mrs. Roesler imported more Old English to the United States than any other individual. She kept few of these dogs herself. Most of them went into private homes and were never heard from again or played a minor role in the breed's development in the United States by whelping or siring a litter or two. Some of the dogs, like Blueberry Blaise, who went to Mrs. Crafts, were shown and actively used in breeding programs.

One very early dog imported by Mrs. Roesler was Downderry Discovery of Merriedip, bred by Miss A. C. Taylor out of Downderry Wakeful by Downderry Dauntless, whelped October 18, 1929. Mrs. Roesler imported him in the fall of 1930 and sold him immediately to Sally Miles. Discovery was later the first dog registered by Sally Miles' cousin, Serena Miles Van Rensselaer and her husband Hendrik.

Over the years Mrs. Roesler bought most of her dogs from four prominent English kennels of the day: the Downderry Kennels of Mrs. Durham-Waite, the Pastorale Kennels of Miss A. Tireman, Henry Tilley's Shepton kennels, and the Lavenderlea Kennels of Mrs. M. Edgar. The dogs Mrs. Roesler used in her breeding were all descended from the same early greats as Kinney's, Jamison's, and Goodsell's. The first four imports she kept, Downderry Vanquisher, Downderry Voyager, Downderry Irresistible, and Snow Bunting of Merriedip, were direct descendants on both sides of their pedigrees of either Tip Toes or Shepton Moonshine. Both of these important English studs of the teens and twenties were sired by Morris Kinney's World War I import, Ch. Tip Top Weather. Her later imports were also descended from the greats of an earlier day, as well as having the important English studs such as Ch. Elkington Squire, Ch. Montford Marksman, and Ch. Southridge Roger of the twenties and thirties in their immediate backgrounds.

Mrs. Roesler took an active part in the activities of her kennel. She personally bought all the dogs, and decided on all matings. She also showed her Bobtails from time to time, particularly after World War II. She had definite opinions on breeding. She told Arthur Frederick Jones when he interviewed her for the 1935 *American Kennel Gazette,* that in her opinion, "satisfactory breeding results only ċan be obtained by judicious outcrosses." Merriedip did no inbreeding, although all the dogs were related at the third or fourth generation removed. Jones wrote of Mrs. Roesler's thinking, "She admits that line breeding intensifies certain strong points—along with the weak points—but she does not think that it is a safe practice to employ from the standpoint of disposition. Ill-tempered dogs, she believes, result always from inbreeding, and she contends that poor disposition is a terrific price to pay for show points." Mrs. Roesler's long experience with purebred dogs made her peculiarly conscious of the fact that although her dogs were exclusively companions and show animals they were intended to perform a specific function. She insisted upon a working conditioned, sturdy, sound Bobtail. As early as November 1930 she returned from England after viewing the specialty show and informed Mrs. Wilbur Kirby Hitchcock English OES were too big. She felt a dog of 25 inches and 80 pounds or so was big enough.

It is difficult to single out any one of the Merriedip dogs in the thirties as being the most important, remembering that many other Merriedip dogs made major contributions to the breed in the show ring and as producers. However, three stand out: Ch. Downderry Volunteer, Ch. Merriedip Master Pantaloons, and Ch. Merrie Dip of Pastorale. The bitch Downderry Voyager was Winners Bitch at Westminster in 1931. Downderry Irresistible was Winners Dog at Westminster in 1933, the same year Merriedip Ethel Ann was Winners Bitch. In 1934, the bitch Snow Bunting of Merriedip was Winners at the Garden. Lucien of Lavenderlea and Mistress Patience of Pastorale were respectively Winners Dog and Winners Bitch and Best of Breed in 1935. Mistress Patience was the second OES bitch to go Best of Breed at Westminster since the system of awarding four Group places had been adopted nearly a decade before. No Old English Sheepdog bitch has been Best of Breed at Westminster since 1935. In 1936, Downderry Volunteer was Winners Dog and Best of Breed at the Garden, while in '37 and '38 the bitches Mistress Petticoats of Pastorale and Merriedip Ethelyn were Winners Bitch. At the 1939 OESCA specialty show Hammerwood Hobbledehoy was Winners Dog and Best of Breed. These wins were just the most important of a string of victories at major Eastern shows during the thirties for Merriedip-owned Bobtails.

Ch. Downderry Volunteer was the first great all-breed special from Merriedip, although he had been preceded by four Best in Show winners. Volunteer was bred by W. N. Tod, by Walleyed Bill out of Glittering Cascade, whelped September 30, 1929. Mrs. Roesler imported him in 1931. Volunteer was handled throughout his show career by George McKercher. In 1934, Volunteer compiled what was considered for the time an unbelievable record. During the year he was shown 21 times, thought to be an amazing total in itself. He was Best of Breed 20 times, first in the Group nine times, second once, and fourth twice. In his entire career in the United States, spanning five years, he was Best of Breed 33 times, first in the Group 14 times, second 4 times, third 6 times, and fourth 6 times. It is difficult to realize just how impressive these totals were for the thirties, when there were few shows and traveling was slow and difficult. Volunteer was widely used at stud. Most dogs that have been bred in the United States since the thirties have Volunteer some place in their background. Among others he sired the Chs. Merriedip Ethelyn, Merriedip Vindex, Merriedip Silverdale, Mistress Merrie O'Merriedip, and Merriedip Master Pantaloons.

Pantaloons was out of Ch. Mistress Petticoats of Pastorale, whelped February 12, 1936. Mistress Petticoats was bred by C. M. Ashford by Beara Leader out of Biddy the Tramp, whelped March 5, 1930. She was an English champion when Mrs. Roesler bought her for $500 in 1934. Petticoats was a great-granddaughter of Shepton Moonshine through her dam's sire Faithful Tramp.

Pantaloons began his show career when a few days less than a year old at Westminster 1937, where he went from best puppy dog to Best of Winners for five points, under all-breed judge Alva Rosenberg. Mrs. Wilbur Kirby Hitchcock in reporting on Westminster observed, "I quite agree with the judge, Alva Rosenberg, in considering him by far the best one of her own breeding that Mrs. Roesler has ever shown." Later that spring Pantaloons completed his championship with two more five-point wins. Pantaloons went on to compile an impressive show record, that included 54 Bests of Breed, 15 Group wins, 36 other Group placements and four Best American-Bred-in-Shows, and one all-breed Best in Show. Pantaloons was Best of Breed at Westminster three times, in 1939, 1940 and 1942. In '39 he was second in the Group, in '40 fourth, and in 1942 he climaxed Merriedip's string of successes by winning the Group, and receiving strong consideration for Best in Show. The 1942 Best in Show judge at Westminster was Herman Mellenthin, who the previous two years had handled his homebred Cocker, My Own Brucie, to Best in Show there. Pantaloons was used at stud, and produced many dogs that contributed to other breeding programs that are immediately in back of contemporary Bobtails including the champions Merriedip Tag-A-Long, Rosmoore Saint John, Rosmoore Fancy Pants II, Rosmoore Tatters of Cartref, Merriedip Flare for Victory, and Merriedip Mistress Monnie, but his impact as a stud was overshadowed by an imported kennelmate, Ch. Merrie Dip of Pastorale.

Merrie Dip of Pastorale (by Peterkin of Halliwick out of Jasmine of Halliwick), whelped April 14, 1937, was bred by Mrs. E. Sanders. Mrs. Roesler imported him in the fall of 1938. He was shown irregularly to a quick championship in the summer of 1939. Mrs. Roesler was confronted with the pleasant dilemma of having four top quality, all-breed specials, all deserving to be exhibited, Pantaloons, Hammerwood Hobbledehoy, Merrie Dip of Pastorale, and Rosmoore Saint John, as well as several excellent bitches and older studs in

Ch. Merrie Dip of Pastorale pictured in his win of Best in Show at Westbury (NY) in 1941, handled by owner Mrs. Renner (then Lewis). The judge was Harry T. Peters, himself so prominently identified with the beginnings of the breed in America. Mrs. William H. Long, club president, presented the trophy.

Ch. Merriedip Master Pantaloons winning Best in Show at Saratoga Springs, handled by George J. McKercher. The judge (behind Mr. McKercher) was David Wagstaff, and Mrs. Renner holds the trophies.

her kennel. Merrie Dip of Pastorale was shown irregularly as a special, winning every time out including Best in Show all-breeds at the important Westbury, Long Island show in 1941. His contributions to the breed as a sire were the most important of any OES in the United States until the late fifties. He sired the champions: Rosmoore Smarty Pants, Gay Lady, Merriedip Bob-A-Long, Rosmoore Claudia O'Merriedip, Royal Price Topper, King's Messenger, Black Baron, Jenny Wren, Cartref Wise Council, Lancashire Lass, Lady Love, Cartref Pandean, Cartref Panjandrum, Royal Prince Peterkin, Lord Peter Whimsey, and Merriedip Mr. Topper. No Old English stud approached his total of champion get until the 1960s, after the boom in popularity had begun.

Beyond the number of champion get was the impact of these dogs, and many others who were not shown, as producers themselves. Of all the Merriedip OES, Merrie Dip of Pastorale has had the greatest impact on the breed in the United States down to the present time. His name appears many times over in the backgrounds of virtually every major American kennel today, from Ambelon to Downeylane to Fezziwig to Greyfriar to Lillibrad to Momarv to Rivermist to Shaggybar to Silvershag to Tamara, and on and on. Of his many offspring a few deserve special mention. Ch. Merriedip Bob-A-Long bred by Merriedip out of Maides Wendy of Merriedip, whelped June 27, 1939 and owned by Dr. and Mrs. George Wiseman of Chicago, was the first OES special to do widespread all-breed winning in the Midwest. Handled by Billy Lang, Bob-A-Long racked up a series of wins in 1941 and 1942 that made him briefly the top winning Bobtail of all-time. Included in his wins were Best in Show at Detroit, and Best of Breed and Working Group second at Westminster in 1941.

Two other Merrie Dip of Pastorale sons surpassed Bob-A-Long's winnings. Chs. King's Messenger and Black Baron were bred by Julius Kraft, Jr. of Cleveland, Ohio. They were whelped May 18, 1940, out of Ch. Mistress Opal of Pastorale. Mistress Opal was bred by Mrs. D. A. Wright out of Caroline by Shaggy Shoes of Pastorale. Eventually six of the 12 dogs in the litter finished. King's Messenger was owned by Julius' brother Stanley Krafts, and shown throughout his career by Julius. He eventually totaled 86 Bests of Breed, nine Bests in show, 33 Group wins, and 39 other Group places. Messenger was Best of Breed and third in the Group at Westminster in 1944, and Best of Breed at the OESCA specialty show that year. In 1946 he was again Best of Breed at the Garden, but did not compete in the Group.

His brother, Black Baron, was sold to Mrs. Howard J. Hickingbotham in California. Baron was handled throughout his show

Ch. King's Messenger, whelped 1940, BIS-winning son of Ch. Merrie Dip of Pastorale, pictured with his breeder-handler, Julius Kraft, Jr. Messenger was owned by Julius' brother, Stanley.

Ch. Black Baron, Messenger's spectacular litter brother, winner of 13 BIS and 39 Groups. Handled by James McManus, Baron was owned by Mrs. Howard J. Hickingbotham of California.

career by James McManus. He totaled 39 Group wins and 13 Bests in Show, as well as Best of Breed and second in the Working Group at Westminster in 1945. In a career of more than 30 years as an all-breed handler McManus considered Baron to be "the equal of any dog I ever had on a lead" and in McManus' opinion as good as the Bobtails he had seen in his judging around the country recently. In the 1960s McManus handled Stan Goldberg's Ch. Shaggybar Bottomsup to several wins including a Best in Show at Reno. Bottomsup was descended from Merrie Dip of Pastorale on both sides of his pedigree.

After the Second World War Mrs. Roesler, now Mrs. Renner, continued to be active in Sheepdogs for a while. From 1942 until 1946 she had been on the West Coast most of the time and inactive in dogs, although she had bred an occasional litter including one out of Merriedip Panda by Master Pantaloons, whelped May 30, 1944 that included Mrs. Crafts' Ch. Rosmoore Fancy Pants II and the bitch Ch. Rosmoore Tatters of Cartref. In the post-war years the Merriedip name was associated with a number of important Bobtails, including the Chs. Merriedip Mr. Personality, Merriedip Mr. Topper, Merriedip Flare of Victory, Merriedip Frilly Petticoats, Merriedip Mistress Monnie, Merriedip Cracker Jack, Merriedip White Pantalettes, and Merriedip Duke George.

It is fitting that the last Merriedip champion, Duke George, was also the greatest winner to bear that kennel's name, and one of the important studs in the breed in the late 1950s. Duke George was whelped April 16, 1952 by Ch. Merriedip Mr. Personality out of Merriedip Pamela. He was bred by Hope Norton. Duke George was doubly descended from both Merriedip Master Pantaloons and Merrie Dip of Pastorale. Mr. Personality's sire, Rosmoore Squire Jim was by Merrie Dip of Pastorale, while his dam Rosmoore Polly was by Master Pantaloons. Pamela's great-grandsire through Towerhill of Mosshaven and his sire Ch. Rosmoore Saint John was Master Pantaloons, while her dam, Merriedip Colleen, was sired by Merrie Dip of Pastorale. Duke George was acquired by Mrs. Mona Kucker (Berkowitz), who showed him to his championship with several big wins including Winners Dog and Best of Winners at Westminster and at the OESCA specialty show in 1955. Interestingly, B. H. and Lillian Lovejoy's Colorado-owned-and-shown Norval Pride King finished his championship at the same time as Duke George. These two dogs in part account for the widespread exposure Old English received in the show world from 1955 until Fezziwig Ceiling Zero began his career in 1959.

Ch. Merriedip Bob-A-Long, another multi-BIS winning son of Ch. Merrie Dip of Pastorale, owned by Dr. G. R. Wiseman, Jr.

Ch. Merriedip Duke George, handled by his owner Mona Kucker (Berkowitz), winning the Old English Sheepdog Club of America Specialty in 1957. Best Opposite was Ch. Patchwork Gillian of Van R, handled by owner Hendrik Van Rensselaer. Between them are Mrs. Milton Erlanger, the judge, and Mrs. Claude Crafts, club president.

81

The great winner of the 1950s, Ch. Merriedip Duke George, had as a great-grandsire on both sides of his pedigree an important winner and producer of the late '30s and early '40s Ch. Merrie Dip of Pastorale. The great winning litter brothers of the 1940s, Champions King's Messenger and Black Baron had as a great-grandsire on both sides of their pedigree, an important producer of a much earlier period yet, Ch. Tommy Tittlemouse of Pastorale. This breeding of generally related dogs has long been the accepted practice in Old English Sheepdogs. Intense inbreeding has been practiced when the right animals have been available. This was true in years gone by, it is true of contemporary breeders. Many of these have used sire to daughter breedings with excellent results.

Pedigree of Chs King's Messenger and Black Baron, whelped May 18, 1940. Bred by Julius Kraft.

sire

Ch. Merrie Dip
of Pastorale

Peterkin of
Halliwick

Corrykin of Pastorale

Peggy of Ringslade

Jasmine of
Halliwick

*Ch. Tommy Tittlemouse
of Pastorale*

Joy's Gift

dam

Ch. Mistress Opal
of Pastorale

Shaggy Shoes
of Pastorale

Ch. Beara Leader

Ch. Biddy the Tramp

Caroline

*Ch. Tommy Tittlemouse
of Pastorale*

Betty Bruin

82

Ch. Merriedip Duke George, owned by Mona Kucker (Berkowitz).

Pedigree of Ch. Merriedip Duke George, whelped Apr. 1, 1952. Bred by Hope Norton.

sire

Ch. Merriedip
Mr. Personality

Rosmoore Squire Jim

    Ch. Merrie Dip of Pastorale

    Ch. Naughty Marietta

Rosmoore Polly

    Ch. Merriedip Master Pantaloons

    Merriedip Panda

dam

Merriedip Pamela

Towerhill of Mosshaves

    Ch. Rosmoore Saint John

    The Platter of Pastorale

Merriedip Colleen

    Ch. Merrie Dip of Pastorale

    Maidie's Wendy of Merriedip

83

Mona Berkowitz is one of the most important figures in the history of American Old English Sheepdogs. She has owned and shown a succession of top winning Bobtails since the late-thirties. Her first show OES was Ch. Crest of the Wave, bred by Mrs. Roland Baker of the Woodland Farm Kennels in Northampton, New Hampshire. Crest of the Wave was whelped August 18, 1933 by Mille Fleurs Major out of Phyllis. He was shown by his young owner to a number of Group placings on the way to his championship in the fall of 1940. Mona's father, Dr. Joseph Saphir, served on the OESCA's Board of Governors in the early forties. Her second show OES, the imported Shepton Guard of Honour, also finished. In the fall of 1941 Guard of Honour was the second Old English Sheepdog to earn a Companion Dog title in Obedience. After the war as Mrs. Marvin Kucker, she had a great deal to do with the revitalization of the OESCA, and the breed in general.

The Kuckers owned and bred a succession of winners and producers from the late 1940s until the late fifties, including Chs. Momarv's Blue Devil, Merriedip Sno-Boots of Momarv, Momarv's Mistletoe, Merriedip Cracker Jack, and Arnue Platinum Penny. As an officer of the OESCA, breed judge, handler, and importer Mona Kucker Berkowitz's importance to contemporary Old English Sheepdogs is manifold. Over the years she has owned and shown more champion Old English Sheepdogs than any person ever associated with the breed. She has long been regarded as one of the finest handlers in all of purebred dogs, and has been honored many times over for her accomplishments including a *Kennel Review* award as best female amateur handler of the year. Living in southern California from the early sixties, she was in large part responsible for introducing Old English Sheepdogs to most of the breed's present West Coast fanciers. Her imported bitch, Ch. Shepton Surprise, was one of the few Bobtail bitches to win an all-breed Best in Show in the United States in the last 20 years, and was *Kennel Review's* top Working Group award winner for 1962. Throughout the sixties and into the seventies Mrs. Berkowitz has owned and shown a succession of winners and producers. One of the more recent of them, the imported Ch. Prospectblue Rodger, was among the top winning Working Group winners from the time he was brought to the United States in the summer of 1967, and was Best of Breed at Old English Sheepdog Club of America specialties in Kansas City in March 1969, and at the largest OES specialty ever held at Anaheim, California in September 1970.

Few handlers, amateur or professional, have enjoyed the success Mrs. Kucker did with Duke George from 1956 to 1959. In all, he won 49 Groups and 12 Bests in Show. He was Best of Breed at Westminster in 1956, '57, '58, and '59, placing second in the Group in '57 and '58, and third in '59. Duke George was also Best of Breed at the OESCA specialty shows in 1956, 1957, and 1958. His career as a special got underway in 1956, the first year the Phillips system of rating all-breed competition was inaugurated. During 1956, George won one Best in Show, 13 Group firsts, 14 Group seconds, nine Group thirds, and seven fourths. He was the third ranked of all Working dogs for the year, and the ninth of all-breeds.

In 1957, Duke George had one of the greatest winning years of any purebred dog, and far and away the greatest year any amateur-handled Bobtail has ever had. He was the top winning Working dog in the United States, and number three of all-breeds, based on his eight Bests in Show, 27 Group wins, 11 seconds, three thirds, and two fourths. He was Best in Show at the Trenton Kennel Club over 1,038 dogs, and the Group winner at Morris and Essex, Westchester, and Philadelphia among other important all-breed events. In 1958, George continued his winning ways, although shown less frequently in order to make room for his Best in Show-winning sons, Chs. Momarv's Hi-Wide and Handsome and Rosmoore Sinney. For the year he was the fourth ranked Working dog in the country with seven Group wins and three Bests in Show, at Greenwich, Somerset Hills, and Westchester. His son, Momarv's Hi-Wide and Handsome, owned and bred by the Kuckers out of Arnue Platinum Penny, whelped November 9, 1954, was Winners Dog and Best of Winners at the 1957 OESCA specialty show, and the only OES other than his sire to win more than two Groups in 1958. He won five, and two Bests in Show at the Putnam and Berks County Kennel Clubs.

Mona Kucker (Berkowitz) continues active in the breed in California today, of which we'll report in the following chapter.

It is from the Merriedip breedings of the thirties, particularly as descended through Duke George and the Patchwork Kennel's Merriedip Mopsie Merrie, that the American-bred antecedents of the Old English Sheepdog in the United States today can be traced. One of the most important contributions of Merriedip was the large number of people who acquired their first dogs from this kennel and became serious breeders themselves. Mrs. Roesler was the principle force in stimulating interest in the breed in New England in the early thirties.

The New England fanciers kept the breed going during the bleak years of World War II. The New England Old English Sheepdog Club was founded in 1933, largely because of Mrs. Roesler's encouragement and support. The NEOESCA became officially asso-

Miss V. Crofts, of the "Robbery" Kennels in England, with Robbery in Broad Daylight (later exported to Mrs. Roland Baker in New Hampshire) and Sunshine Bogie.

Two of the imports featured in the Mobla Kennels of Mrs. Mary H. Schloss c. 1940. At left, the Group-winning bitch, Eng. & Am. Ch. Shepton Dolly Grey of Mobla. At right, Crede Mac Midi of Mobla.

ciated with the American Kennel Club in 1944. It is not connected with the OESCA in an official manner, although of course the goals and purposes of both clubs are the betterment of the breed. The NEOESCA is considered one of the breed's two parent clubs. No other local or regional OES club was formed in the United States until the middle-sixties. The New England club's presidents from 1933 to 1948, Mrs. Roland Baker, Miss Edith Buckingham, Mrs. C. M. Crafts, Mrs. D. Mather Briggs, Mrs. Alonzo P. Walton, Jr., and Mrs. William B. MacColl, were among the most important names in keeping Bobtails going in this country during the 1940s.

Woodla Kennels

Mrs. Roland M. Baker of Woodland Farm Kennels in Northampton, New Hampshire, holds the record for an American of longest continuous activity in the breed. P. Hamilton Goodsell, from first ownership to his death had Bobtails for more years, but he was not active to any appreciable extent during his last twenty years. Mrs. Baker bought her first Bobtail in England in 1908. This was the dog English Charter, whelped September 17, 1907 by Ch. Shepton Hero out of Fair Ellen, a granddaughter of Watch Boy. For the next forty years, Mrs. Baker seldom bred less than two litters a year, and occasionally had four or more litters. Because of her relative isolation from the mainstream of the dog show world from 1909 until 1930, she did not attend many shows and finished no champions. However, dogs of her breeding found their way into the breeding programs of all the major kennels of the day including those of Morris Kinney and P. Hamilton Goodsell. She was one of the most prolific American OES breeders.

Mrs. Baker, however, finished only three Bobtails. They were all imported, the dogs McAlister and Robbery in Broad Daylight and the bitch Hush Money for Robbery. McAlister was widely used at stud, sired a number of champions, including Edith Buckingham's studs Wuffa and Oswald, and was a multiple Group winner. His name can be found in back of many American OES today. He was bred by F. Farquharson, and was by Brisk Weather out of Pendley Snowball, whelped October 1, 1926. Mrs. Baker imported him in 1929, when he had already been proven at stud in England. Brisk Weather was sired by Glorious Weather who was in turn out of Shepton Moonshine, while Pendley Snowball was sired by Shepton Moonshine. Robbery in Broad Daylight and Hush Money for Robbery were both bred by Miss V. Croft of the celebrated English "Robbery" Kennel. Robbery in Broad Daylight was whelped October 12, 1929, by Highroad Robbery out of Determined Robbery. Both Highroad and

Determined Robbery were grandchildren of Shepton Moonshine. Mrs. Baker did not import Robbery in Broad Daylight to the United States until the summer of 1935, when he was nearly six. He had been used widely at stud in England before coming to this country. He figures prominently in the backgrounds of many contemporary OES in England and the United States. Hush Money for Robbery was whelped December 10, 1933, also by Highroad Robbery out of Rough Diamond Robbery, who was herself a daughter of Robbery in Broad Daylight. Mrs. Baker was long considered one of the most knowledgeable and interesting Bobtail fanciers in the United States. She was a licensed judge of the breed, and the first OES judge to fly to an assignment, when she flew from New Hampshire to Orange, New Jersey to judge there in 1939.

Cleoftaegel Kennels

Miss Edith Buckingham, of the Cleoftaegal Kennels in Massachusetts, was another of the important Bobtail fanciers in New England during the thirties. She was a judge, club officer, and writer on the breed. Over the years she bred many Sheepdogs that were used in other breeding programs. The names of her three homebred champion studs, Wuffa, Oswald, and Cleoftaegel Grimbald CDX, can be found in back of many American-bred OES today. Wuffa and Oswald were whelped September 16, 1931 out of Miss Buckingham's Lady Jinx by Mrs. Baker's Ch. McAlister. Grimbald was whelped September 12, 1935 by Wuffa out of Glenvalley Valois. He was the first Bobtail to compete in Obedience in the United States and the first to earn a Companion Dog (CD) title, in the fall of 1939, as well as the first to earn a Companion Dog Excellent (CDX) title in September, 1942. Miss Buckingham also owned the imported bitch, Ch. Shepton Maid of the Mountains, (out of Dextress by Henry Tilley's great stud of the thirties Ch. Southridge Roger), whelped March 13, 1932, bred by Mrs. N. Freeth. Southridge Roger was the most important stud in England during the thirties. He had a wide impact on the breed there, and through a great many imports on the breed in this country. He was sired by Hammerwood Jolly Roger out of Nancy. Roger was sired by Elkington Squire. Dextress was also sired by Elkington Squire. Shepton Maid of the Mountains was widely admired. She enjoyed considerable success at the shows, going Best in Show at the Brockton, Massachusetts all-breed event on September 16, 1937.

Maid of the Mountains was one of the first of a procession of English Bobtails that came to the United States from the middle thirties until the war made shipping impossible. The depression and war had a widespread devastating impact on the breed in England. Like the First World War this initially resulted in many Bobtails coming to the United States. In the long run, it nearly finished the breed in both countries. Henry Tilley was principally responsible for attempting to get the best breeding potential Bobtails out of England once the international situation had deteriorated to the point where war was only weeks or months away. At one point he wrote to all members of the OESCA offering the best English breeding from all lines and kennels at little more than the cost of transportation to the United States. Unfortunately, the situation in the United States prevented many Americans from acquiring any dogs. Only three individuals were able to import several good dogs: Mrs. U. Cline Lyndley of Lynnhaven Kennels in Dubuque, Iowa; Mrs. Harold Schloss of Mobla Kennels, Baltimore, Maryland; and Mrs. James H. Hughes of Round Table Kennels in Middletown, Delaware.

Three New Englanders, all of whom got their first breeding and show OES from Merriedip, served the New England and national OES clubs in varying capacities, and have left a marked influence on the breed in the United States today. These are Mrs. D. Mather Briggs of the Cartref Kennels, Mr. and Mrs. Alonzo P. Walton of the Royal Kennels, and Mrs. Claude Crafts of the Rosmoore Kennels. These fanciers owned, bred, and showed important Old English Sheepdogs. They in turn provided the dogs with which others contributed to the breed's development in this country in the late 1940s and '50s. However, before turning to them it is necessary to look at the impact of a number of Canadian dogs on the breed during the 1930s, and a few other American breeders who made major contributions before World War II.

Canadian Impact

In the opinion of many Old English fanciers, including Freeman Lloyd and P. Hamilton Goodsell, the greatest litter of any breed whelped before World War II was an English-bred, Canadian-born litter of five Old English Sheepdogs. The litter was the property of F. T. James of Red Gables, Lambton Mills, Ontario, Canada. James was the first Sheepdog fancier in Canada, having become active at the end of World War I. In the spring of 1929, he imported from Miss Palmer the bitch Bhurra Snow Bunting, in whelp by Tenet Spook. Both Spook and Snow Bunting were grandchildren of Shepton Moonshine, as well as Right Sort O'Weather and Old Fashioned Weather, and through these dogs to the famous names of the World War I era. Snow Bunting's litter was whelped June 19, 1929. There were three bitches, Snowball, Snow Lady, and Snow Bunting of Merriedip, and two dogs Snowman and Snowflake. James kept Snowman, Snowball

Ch. Snowman, Best in Working Group at Westminster 1932. Owned by F. T. James of Canada.

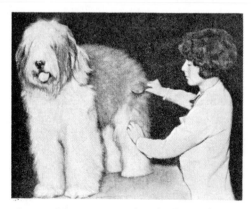

Ch. Snowflake, Snowman's litter brother, and winner of the Group at Westminster 1934, pictured here being readied for the show ring by his owner, Miss Helen Cluff.

and Snow Lady. He sold the bitch, Snow Bunting of Merriedip, to Mrs. Lewis Roesler in the United States, and the dog Snowflake to Helen Cluff of the Clearbrook kennels of Caledon, Ontario, Canada. All five dogs became champions. All except Snowball were multiple Group winners, and Snowman, Snowflake, and Snow Lady were Best in Show winners. Snowman and Snowflake also have the distinction of being the only litter brothers to win the breed and Group at the Westminster Kennel Club show, Snowman in 1932, and Snowflake in 1934. Snowman was the youngest of the five OES that have won Groups at the Garden, winning at two years and seven months.

In addition to their winnings these dogs all contributed to the breed as producers. James bred his Snow Lady to Mrs. Roesler's Downderry Irresistible and produced a litter on April 18, 1930, containing the dog Walleyed Snow Bobs O'Merriedip. Mrs. Roesler took this dog for her own kennel. He appears prominently in the backgrounds of many American OES today. In a subsequent breeding to Boxer of Vacoas, Snow Lady produced among others, the Cluff's champion dog and bitch Snowdrift and Snowflurry. Snowflurry was in turn bred to her dam's litter brother, Snowflake, and produced on February 16, 1932 the Best in Show winnings dogs, Blue Bill of Clearbrook and Smokey of Clearbrook. Both of these dogs, together with their littermates and relatives, as well as Leonard Collins of Toronto's OES, were widely admired in the United States, even by such a rigorous critic of foreign Bobtails as Mrs. Wilbur Kirby Hitchcock. Mrs. Hitchcock thought Smokey of Clearbrook was the greatest young Old English Sheepdog she had ever seen, after having gone over him at the 1933 Westminster show. Smokey was later sold to Mrs. Roy Del Ruth of Hollywood, California, wife of the famous early movie producer and director. Mrs. Del Ruth showed Smokey infrequently, but always with success, including Best in Show at Santa Barbara. The only other breeding James was able to get out of Bhurra Snow Bunting before her death in the fall of 1930, was by her son Snowflake. From this breeding came T. L. Clayton's Snobobs, who among other victories in the United States was Best of Breed and fourth in the Working Group at the Detroit Kennel Club show in 1934, an important early win for a Bobtail in the Midwest.

The most important Old English Sheepdog ever to come out of Canada, and in the opinion of some authorities the greatest Old English Sheepdog of all-time, was American, Canadian Ch. Ideal Weather, owned and bred by Leonard Collins of Toronto. Ideal Weather was one of two dogs in the first litter Collins ever bred by his imported stud Lucky Jean, out of his imported bitch Moonbeam Weather's first litter, whelped May 17, 1932. Lucky Jean and Moonbeam Weather were both descended from the earlier greats, through Old Henry, Blue Knight and Glorious Weather on both sides of their pedigrees.

Ideal Weather was shown throughout his career, in the United States and Canada by Alf Loveridge, later a noted judge. His show career began in the fall of 1936, blossomed in both countries and ended with his retirement on May 29, 1938, after going Best in Show at the largest one day show ever held to that time. In Canada he was shown 12 times between November 23, 1936 and May 24, 1938, going Best of Breed every time, first in the Working Group ten times (placing second at the other two shows), best Canadian-bred Dog in Show ten times, and Best Dog in Show six times. In the United States between September 12, 1936 and May 29, 1938, he was shown 19 times, going Best of Breed every time, winning the Working Group nine times, placing at the other ten shows, and was Best in Show five times. He was second in the Working Group at the 1937 and 1938 Westminster shows. The group judge at the '38 show was O. C. Harriman. Later in 1938 he was Best in Show at the Chicago International Kennel Club event.

Then on May 29th Ideal Weather climaxed his career by going Best in Show at Morris and Essex. The other finalists at that event included some of the greatest all-breed winners in the history of purebred dogs in the United States. The Terrier Group winner was Nornay Saddler, the greatest winning Smooth Fox Terrier of all-time, and considered by many the greatest show dog of the late thirties and early forties. The winner in the Hound Group was Louis Murr's Borzoi, Vigow of Romanoff, while the Sporting Group winner was the English Setter Maro of Maridor, and the Non-Sporting winner was the white Standard Poodle Blakeen Jung Frau. The Best in Show judge was one of America's most distinguished dog fanciers, Harry T. Peters, who just after the turn of the century had owned and bred Old English and served as an officer of the OESCA. Mrs. Dodge had every breed winner at Morris and Essex weighed and measured. Ideal Weather was in the best possible condition for a show Bobtail. He weighed 76 pounds and was 25 inches at the withers on the day he won Best in Show.

Mobla Kennels

Mrs. Harry O. Schloss of Baltimore, Maryland was one of the most active OES fanciers in the United States between 1937 and 1940. In those years she imported, showed, and bred extensively. One or another of the dogs she imported or bred can be found in the background of most American OES today. Her kennel, Mobla, was managed by James McNaull. He also showed the dogs. Among the many

Ch. Ideal Weather and his handler, Alf Loveridge. Ideal Weather, rated by some as the greatest Old English Sheepdog of all time, was owned by Leonard Collins, of Toronto.

Ch. Ideal Weather in his greatest win, over an entry of 4,850 at the 1938 Morris and Essex Kennel Club show on the estate of Mrs. M. Hartley Dodge at Madison, New Jersey. Pictured are the judge, Harry T. Peters, handler Alf Loveridge and Mrs. Dodge.

dogs she imported were the champions, Shepton Dolly Grey of Mobla (finished in 1937), Cairbre Mac Ana Life of Mobla (finished 1938), Segda Mac an Dav of Mobla (finished 1939), Crede Mac Midna of Mobla, Broadlands Blue Bob, and Rigru Mac Vail of Mobla (all finished in 1940).

Cairbre Mac Ana was bred by the Rev. W. B. C. Buchanan, by Southridge Roger out of Lady Pamela, whelped November 24, 1934. Cairbre was the sire of Mrs. Schloss's Sedga Mac an Dav and her Crede Mac Midna. Buchanan was the secretary of the Scottish OES club, and the first man from Great Britain to judge Old English Sheepdogs in the United States at the 1939 Morris and Essex. At the show Buchanan put Ch. Merriedip Master Pantaloons Best of Breed, Hammerwood Hobbledehoy Winners Dog and Best of Winners, and Merriedip Tag-A-Long Winners Bitch. In commenting on his impression of the 27 dogs he judged, Buchanan said he liked the type and found no major faults, but he thought there were too many light eyes and irregular teeth.

Broadlands Blue Bob bred by Miss E. M. Brazq, whelped July 5, 1937 in Canada, by Ch. Snowflake out of Blue Bunting, was the top winning Bobtail in Canada following Ideal Weather's retirement. He was never defeated by another OES in Canada until he came up against Mrs. Schloss' great imported bitch Shepton Dolly Grey. Dolly Grey had been bred in England by F. T. Saunders, by Southridge Rodger out of Pensford Blue Mist, whelped January 14, 1935. Mrs. Schloss acquired her from Henry Tilley in the summer of 1937. She arrived in the United States on Labor Day that year. Dolly Grey began her show career in the United States at the Storm King Kennel Club show at Cornwall, New York on September 25, 1937, under Edith Buckingham by going Winners Bitch, Best of Winners, and Best of Breed for two points and then on to fourth in the Working Group. She completed her championship in October and November with three consecutive Group firsts, at Annapolis, Old Dominion, and Western Maryland. Dolly Grey was Best in Show at the Tri-State Kennel Association's show in Wheeling, West Virginia on April 24, 1938. Before her retirement in early 1940 she went on to compile a record of 23 Bests of Breed in 30 shows, 16 Group placements, including seven firsts. For many years she was the Bobtail pictured in the AKC's official all-breed book.

Lynnhaven Kennels

At the same time that Mrs. Schloss began importing Bobtails, another American, Mrs. Mildred Lyndley from Dubuque, Iowa, was becoming extensively involved with the breed. Between 1937 and 1950, Mrs. Lyndley imported, bred, and showed a large number of

Ch. Lynnhaven Great Son, multiple BIS winner owned by
Mrs. Mildred Lyndley.

Ch. Norval Pride King, owned by B. H. and Lillian Lovejoy,
winning under judge Wm. L. Kendrick. Together with his grandsire Ch. Shepton Noble King, his sire Ch. Lynnhaven Great Son,
and his son Ch. Lillibrad Prince Charming, Pride King was of a
four-generation father-to-son line of Best in Show winners.

Old English Sheepdogs. Between 1946 and 1950 she bred more OES than anyone in England or the United States. Her first champion was the Tilley-bred bitch, Shepton Attraction, who had been imported in whelp by Shepton Chief in the summer of 1936. Attraction was by Shepton Alarm out of Shepton Pamela, whelped July 1, 1933. Shepton Alarm was out of Miss Croft's Robbery line, while Pamela was sired by Southridge Roger. Her litter was whelped August 5, 1936, and contained among others the dog Shepton Commander, who Mrs. Lyndley kept and finished in 1938. Attraction was taken to the shows three months after whelping her litter, and in six appearances became a champion with six Bests of Breed, and two Group seconds, two Group thirds, and two Group fourths. In subsequent appearances Attraction won several Groups and placed whenever out. She was Best in Show at Ottumwa, Iowa in 1938, and at Mankato, Minnesota in the fall of 1939.

In 1940, Mrs. Lyndley was able to get, through Tilley, Shepton Noble King. Noble King and Shepton Guard of Honour who went to Mona Saphir, and Shepton Blue Prince of Round Table who went to Mrs. James H. Hughes of Round Table Kennels in Middletown, Delaware, were among the last Bobtails to get out of England before World War II made it impossible to ship across the North Atlantic. Noble King was bred by Mrs. E. Smith by Shepton Wall-eyed Wonder out of Lady Gloria, whelped September 21, 1936. He was Best in Show at the Waterloo, Iowa all-breed event in the fall of 1940. His son Lynnhaven Great Son was Best in Show at Cheyenne, Wyoming in 1950.

Lynnhaven Great Son was the sire of B. H. and Lillian Lovejoy's multiple Best in Show winner, Norval Pride King. Pride King was the sire of the Lovejoy-bred Lillibrad Prince Charming, owned by the Arthur Gustafsons of Chicago, Illinois, who was a multiple Best in Show winner, as well as Best of Breed from the classes at the OESCA specialty show in 1960, and Best of Breed and Group second at Westminster in 1961. These dogs represent the only four generation of father-to-son OES Best in Show winners in the United States.

After the Second World War the Lynnhaven kennel name was associated with many Bobtails that played an important part in almost all Sheepdog breeding done in the Midwest, and in most other sections of the country. Lynnhaven appears prominently in back of most contemporary Double JJ, Downeylane, Greyfriar, Lillibrad, and Silvershag breedings. Among Mrs. Lyndley's post-war champions were Lynnhaven Punchinello, Pride of Lynnhaven, Lynnhaven Silvery Lace a Best in Show winning bitch at Minneapolis in 1948, Lynnhaven Glamour Girl, and Lynnhaven Starlight. Punchinello was the sire of Pride of Lynnhaven, Silvery Lace, and many others.

96

Lynnhaven Silvery Lace, handled by her breeder-owner Mrs. Mildred L. Lyndley, winning BIS at Minneapolis 1948 under judge Walter H. Reeves.

Ch. Lillibrad Prince Charming, owned by Mr. and Mrs. Arthur Gustafson and handled by Jack Funk, winning BIS at Kankakee 1960 under judge Percy Roberts.

Ch. December Snow winning 1950 BIS under judge James W. Trullinger. Handled by Charles H. Meyer for owner William T. Houston.

Ch. Umm Pa's Surprise Snowfall winning 1953 Best in Show under judge Alva Rosenberg. Owned by George Depp.

		Ch. Merrie Dip of Pastorale
	Ch. King's Messenger	
sire		Ch. Mistress Opal of Pastorale
Ch. December Snow		Ch. Cartref Panjandrum
	Ch. Shadow Girl	
		Ch. Mobla Lady Mary- land
		Ch. Merrie Dip of Pastorale
dam	Ch. King's Messenger	
		Ch. Mistress Opal of Pastorale
Ch. Umm Pa's Glamour Girl		Ch. Cartref Panjandrum
	Shadow Girl	
		Ch. Mobla Lady Mary- land

Pedigree of Ch. Umm Pa's Surprise Snowfall, whelped November 2, 1950. Bred by Mrs. Cyrus Carey

One of the few bitches to win more than one Best in Show since World War II and Best of Opposite Sex at the Old English Sheepdog Club of America's Specialty show in 1953 was Ch. Umm Pa's Surprise Snowfall, the product of a full brother sister breeding. She represented the product of inbreeding on dogs of exceptional merit. This is the only intense inbreeding that should be made. Her sire was a specialty Best of Breed winner, Ch. December Snow, and his sire was both a great all breed special and specialty show Best of Breed winner, Ch. King's Messenger.

Cartref Kennels

Mrs. D. Mather Briggs of Bramble Hill, Rehoboth, Massachusetts, was one of the New Englanders that got their first OES from Merriedip and subsequently made major contributions to the breed in their own right—she as a writer, judge, exhibitor, importer and breeder. Mrs. Briggs' first Bobtail was the bitch Merriedip Silverdale, whelped April 25, 1935 by Ch. Downderry Volunteer out of Ch. Mistress Patience of Pastorale. Mrs. Briggs, although past 50 when she became active in OES, always showed her own dogs. In the bleak years at the end of the Second World War she was almost the only regular exhibitor in the United States. Merriedip Silverdale finished her championship in 1938. She produced many Cartref Bobtails for Mrs. Briggs in two litters out of Merrie Dip of Pastorale, including the champion studs, Cartref Wise Council, Cartref Pandean, and Cartref Panhandrum. Mrs. Briggs showed all three to their championships. They were used at stud, and merged into the background of many important American Bobtails in the years after the Second World War. Panjandrum, for example, was bred to Martha Rees' Penelope of Mol Kiah, and produced on April 30, 1944, a litter that among others included the bitch Calamus Gillian, who was acquired by Marion Osborne, shown to a championship and bred to her Calamus Blue Boy. From this litter, whelped July 9, 1946, came Mona Kucker's Ch. Momarv's Blue Devil. Panjandrum's litter, whelped October 2, 1943 out of Mrs. Brigg's Mobla Lady Maryland, contained several champions including the bitches Panache Encomium Skippy owned by Cleopatra P. Finch and Shadow Girl owned by William T. Houston of Mercer, Pennsylvania.

Houston bred Shadow Girl to the Krafts' King's Messenger and in two litters, whelped January 24, 1947 and July 27, 1948, produced several important Bobtails, including the champions, December Snow, Peter Pan IV, owned by George Depp of Wexford, Pennsylvania, and Umm-Pa's Glamour Girl, owned by Mrs. Cyrus Carey of Cincinnati, Ohio. December Snow was kept by Houston. He was Best of Breed at the OESCA specialty shows in 1950 and 1951, as well as a multiple Best in Show winner, always handled by Charlie Meyer. Mrs. Carey used December Snow on his full sister, Glamour Girl, and produced her multiple Group, Best in Show winning, OESCA specialty show Best of Opposite Sex bitch, Ch. Umm-Pa's Surprise Snowfall, whelped November 2, 1950. Cartref Wise Council also produced many Bobtails that appear in the immediate backgrounds of today's OES, including four champions from one litter out of Kathryn S. Wynne's Juno CD, whelped May 16, 1947: Lady Lewis Burwell owned by Mrs. Arthur T. Mahoney, Royal Prince Crestwood and Royal Princess of Crestwood owned by Alonzo P.

h. Rosmoore Tatters of Cartref, helped 1946, owned by Mrs. D. athers Briggs.

Ch. Cartref's Career Girl, bred by Mrs. Briggs, and later acquired by Mr. and Mrs. H. S. Dunning's Waterfall Kennels.

Ch. Waterfall Rippling Rythym II, owned by Mr. and Mrs. Dunning.

Walton, Jr., and Marksmans Bing owned by Fred La Crosse. All of these dogs made an impression on the breed as producers and winners. Bing was a Group winner and Best of Breed at the 1953 OESCA specialty show, while Lady Lewis was Best of Opposite Sex at Westminster in 1952.

The Cartref name was associated with many other Bobtails that appear prominently in the background of contemporary Sheepdogs in the United States including Cartref Hurdy Gurdy, Cartref Guard of Honour, Cartref's Lucky Piece, and the champions Rosmoore Tatters of Cartref, Cartref's Career Girl, Cartref Toggery, Cartref Pinafore II, and the imported English and American Ch. Shepton Home Guard. Home Guard was whelped October 11, 1943 by Nosey Parker of Pickhurst out of Snowwhite of Pickhurst. His breeder was Mrs. T. E. J. Shanks. As one of the few Bobtails to be bred during the war years, Home Guard had an important impact on the breed in England and through his get in Europe and the United States in the post-war years. He was one of the first OES to make an English championship after the war, winning his third challenge certificate in 1947.

Home Guard was the sire of English Ch. Shepton Wonder. Wonder was one of the most prolific sires in England after the war. Among Wonder's get were International Champions Shepton Grey Idol and Shepton Sally Ann. Grey Idol was the sire of Ch. Reeuwijks Cupid. Cupid was the sire of the Swedish-bred Unnesta Pim. Pim was out of Sally Ann. In this country Home Guard was the sire of Cartref Guard of Honour, out of Rosmoore Tatters of Cartref, and through him and his littermates and other get, can be found three or four generations removed from many prominent American OES kennel names.

Waterfall Kennels

One of Guard of Honour's sons was Cartref Toggery, who together with the bitch Ch. Cartref Career Girl, was acquired by Mr. and Mrs. H. S. Dunning following Mrs. Briggs' death in the late spring of 1953. The Dunnings of Waterfall Kennels in Ridgefield, Connecticut had owned and bred Bobtails since the early forties. They were among those principally responsible for the resuscitation of the Old English Sheepdog Club of America in the late forties and fifties. They served the club as officers throughout the fifties. Mr. Dunning was president for several years while Mrs. Dunning wrote regularly for the *American Kennel Gazette*. The Dunnings' first Bobtail was the dog, Charlie of Chanticleer, bred by Edward Clark of the Ackerson Farm kennels in Pompton Plains, New Jersey, by Patriot of Ackerson Farm out of Ackerson Farm Tiny, whelped December 20, 1941. Clark was one of

Ch. Cartref Toggery, winner of the 1954 and 1955 OESCA Specialties.
Owned by Mr. and Mrs. H. S. Dunning.

Ch. Tara Wood's Blue Baron winning 1964 OESCA Specialty under
Mona Kucker (Berkowitz). Owned by Mrs. Adeline H. Isakson, and
handled by Howard Tyler, Blue Baron scored 9 Bests in Show.

the oldest Sheepdog fanciers in the United States, having started at the end of World War I, with Morris Kinney's-bred bitch Kinnelon Fleda, whelped February 21, 1917 by Right Sort O' Weather out of Spring Weather. On October 28, 1922, Clark produced his first Ackerson Farm litter out of Fleda by Kinnelon Tower, including Ackerson Farm Boy, A. F. Luna, A. F. Parthenia and A. F. Sleepless Night. Thereafter Clark bred a litter or two, year in and year out. Patriot of Ackerson Farm was the Winners Dog at the 1944 OESCA specialty show.

Over the years, the Dunnings owned and showed several prominent winners. They finished Cartref Toggery's championship. Toggery was Best of Breed from the classes at the 1954 Westminster show under Mona Kucker, a win he repeated in 1955. He was also Best of Breed at the Old English Sheepdog Club of America specialty shows in 1954 and 1955. At the 1955 OESCA specialty, Ch. Cartref's Career Girl was Best of Opposite Sex. The Dunnings imported the bitch. Shepton Bridewell Bo-Peep (by Ch. Shepton Wonder out of Ch. Shepton Lovely Memory, whelped July 12, 1954), bred by Mrs. W. Randell. Bo-Peep was Best of Opposite Sex at Westminster and the OESCA specialty shows in 1959 and 1960. During the fifties, the Waterfall Kennel name was associated with a succession of winners at Westminster and OESCA specialty shows, including Waterfall Chore Boy, Waterfall Rippling Rhythm II, Waterfall Leap to Glory, Waterfall Rollicking Rousty, and Waterfall Lord Cholmondley. Lord Cholmondley was Winners Dog at Westminster in 1959. He was a litter brother of Fezziwig Ceiling Zero, bred by the Van Rensselaers, whelped March 17, 1959. The Dunnings continued to breed and infrequently exhibit their Bobtails in the late 1960s.

Rugbridge Kennels

Adeline Hewitt Isakson of Rugbridge Kennels in Bridgewater, Connecticut acquired her first OES from the Dunnings, the litter-mates Waterfall Rippling Rhythm and Waterfall Thunderdawn Nana, whelped June 24, 1952, by the Achesons' Ch. Laddie of Bashurst out of Rosmoore Polly. Mrs. Isakson subsequently acquired and bred several notable winners, as well as writing for the *American Kennel Gazette* and serving as president of the OESCA before her early death after a long illness in the mid-sixties. Mrs. Izakson owned and finished the bitch Fezziwig Bridget of Gaytrees, another littermate of Ceiling Zero who produced the bitch Rugbridge Bluejeans by her Rippling Rhythm on April 13, 1959. Bluejeans was Winners Bitch and Best of Winners at the 1962 OESCA specialty show. The Winners Dog at that show was Fezziwig Raggedy Andy.

Ch. Ramsrock Defender, a 1937 champion of Alonzo P. Walton's Royal Kennels.

Ch. Dulce Duchess of Davdon, 1947 Royal Kennels' champion.

Ch. Royal Prince Victor, a five-time Best of Breed winner at Westminister, owned by E. Herbert Gilg.

Mrs. Isakson also imported from Canada Tara-Wood's Blue Baron, bred by Diane Buckland of the foremost contemporary Canadian OES kennel. Baron was whelped June 18, 1961 by Tara-Wood's Flannel Pants out of Tara-Wood's Rags n' Tatters. Baron eventually compiled a record of 115 Best of Breeds, 34 Working Groups firsts, and nine all breed Bests in Show. He was Best of Breed at the 1964 OESCA specialty show, judged by Mona Kucker Berkowitz.

Royal Kennels

The Alonzo P. Waltons of the Royal Kennels in Schenectady, New York, also acquired their first Bobtail from Merriedip in the late-thirties. This was the litter sister to Merriedip Master Pantaloons, Mistress Merrie O'Merriedip, who finished her championship in 1938, and in the next few years proved a formidable contender in the breed ring, frequently going up over more renowned dogs. She was a multiple Group and Best American-Bred in Show winner, as well as being the dam of several champions by Merrie Dip of Pastorale, including the Walton-owned, Group-winning studs Royal Prince Topper and Royal Prince Peterkin, whelped February 29, 1940. Over the years the Waltons owned a succession of champions, including Ramsrock Defender, Dulce Duchess of Davdon, Royal Prince Crestwood, Royal Duchess O'Bobby Dell, Royal Princess of Crestwood, Royal Princess Bonnie, Merriedip White Pantalettes, Royal Prince Snowman II, and Royal Prince Topper II. Royal Prince Topper was the sire of Royal Prince Victor, whelped May 8, 1945, out of Dulce Duchess of Davdon.

The Gilgs

Victor was bought by Mr. and Mrs. E. Herbert Gilg of Pittsburgh, who showed him widely in their area to several Group wins and a Best in Show. Prince Victor was Best of Breed at Westminster in 1948, 1949, 1950, 1951, and 1953, a record five times since the modern system of judging has been used at the Garden. Victor's sire Prince Topper was Best of Breed at Westminster in 1943, while his son Marbert Highland Tuffy defeated and interrupted his sire's string of victories by going Best of Breed in 1952. This is the only case of three generations of father-to-son Best of Breed winners at Westminster; none of the three placed in the Group.

The Gilgs, like so many others, got one of their first Bobtails from Merriedip. This was the bitch Merriedip Flare for Victory, whelped November 4, 1946 by Ch. Merriedip Master Pantaloons out of Mer-

106

riedip Colleen. Flare for Victory in turn produced three champion studs for the Gilgs, all sired by Royal Prince Victor, Marbert Spooky, Marbert Highland Tuffy, and Marbert Tommy Atkins.

The Gilgs were among those most responsible for establishing the Old English Sheepdog Club of America on a firm foundation during the 1950s. They served the club in many capacities. Mr. Gilg was president of the OESCA in 1953, when the decision was made to delete the sentence from the standard that a height of more than 26 inches was objectionable. Unfortunately, no record of the reasons for this decision have survived and no discussion of the decision was ever published in the *Gazette*. At the time of his death in 1963, Mr. Gilg was treasurer. Mrs. Gilg contributed many articles on the breed to the *American Kennel Gazette* during the fifties.

Largely through the prompting of Herb Gilg the OESCA decided to hold its 1962 specialty show in Pittsburgh, the first time a club specialty show was held outside the New York metropolitan area. The Gilgs wanted the OESCA to be a national club in fact as well as in name. Their hopes were fulfilled when through Hendrik Van Rensselaer's efforts there was a reorganization of the club's by-laws, and a stress on increasing club activities and opportunities for competition westward.

Rosmoore Kennels

The most well-known of all the people who got their start in Sheepdogs through Merriedip was Mrs. Claude Crafts of Rosmoore Farms in Grasmere, New Hampshire. Mrs. Crafts apparently owned Sheepdogs from the end of the first World War, but never bothered to register them with the AKC. She began breeding and exhibiting seriously in the early '30s with stock acquired from Merriedip, including the bitches Merriedip Mary and Merriedip Trouble. At Mrs. Crafts' second show with Mary, on March 25, 1933 at the Manchester Kennel Club, Mary went to Best of Breed over Mrs. Roesler's imported Downderry dogs, and then fourth in the Working Group. In 1935 the Merriedip imported dog, Blueberry Blaise, was the first Bobtail Mrs. Crafts finished. Blaise was bred by M. Flangton by Courtesy out of Downderry Damsel, whelped August 6, 1931. He was descended from Elkington Squire on both sides of his pedigree. Mrs. Crafts' first registered litter was sired by Blaise out of Merriedip Trouble, whelped October 20, 1934. From this litter came the bitch Naughty Marietta, who finished with a couple of Group placements, and on November 8, 1937 whelped the first registered Rosmoore litter, by Merriedip Master Pantaloons. Mrs. Roesler took the multiple Best in Show winner Rosmoore Saint John from this litter.

Naughty Marietta later produced Rosmoore Smarty Pants by Mer-

Ch. Rosmoore Smarty Pants, handled by her breeder-owner, Mrs. C. M. Crafts, winning Best American-Bred at the New England Old English Sheepdog Club's 1941 show, under judge Percy Roberts. A few months later, Mrs. Crafts handled Smarty Pants to win of Best in Show at Portland, Me.

Ch. Marksman's Bing, owned by Fred LaCrosse and handled by Barbara Partridge, winning the 1953 New England Old English Sheepdog Club Specialty.

rie Dip of Pastorale. Mrs. Crafts handled Smarty Pants to her first Best in Show win at Portland, Maine in the fall of 1941. Over the years Mrs. Crafts produced several winners and producers for herself and others including: Rosmoore Fancy Pants II, winner of the Group at the Eastern Dog Club's show in 1947; Rosmoore Smarty Pants II; Rosmoore Joy's Gift; Rosmoore Sinny, whelped March 16, 1957 and Best in Show from the classes at the Framingham District Kennel Club on June 1, 1958, handled by Mrs. Crafts; Rosmoore Blue Kate; Rosmoore Ole Bill, winner of the OESCA specialty show in 1961 and one of only three dogs ever to defeat Fezziwig Ceiling Zero; and Rosmoore Miss Dior. Miss Dior owned by Mr. and Mrs. Richard Rawls was the last Rosmoore Bobtail to finish a championship (1966). She was whelped June 27, 1960 by Reculver Billie Buster out of Rosmoore Pink Lady. Pink Lady subsequently went to Mr. and Mrs. Harold Richards in Canada and in two litters by Mrs. Crafts' imported stud Beckington Reprint, produced several champions with the Shayloran prefix, including Mona Berkowitz' top-winning Shayloran's Billy Hayseed. Mrs. Crafts served the New England and OESCA in many offices in the 1940s and '50s. She was a licensed judge of the breed.

Patchwork Kennels

The Patchwork kennels of Barclay and Louise Acheson of Briarcliff, New York are the most important single link between the pre-World War II Old English Sheepdogs, the difficult times after the war, and the boom of the sixties. They were already well into their middle years when they took up importing, exhibiting, and breeding Old English in 1948. In the fall of that year they imported three English Bobtails, Laddie of Bashurst, Peggy Ann of Bashurst, and Shepton Blushing Maid. They all finished their American championships handled by E. J. Carver. Laddie and Peggy Ann were both out of Ch. Bashurst Sally Ann of Pichurst. Peggy Ann was by Watchers Warrant, whelped October 30, 1946, while Laddie was by Ch. Watchers Boulgehall Toby, a son of Watchers Warrant, whelped June 26, 1948, both bred by Mrs. P. V. Maidment. Laddie was the sire of Patchwork Bluebirds out of Shepton Blushing Maid, and Patchwork Phoebe out of Merriedip Mopsie Merrie. Bluebirds was bred to Pheobe in the fall of 1953, and given to Mr. and Mrs. Hendrick Van Rensselaer to whelp. The pick bitch from this litter, whelped October 29, 1953 was Patchwork Gillian of Van R, the foundation brood of the Van Rensselaers' Fezziwig kennel.

The Achesons were devoted workers for the OESCA. They had a great deal to do with getting the club going in the early fifties. Barclay Acheson was voted an "Outstanding Service to Dogs Award," for his part in getting out the first OESCA yearbook in fifteen years in 1950. In 1952 the Achesons imported Ch. Paul of Squarefour, considered the best Old English Sheepdog of the day in England. Paul had won his third challenge certificate and championship under Mrs. Edward P. Renner in late 1951. He won five Groups and a Best in Show in the U.S. in 1952, with E. J. Carver handling.

The Changing Trend

It is possible to trace the development of the Old English Sheepdog in the United States without interruption from the late nineteenth century until the present day. However, this is to a large extent misleading. The breed's history has two distinct periods, roughly separated by the Second World War. The War itself nearly destroyed the breed in England. In a series of letters to Mrs. D. Mather Briggs and Laura Dohring Hitchcock among others, during and after the war Henry Tilley detailed the devastation. The English Kennel Club's official policy was to encourage only as much breeding as needed to prevent the extinction of a breed. Restrictions and shortages of food made it almost impossible to feed more than one Bobtail. Many had to be destroyed or face slow starvation. Tilley became a scavenger in his district, carting off dead bodies of farm animals in order to feed his dogs. He reported that "two or three (Old English Sheepdog) kennels (were) completely wiped out through enemy action." The impact on dog fanciers was not as critical in the United States, but Old English Sheepdogs as a breed suffered more severely than most for several reasons. Americans had always acquired new blood from England; this was cut off by the war. The devoted fanciers of the World War I era were either dead or no longer active. The most active importer, breeder, and exhibitor during the thirties, Mrs. Lewis Roesler, was involved in other affairs, which took her to the West Coast and away from dogs altogether for extended periods from 1938 to 1946. The result of this combination of circumstances was that the breed went into decline in the United States. The quality of animals continued high for the most part, and the number of annual registrations remained nearly what it had always been, few, mostly in the Northeast. But, the nature of the fancy changed. Virtually all of the trends present in Old English Sheepdogs as a breed today began to emerge in the late thirties and continued to develop through the fifties. Only popularity was missing.

The major differences between Old English Sheepdog fanciers today and before the Second World War are obvious. Today there are almost no large kennels. Thirty years ago or so there were almost

Ch. Paul of Squarefour, English import owned by Mr. and Mrs. Barclay Anderson and handled by E. J. Carver, winning 1952 Best in Show at Sewickley Valley. Ch. Paul later became a regular on the Howdy Doody Television show.

Ch. Patchwork Mother Machree, a homebred of Mr. and Mrs. Anderson's Patchwork Kennels, winning ribbon at the 1955 Morris and Essex show under Mrs. Renner, with Ed Carver handling.

nothing but a few large kennels. Then the breed was located entirely in the Northeast. Today it is nationwide. It is impossible to adequately account for the sudden, rapid rise in popularity of the Old English Sheepdog. The breed has been in this country since purebred dogs have become in any way a widespread sport. During the first 40 years of the twentieth century the Morses, Kinney, Goodsell, Hitchcocks, and Merriedip had a succession of Bobtail winners in the toughest all-breed competition year in and year out. At the end of the Second World War the early glory days were over. From 1945 when Ch. Black Baron went second in the Group at Westminster until 1957, when Ch. Merriedip Duke George went second, no Old English Sheepdog placed in the Group at the Garden. Since then Bobtails have won a Best in Show and placed in the Group 14 times, including 4 Firsts and 8 Seconds. In 1945 Old English Sheepdogs were exhibited at 43 shows for the entire year. At 15 of these shows only a single Special (champion) was entered, while at another 11 shows only one class dog was entered. Of the 17 shows where it was possible to win points in the breed, at only four, Westminster with the sexes combined, Tuxedo, Des Moines, and the Mohawk Valley Kennel Club was it possible to earn more than one point. The only major was at the Mohawk Valley show on November 24th, where the Alonzo P. Walton's bitch Dulce Duchess of Davdon went Winners Bitch, Best of Winners, and Best of Opposite Sex in an entry of five bitches, including three puppies, for four points. While there was usually more than one multiple point entry a year during the next decade, entries at shows remained distressingly small. The breed did not attract fanciers.

The Old English Sheepdog Club of America, which itself had almost disappeared toward the end and just after the war, was revived in the late forties and early fifties. In 1950 the club began holding annual specialty shows again. In order to get as many Bobtails as possible out for the important shows, it was decided to support entries at several shows as well as offering the Challenge Bowl at both Westminster and the OESCA specialty show. At one point in the early fifties it was decided to form a publicity committee within the OESCA, in an attempt to stimulate interest in the breed. The result saw Bobtails appearing prominently in several nationally circulated magazines. The Barclay Achesons even sold their Best in Show-winning, imported English Champion stud Paul of Squarefour in early 1953 to the Kagran Corporation, who produced the Howdy Doody children's television show. Paul was thereafter a regular on the show, as well as going to shows occasionally with his handler, E. J. Carver.

However, the breed continued on its placid level of about 100 registrations a year. In 1959, there were 112 Old English Sheepdogs registered with the American Kennel Club, only six more than in 1958. In 1960, there were 149 registered. Since then annual registrations have zoomed. In 1965 there were 809 Bobtails registered for the year. In 1970 there were 6,782 Old English Sheepdogs registered and by 1975, these annual registrations had multiplied to 15,623 and the breed was 21st in popularity of all breeds. The breed thus shared honors with the Lhasa Apso for the greatest vault in popularity over the last decade: the Lhasa going from 53rd in 1965 to 19th in 1975, and the Old English from 55th in 1965 to 21st in 1975.

Suggestions for Further Reading:

The basic sources for the history of the breed are the official publications of the American and English Kennel Clubs. The *American Kennel Gazette* and the Kennel Club's official *Stud Books* are invaluable reference sources, as is the English Kennel Club's official *Stud Book and Calendar.*

E. C. Ash, *Dogs: Their History and Development* (n.d.); H. P. Davis, *Modern Dog Encyclopedia* (1958); Richard and Alice Fiennes, *The Natural History of Dogs* (1970); Walter J. Graham, "Dogs Inherit Characteristics: Experiment with Old English Sheepdogs Proves Herding Instincts Are Transmitted,"; *American Kennel Gazette,* Volume 48 (February 1931); Aubrey Hopwood, *The Old English Sheep Dog From Puppyhood to Championship: A Handbook for Beginners* (1905); W. Hutchinson, *Hutchinson's Dog Encyclopedia,* Volume 11 (1935); S. N. Vewot "Do You Recognize the Breed? Experts Disagree Regarding Gainsborough's Famous Painting of the Buccleugh Dog," *American Kennel Gazette,* Volume 58 (June 1941); Rowland Johns, *Our Friends the Old English and Shetland Sheepdogs* (1935); Arthur Frederick Jones, "Letting the Bobtail Follow Nature, Kinnelon Dogs Raised True to Type Without the Aid of Folderols or Theories," *American Kennel Gazette* Volume 43 (January 1926); Arthur Frederick Jones, "Merriedip Bobtails Have True Quality In and Out of Ring," *American Kennel Gazette* Volume 52 (January 1935); Rawdon Lee, *A History and Description of the Collie or Sheep Dog in His British Varieties* (1890); Rawdon B. Lee, *A History and Description of the Modern Dogs of Great Britain and Ireland, Nonsporting* (1899); Arthur Frederick Jones, "Pembroke Welsh Corgis of Merriedip Now Rank Close to Its Bobtails" *American Kennel Gazette* Volume 57 (April 1940); Freeman Lloyd, "The Bobtails of Great Britain: Author of First Old English Sheepdog Standard Relates History of the Breed", *American Kennel Gazette* Volume 46 (April 1929); Freeman Lloyd, "Dog Breeds of the World; Their Origin, Development and Use Throughout the Ages: Old English Sheepdogs," *American Kennel Gazette,* Volume 51 (April, May, and June 1934); Freeman Lloyd, "The Old English Sheepdog," *Turf, Field and Farm* (1889); *Official Kennel Blue Book* (1909); Old English Sheepdog Club of America *Yearbooks* (1906, 1907, 1908, 1909, 1922, 1923, 1925, 1935, 1950, 1955, 1963); Walford Graham Robertson, *Life Was Worth Living: The Reminiscences of W. Graham Robertson* (1931); Phyllis Robson, *Popular Dogs* (England) (1934); Albert Payson Terhune and Lillian Gatlin, "What We Two Dogs Did, Incidentally We Saved the Lives of 1062 Soldiers;" *The Ladies Home Journal* (September 1919); Henry Arthur Tilley, *The Old English Sheepdog* (1933 and 1937); William Wade, "The Old English Sheep Dog," in G. O. Shields ed., *The American Book of the Dog* (1891); A. S. L. Wallis, "The Old English Sheepdogs," in Brian Vesey-Fitzgerald, ed., *The Book of the Dog* (1948); James Watson, *The Dog Book* (1905).

Serena Van Rensselaer and Sheepdogs in a 1930s photo.

Mrs. Van Rensselaer with "Barty" (Am. & Can. Ch. Farley-dene Bartholomew).

Into the 1970s

THE RECENT phenomenal growth in Old English popularity has many parallels with the increased popularity of purebred dogs in general. Large kennels with substantial breeding and exhibiting programs were the backbone of the sport in its formative years. This remained true for most breeds through the Second World War. After the war, ownership of purebred dogs became far more common. Large kennels gradually disappeared and the "small" breeder-exhibitor became the rule.

Because Old English were very rare until well into the 1960s the breed remained in the hands of a relatively few breeders and exhibitors through the 1950s. Even in the mid-1960s it is possible to point to a few kennels as having the predominate role in shaping the breed's development. But by the end of the decade this was no longer the case.

From scarcely a hundred registrations a year in 1960 Old English have skyrocketed to 15,000 registrations a year in the mid-1970s. With this vast growth in numbers has come the rise of many dedicated small breeders. These serious fanciers, seldom having more than a litter or two a year and finishing a champion from time-to-time, are now the backbone of the breed. This trend makes it difficult to single out individual kennels as making a significant contribution to the breed's development, for the reason that many, many individuals are making small but important contributions. The net impact of these many small breeder-exhibitors is the contemporary history of the breed.

Increased popularity has meant several things for Old English Sheepdogs as a breed. There are now a large, and ever increasing, number of Sheepdogs that are purebred and AKC registered, but in terms of the ideal called for in the Standard, of shockingly low quality. Many, if not most, Old English Sheepdogs in the United States today

Fezziwig Ceiling Zero and Fezziwig Black-Eyed Susan, littermates, pictured at left as puppies, and below as 26-mos. old champions at the New England Specialty held with Framingham District all-breeds show, May 1959. "Ceilie" (at right, handled by E. J. Carver) won the Specialty, and went on to win Best in Show. Susan (handled by Mr. Van Rensselaer) was BOS at the Specialty.

are not show quality dogs. This does not mean they are not good pets. Any even-tempered, well-behaved dog can be a good pet. But, if it were not for the expanse of hair, many Bobtails today would scarcely be recognizable as such by the breed's mainstay of a half-century ago.

The comparative decrease in total breed quality is the natural product of a situation in which demand has far exceeded supply. But the situation is not altogether dismal. It is agreed at the same time that there are more poor-quality Bobtails than ever before, there are also more good OES than ever before.

Fezziwig Kennels

The most prominent name in Old English Sheepdogs throughout the 1960s was Fezziwig. Fezziwig is the jovial character out of Christmas past in Dickens' classic *A Christmas Carol.* It is also the apt name of the Old English Sheepdog kennel of Hendrik and Serena Van Rensselaer of Basking Ridge, New Jersey.

The Van Rensselaers have owned, shown, and bred Old English Sheepdogs since 1932. They received their first Bobtail as a wedding gift from Mrs. Van Rensselaer's uncle, Roy Miles, on October 25, 1932. Roy Miles and his daughter, Sally Miles Grey, were breeders of Old English under the Milenick Kennel prefix in the late 1920s and '30s. The Van Rensselaers' first Sheepdog was imported by Mrs. Helen Roesler of Merriedip fame, from the Downderry Kennels of Mrs. Durham-Waite. In 1936 the Van Rensselaers registered their first kennel prefix, Van R., with the American Kennel Club.

Following World War II, Mr. Van Rensselaer's work as a water engineer took him to all corners of the world, from South America to South Africa to Russia and back. A year's stay in Brazil in the late 1940s occasioned what may have been the first immigration of the Old English Sheepdog into that country.

Upon their return to the United States (at Summit, New Jersey) the Van Rensselaers resumed active interest in breeding Old English. In 1953 Louise and Barclay Acheson of Patchwork Kennels asked Hendrik and Serena to take Patchwork Phoebe and deliver a litter by Patchwork Bluebirds. Phoebe whelped her litter on October 29, 1953.

Patchwork Bluebirds and Patchwork Phoebe were both sired by the Achesons' imported stud Ch. Laddie of Bashurst. (Ch. Watchers Boulgehall Toby ex Ch. Bashurst Sally Ann of Pickhurst.) These dogs were descended from the celebrated pre-World War II Pickhurst Old English Sheepdogs and through them from the important dogs of the 1920s and earlier, including Shepton Moonshine and many of Mrs. Fare Fosse's Weather dogs.

117

Patchwork Bluebird's dam was Ch. Shepton Blushing Maid, bred by F. C. Padfield in England. She was whelped July 10, 1948 by Ch. Shepton Surf King out of Shepton Bluette. On her sire's side, she was descended from the Boldwood dogs, and in turn from the famous pre-World War II Pastorale dogs of Miss Tireman. On her dam's side she was descended from several Shepton dogs, including Rajah and Wall-Eyed Wonder, and in turn from Shepton Moonshine. Handled by E. J. Carver, Blushing Maid had a distinguished show career in the United States and Canada. She was Winners Bitch and Best of Opposite Sex at the 1952 Old English Sheepdog Club of America specialty show, and was a Canadian Best in Show winner and a multiple Group winner in the United States and Canada.

Patchwork Phoebe's dam was Merriedip Mopsie Merrie, who was descended from the Merriedip Kennel's great pre-World War II dogs including Ch. Merriedip Master Pantaloons and in turn from the Downderry dogs of the '20s.

The Van Rensselaers selected the pick bitch from this litter as the basis of their breeding plans. They named her Patchwork Gillian of Van R. Gill represented to the Van Rensselaers correct type, soundness, and substance as they had seen it in pre-World War II dogs. She was finished to championship in the summer of 1956. As a special she was Best of Opposite Sex at the Old English Sheepdog Club of America specialty show in June 1957, two and a half months after her first litter was whelped.

A business trip to South Africa, with return by way of England in the spring of 1956, gave the Van Rensselaers an opportunity to look for a stud to breed to Gill. After visiting various kennels, the Van Rensselaers were convinced only one dog they had seen would do. This was George Gooch's Farleydene Bartholomew, bred by W. Fowler, whelped May 25, 1954.

Barty had won classes at various shows including Crufts. He was a promising youngster. Gooch was reluctant to let him go. However, a return trip to Gooch's, combined with a convincing argument of Barty's worth, persuaded Gooch to sell him to the Van Rensselaers for seventy pounds. Gooch's sale of Barty to the Van Rensselaers was a momentous decision for the history of American Old English.

Barty was sired by Farleydene Rudolph who was in turn descended from the Pickhurst and Watchers dogs of an earlier day. His dam was Shepton Misty Light who was sired by Ch. Shepton Surf King. Barty and Gill were both descended from the same pre-World War II stock the Van Rensselaers considered the best Old English Sheepdogs in their experience.

Following his arrival in this country Barty was shown by E. J. Carver to his American and Canadian championships, undefeated in

118

Ch. Fezziwig Ceiling Zero, all-time greatest sire of the breed with 63 champions. Bred and owned by Fezziwig Kennels.

Ch. Fezziwig Raggedy Andy, prime Sheepdog of the mid-60s. Bred and owned by Fezziwig Kennels.

119

Ch. Fezziwig Peeko Hannaford, one of 11 champions of Barty-Gill matings. Owned by Joyce Anderson.

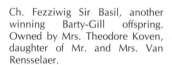

Ch. Fezziwig Sir Basil, another winning Barty-Gill offspring. Owned by Mrs. Theodore Koven, daughter of Mr. and Mrs. Van Rensselaer.

Ch. Fezziwig Bonnie Blue Flag, impressive Barty-Gill daughter. Owners, Mr. and Mrs. Joseph McCabe.

the classes. He was a multiple Group winner in the United States and Canada and a Best in Show winner in Canada.

The importance of Barty and Gill to the breed has been as producers. Barty sired 13 litters, six of them by Gill (only three of them outside the Fezziwig family). Barty and Gill produced 11 champions: Fezziwig Ceiling Zero, Black-Eyed Susan, Bridget of Gaytrees, Isle of Wight Vici, Nannie, Easter Bonnet, Sir Basil, Fainthart Falstaff, Bonny Blue Flag, Phoebe and Peeko Hannaford. Barty also produced four other champions, Fezziwig Raggedy Andy, Raggedy Anne, Bartholomew, and Lord Higgins of Wyncote.

The first litter of Barty and Gill and the first Fezziwig litter was whelped March 17, 1957. From this litter came Fezziwig Ceiling Zero and Black-Eyed Susan. Ceiling Zero was named in deference to the breed's characteristic face coat and Mr. Van Rensselaer's globe-trotting, which frequently found him delayed at some remote spot when flying conditions were "ceiling zero." Ceilie was shown intermittently as a puppy at important shows, including Westminster. His early promise was fulfilled at the 1958 Old English Sheepdog Club of America Specialty in June, when he went Best of Winners at 15 months. This was followed by a Group first from the classes and a Best American Bred in Show and his championship later that summer, while still less than 17 months old.

Ceilie's career in Specials began in earnest in the spring of 1959. At Trenton he went Best of Breed over a Best in Show winning Old English. Then with Anne Rogers (Clark) handling he went on to win the Working Group under Percy Roberts. Ceilie rounded out the month by going Best of Breed at the New England Old English Sheepdog Club specialty show held in conjunction with the Framingham District Kennel Club show on May 31, 1959, then on to Group first and Best in Show over more than 1,000 dogs for his first top win. E. J. Carver handled Ceilie to this first Best in Show. Percy Roberts, long considered one of the great authorities on purebred dogs in the world, found Ceilie at two years of age to be "almost perfect, even in the finest points," and predicted that a dog of his strength and soundness would last indefinitely, a prediction that proved accurate. Ceilie dominated the show ring until his retirement a few weeks short of his seventh birthday in February 1964. From his retirement until his death in May 1969, Ceilie dominated Sheepdog ranks as a producer.

Ceilie won six Bests in Show in 1959 and '60, and then disappeared from the show ring for a year. It is not generally known, but at the height of his show career Ceilie broke his left hind leg and was forced into retirement. The leg healed perfectly, except for a bone burr. If anything, Ceilie was more impressive following his return to the ring.

Judges' comments remained exceptional through his sixth year in the ring: "So balanced and sound he cannot stand wrong;" "One of the best movers I've ever seen;" "The head, bone and substance the breed should have;" "Always exciting, showing with great style and in working condition." During the last 25 months of his career Ceilie was undefeated in the breed. From the time he entered the ring as a special in 1959 until his retirement after his second consecutive Group second at Westminster in 1964, only three other Old English Sheepdogs defeated him: Ch. Blue Admiral of Box, Ch. Lillibrad Prince Charming, and Ch. Rosmoore Ole Bill, all of whom he in turn defeated.

Ceilie was the greatest winning Old English Sheepdog of all time at his retirement with 15 Bests in Show, 50 Group wins, two American-Bred Bests in Show, six specialty wins, and seven wins of the Old English Sheepdog Club of America's Challenge Bowl. In the Phillips System ranking for show dogs of all-breeds, Ceilie was the fifth ranked Working Dog in 1959, sixth in 1960, seventh in 1962 and second in 1963 (also ranking fifth of all-breeds that year).

(The Phillips System is an unofficial rating system that awards dogs points in accordance with the number of dogs they win over. A Best in Show winner gets a point for every dog in the show. A Group winner gets a point for every dog in the Group. A Group placement win entitles a dog to a point for every dog in the Group, less the number of dogs in the breeds that placed above it in that Group.)

Ceilie's records as a show dog and the widespread publicity he brought an almost unknown breed are of less significance in evaluating his total impact on Sheepdogs than his career as a producer. In his first years he had to take a back seat to his sire as the chief stud at Fezziwig. His first litter was whelped February 1, 1961, when he was six weeks short of four years of age. This litter contained the Best in Show winner and sire of Best in Show winners, Ch. Shagbourne's Messenger. Ceilie was the sire of the celebrated Rivermist litter of nine champions including four Group and two Best in Show winners.

At start of 1975, six years after his death, Ceilie's total champion get stood at 63, with one or two dogs from his last litters still seen at shows occasionally.

Ceilie's champion get have not only been numerous but significant in their own right as winners and producers. Ceilie was on the Phillips Honor Roll as a top producer for 1965, 1966, 1967 and 1968. His sire, Farleydene Bartholomew is one of the breed's all time top producers, while his son, Dan Patch, and Dan Patch's son, Ch. Rivermist Dan Tatters are now among the breed's top producers. Other sons, daughters, grandsons and daughters, and even great and great-great offspring are producing champion get.

122

The Van Rensselaers inbreed as long as the dogs being used warrant the matings. They have used a few basic inbreeding patterns and from time to time have introduced new blood through outcross bitches. The first inbreeding the Van Rensselaers did was to take their bitch Ch. Fezziwig Black-Eyed Susan back to her sire Ch. Farleydene Bartholomew. This litter, Susie's only, was whelped April 16, 1960. From it came Ch. Fezziwig Raggedy Anne and Ch. Fezziwig Raggedy Andy.

Raggedy Andy made an unparalled mark on the show world. Andy was a much different dog than Ceilie. Ceilie was bigger, and had an all-white head and front. Andy had black ears. Most observers feel Ceilie was a more striking dog. He had a more elegant bearing with better reach of neck. On the other hand, Andy had tremendous bone and substance, and a great head. Both Ceilie and Andy were spirited showmen. Andy was shown intermittently to his championship at two. Thereafter he lived in semi-retirement coming out at specialty shows and Westminster and occasionally as a brace with his dam Susie.

Andy's career as a special began in earnest a week after Ceilie's retirement in February 1964, with a Group win. He was shown throughout his career by Bob Forsyth, who had handled Ceilie during the last year of his career. Andy scored 22 Group wins and three Bests in Show in 1964, and was the second ranking Working Dog for the year, and fifth ranking of all-breeds according to the Phillips System.

Throughout the three years Andy was shown (1964, '65, and '66) he was never shown before Westminster or in the summer months; nor was he shown week in and week out the rest of the year. Andy went to less than 50 shows a year, whereas other top winning dogs attend 70 to 90 shows a year—which made his high Phillips System ratings all the more significant. In 1965, Andy added four more Bests in Shows and 23 Group wins, to make him third ranking Working dog and fifth ranking all-breed winner.

He had his greatest winning year in 1966. He began by winning the Group at Westminster, the first Old English to do this since Ch. Merriedip Master Pantaloons in 1942. He followed with Group and Best in Show wins at the largest all-breed shows in the country, including Best in Show at Detroit, Chicago, Trenton, and Greenwich. His winnings for the first half of the year moved him far in front of all Working and all-breed contenders in the Phillips ratings. Even with time out for summer vacation, he ended the year as top Working dog and a very close second in all-breed competition to the California-campaigned Miniature Poodle, Ch. Frederick of Rencroft. In the 48 times he was shown in 1966, Andy won the breed 47 times, going Best

123

of Opposite Sex in a bittersweet loss on the last show weekend of the year at the Eastern Dog Club in Boston, a loss which almost certainly cost him the ranking of number one dog all-breeds by the Phillips System. He was only 114 points behind Frederick, and more than 7,000 points ahead of the second ranked Working dog. Of the 47 times Andy was Best of Breed he placed in the Group 46 times, winning 28 times, going second 13 times, third three times and fourth twice. He was Best in Show at 11 all-breed shows in 1966.

Andy was shown twice more, in 1967, winning the Group both times, one a repeat of his 1966 win of the Group at Westminster. His career totals were 18 Bests in Shows, 75 Group wins and 63 other Group placements. His winning included three Bests of Breed and two Group firsts at Westminster, as well as four Bests of Breed at the Old English Sheepdog Club of America's specialty shows.

While Andy's great show winnings surpassed those of his half-brother and kennelmate, Ceiling Zero, he remained in Ceilie's shadow as a producer. During his show career, from 1964 to February 1967, Andy was not widely used at stud because of the demands of his show going. He died in February 1969, from poisoning as a result of orchard spraying.

However, one of Andy's matings proved invaluable to the Fezziwig program. Milton and Charlene Semer bred their bitch Amblehurst Daisy to Andy in the summer of 1966. From this litter, the Van Rensselaers bought Ch. Fezziwig Andrea, who was planned for breeding back to her sire at the appropriate time. Andrea produced three puppies in August 1967. These became Chs. Fezziwig Vice Versa, Artful Dodger and Andorra. Vice Versa and Artful Dodger are both Best in Show winners and owned by the Van Rensselaers while Andorra is co-owned by Serena Van Rensselaer and Jacqueline Lamb. Artie was handled to early wins by Jim McTernan, finishing his championship at the Hartford all-breed show with a Best in Show from the Open dog class.

In the 1970s Vice Versa has been the principal show and stud dog at Fezziwig. In the show ring he has compiled a record of more than 90 Best of Breeds, including Westminster where he was second in the Group in 1974, and the Old English Sheepdog Club of America specialty show in New Orleans in 1973. Vice Versa has placed in the Group more than 40 times including 13 firsts and he has four American Bests in Show. On a trip to Canada in 1971 he garnered his Canadian championship, two all-breed Bests in Show, and the Canadian Old English club's specialty show. He also earned his Bermuda championship.

Vice Versa's final impact as a producer will be many years in assessing, but it is already monumental. He is the foremost living

Am. Can. & Berm. Ch. Fezziwig Vice Versa, multi-BIS winner and one of the all-time top sires. Bred and owned by Fezziwig Kennels, and handled by Mr. Van Rensselaer.

Ch. Fezziwig Artful Dodger, litter brother of Vice Versa, pictured winning Best in Show from the classes at Hartford 1970 under judge Frank Foster Davis. Bred and owned by Fezziwig Kennels, handled by Jim McTernan.

Am. Can. & Berm. Ch. Fezziwig Fringe Benefits, multi-BIS winner, a Ceiling Zero son out of Silvershag Sweet Sue. Bred and owned by Fezziwig Kennels.

Ch. Fezziwig Ruffle and Flourish, a Ceilie-Sweet Sue daughter. Owned by Mr. and Mrs. Joseph Saunders.

Ch. Fezziwig Bluejohn Wilhemina, another Ceilie-Sweet Sue winner. Owned by Mr. and Mrs. Lawrence H. Conklin.

producer of Old English champions (with 32 at this writing). The quality of his get has been outstanding. One of his daughters, Ch. Langley Snowmaiden, is now the all-time Old English Best in Show winner with 19.

Snowmaiden was whelped December 26, 1969, by Vice Versa out of Fezziwig Bonnie Blue Belle. Blue Belle is a double granddaughter of Ceiling Zero. Snowmaiden was bred in Maryland by Joan and Roy Butler, Jr., and eventually was campaigned by Kathy and Don Bedford.

In little more than a year's time from mid-1972 until November 1973, Snowmaiden totalled some 138 Bests of Breed, 47 Group firsts, 27 seconds, 19 thirds, 8 fourths, and 19 Bests in Show. She was handled throughout her career by Don Bradley.

One of the most successful producers the Van Rensselaers had in the 1960s was Silvershag Sweet Sue. "Taffy" was bred by Dr. Louise Forest out of her Greyfriar's Jennie by Ch. Shepton Bobbibingo. In two litters by Ceilie and a third by Sir Basil, Taffy produced seven champions: Fezziwig Sir John Falstaff, Bluejohn Wilhelmina, Nosey Pepper, Ruffle and Flourish, Fringe Benefits (all by Ceilie); Gillian and Kara (by Basil). Fringe Benefits was a multiple Group and Best in Show winner as well as a champion in Canada and Bermuda. "Benny" has produced some important dogs for Fezziwig.

Over the years the Van Rensselaers have served Old English Sheepdogs in many capacities. They have been members of the Old English Sheepdog Club of America since 1936. Hendrick Van Rensselaer served several terms as treasurer, president and AKC delegate. Largely through his efforts in the middle 1960s, the Club was reorganized and put on an effective basis for serving a breed that is now national in scope. Serena Van Rensselaer has a special knack for capturing the personality of the breed in her excellent drawings of OES dogs and puppies. Her drawings have been used on the official Old English Sheepdog of America stationery for more than a decade. She also wrote for the *American Kennel Gazette* and *Popular Dogs* over a ten year span from the mid-'50s to the mid-'60s and contributed to the OESCA's monthly bulletin.

Rivermist Kennels

A most prominent name in American Old English Sheepdogs during the last half of the sixties was Rivermist, the kennel of Mr. and Mrs. Barry Goodman of Brinklow, Maryland. The Rivermist experience is an example of the judicious combination of purchased stock, here and abroad, use of other kennels' studs, and successful breed-

127

Int. and Am. Ch. Unnesta Pim, sire of 46 champions. Swedish bred. Owned by River-mist Kennels.

Ch. Baroness of Duroya, English import BIS winner and foundation bitch of the River-mist Kennels.

128

ings. Rivermist produced more champions in a shorter period of time than any American OES kennel.

The first Rivermist OES was acquired from Mona Kucker (Berkowitz). This was the bitch Momarv River Mist. She finished her conformation championship in 1960, after having earned an obedience Companion Dog degree. She was bred by the Kuckers out of their Ch. Arnue Platinum Penny by Ch. Merriedip Duke George, whelped December 26, 1957. Platinum Penny was by Ch. Momarv's Blue Devil out of Patchwork Pleasure Plus. Her litter, the first Rivermist litter, was whelped May 20, 1962, by Louise Forest's imported Ch. Shepton Bobbibingo, and included among others Chs. Rivermist Robber Baron and Rivermist Frostflower CD, who have made important contributions to the breed.

Robber Baron was owned by Beverley Katchmar Hildrith of Silvermist Kennels in Brooklyn, Wisconsin. He sired several champions, including Beowulf Tyrone, Silvershag Miss Debonair, Silvershag Miss Bustle N' Bows, Silvershag Robbin' Rascal, Silvermist Snow Dance, and Silvermist Snow Sprite. Silvermist has produced other champions, including S. Peek-a-Boo, sired by Ch. Greyfriars Lord Fauntleroy out of Ch. Silvershag Sally Snow Boots (the dam of S. Snow Sprite) and Ch. Silvermist Southern Belle and S. Striker out of Silvermist Mary Poppins (a daughter of Ch. Rivermist Dan Patch, by Ch. Prince Andrew of Sherline, the top winning OES in the United States in 1968, '69, and '70.)

Ch. Rivermist Frostflower CD was owned by Ann Penn, then of Dayton, Mayland, now of Colorado Springs, Colorado. Frostie became the foundation of the Penns' Sunnybrae Kennels, which has produced several champions and winners. From an early litter by Ch. Holloways Downright, Frostie produced Sunnybrae Bobby the Bruce, who in turn sired Ch. Happihill Ringo Ragbag CD, whelped April 1, 1966, out of Round Table Damoiselle. Ringo Ragbag was shown by Barbara Getty Hill of Claymont, Delaware. He sired several winners including champions with the Littlejohn prefix out of Buechler's Joan of Arc. The influence of Fezziwig breeding in contemporary OES is seen in these dogs. Round Table Damoiselle is a granddaughter of Ceiling Zero through her dam Round Table Lady Bess, while Joan of Arc is a daughter of Fezziwig John Silver, himself a son of Ceiling Zero. In two litters by Ch. Rivermist Dan Patch, Frostie has produced several champions, including Sunnybrae Gunsmoke and S. Jack Frost, with others pointed.

Jack Frost attracted widespread favorable comment for his owners, Robert and Louise Lopina of Colorado Springs. He was a Group winner and sire of champions. Louise is a talented artist, whose OES drawings have added much to our book.

129

Beckington Reprint, an imported stud, was acquired by the Goodmans from Mrs. Crafts of the Rosmoore Kennels in the early 1960s. Reprint was by English Ch. Beckington Tom Tod out of Eng. Ch. Beckington Lady of Welby House, who is the all time top Challenge Certificate winning Bobtail in England with 35 CC's. Unfortunately, Reprint was never shown in the United States, and lived only a short time, but he had a marked impact on the breed's development in the few litters he sired. Goodman was forced to clip him down, but rates him a great OES. His get indicate this is the case. In two litters out of Rosmoore Pink Lady, whelped in Canada, bred by Mr. and Mrs. Harold Richards, Reprint sired several champions with the Shayloran prefix, including S. Penny Plain Rosmoore, S. Little Beaver, and S. Billy Hayseed. Billy Hayseed was Winners Dog and Best of Winners at the 1964 OESCA specialty show judged by Mona Berkowitz. Mrs. Berkowitz subsequently acquired Billy and campaigned him to numerous important wins, and used him widely at stud on the West Coast. One of the few OES Reprint produced for Rivermist before his death was the bitch Rivermist Laurel out of Nana of Rokeby, owned by Constance Chipp Lowden of Laconia, New Hampshire. She was Winners Bitch, Best of Winners, and Best of Opposite Sex at seven months of age at the New England Old English Sheepdog Club specialty show on June 5, 1965, and subsequently finished her championship with a string of major wins.

The basis of the widespread reputation of the Rivermist name begins with the imported bitch Baroness of Duroya, bred by Mrs. A. F. Woodiwiss, whelped January 17, 1962 by English Ch. Fernville Fernando out of Azure Queen of Duroya. During her brief show career prior to her death in 1965, Baroness was the top winning OES bitch. She was Winners Bitch at Westminster in 1964, and Best of Opposite Sex there, as a special in 1965. She was Best of Opposite Sex at the 1964 OESCA specialty show, elsewhere winning two Groups and placing in three others that year. At Salisbury, North Carolina on September 6th, she was Best in Show, making her one of only three OES bitches to win a Best in Show in the United States in the 1960s. Her Best in Show came almost four months to the day after she whelped her only litter, the most famous OES litter ever produced.

This litter of 11, sired by Fezziwig Ceiling Zero and whelped May 5, 1964, eventually included two Best in Show winners, four Group winners, nine champions, and a tenth with both majors: Ch. Rivermist Dan Patch, Galahad, Marco Polo, Gulliver, Hollyhock, Gentian, Indigo, Bellflower and Nosegay. The combined total of champion get out of these nine champions and the sister, Rivermist Heather, who has two majors, is more than 50, with some still in the rings. Galahad and Dan Patch were Best in Show winners. Galahad, handled by Roy

Ch. Rivermist Dan Patch, a top winner and sire of the mid-60s. Owned by Howard and Celeste Payne.

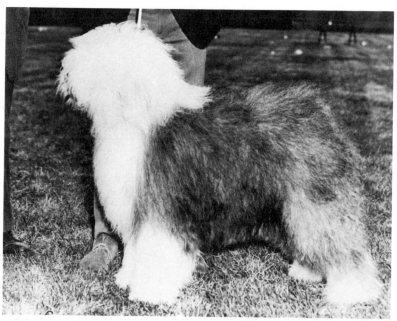

Ch. Rivermist Gentian, the all-time top producing Bobtail dam, foundation bitch of Captain and Mrs. F. E. Rich's Jendower Kennels.

Ch. Rivermist Marco Polo, by Ceiling Zero ex Baroness of Duroya, pictured winning the Group at Wilmington 1967 under Wm. L. Kendrick, handled by Lina Basquette. Owned by Mr. and Mrs. Louis Loeb.

Ch. Rivermist Galahad, Best in Show and Specialty winner, also out of the historic Ceilie-Baroness litter. Pictured winning 1967 Best in Show under Major Godsol, Roy Holloway handling. Owned by Henry Hecht.

Holloway, won several Groups, was Best in Show at Woodstock, Vermont in July 1967, and in September of that year was Best of Breed at the OESCA specialty show held in conjunction with the Westchester Kennel Club, narrowly defeating his littermate Dan Patch. The Best of Opposite Sex at that specialty went to Hollyhock, while the Winners Dog was Knightcap Moody Blue and the Winners Bitch was Fezziwig Ruffle and Flourish, making all four top spots in the largest specialty ever held in the East to that time, the sons and daughters of Fezziwig Ceiling Zero.

Dan Patch compiled one of the most impressive show records of any Working dog between 1966 and June 1968. In all he won 183 Bests of Breed, 17 Bests in Show, 52 Group firsts, and 79 other Group placements, for his owners Howard and Celeste Payne of Kankakee, Illinois. Danny was handled to almost all of these wins, including Best of Breed and second in the Group at Westminster in 1968, by Jack Funk. Danny's first Best in Show was at Manitowoc, Wisconsin on September 18, 1966. For 1966 he was the No. 2 winning OES in the United States, trailing only Fezziwig Raggedy Andy. In 1967, with six Bests in Show, 28 Group firsts, and 43 other places, Danny was top winning OES, the number three Working dog and number five all-breeds. He was only shown during the first five months of 1968, but his winnings, including ten Group firsts and nine Bests in Show, made him the No. 2 Sheepdog and No. 9 Working dog for that year.

Dan Patch's influence has already been widely felt as a producer. He sired more than 15 champions, and many sons and daughters are with majors. Many of Dan Patch's offspring have in turn begun to produce top winning get of their own. In addition to Rivermist and Sunnybrae, Dan Patch's champion get include the prefixes Briarmead, Downeylane, Droverdale, Graceland, and Silvershag, as well as many Bobtails with no kennel prefix.

One of Danny's first litters has had a marked influence on Sheepdogs. This was out of Gail Janoff's Miss Muffit of Tatters, who in litters by Dan Patch and Int. Ch. Unnesta Pim has become one of the greatest producing bitches in the breed's history. Miss Muffit was leased for breeding purposes by the Goodmans. She was sired by Marksman's Guardsman, who although not a champion himself, has sired many winners and producers in addition to Miss Muffit, including Chs. Ambelon's Ole King Cole, Marksman's Sir Winston, Darling Dolly of Trynlaw, Marian of King Oak Hill, Marksman's Morgan C.D., and Lady Stephanie of Cartree.

Guardsman was sired by Ch. Merriedip Duke of George out of Ch. Cartree Pinafore. His get represent one of the principal lines of descendants among contemporary OES of the famous American and English imported OES of the pre-World War II period. Miss Muffit's dam was Fellscove Caprice, sired by Ch. Fellscove Mr. Wonderful out of the imported bitch Ch. Miss Muffit of Tansley. Mr. Wonderful (by Ch. Marksman Bing out of Sweet and Lovely) is also descended from the pre-World War II New England OES, while Miss Muffit of Tansley is a great-granddaughter of Ch. Shepton Home Guard.

Miss Muffit's litter by Dan Patch, whelped September 9, 1965, included the Chs. Rivermist Hornblower, R. Horatio, R. Wildflower, and R. Dan Tatters. In subsequent breedings to Ch. Unnesta Pim and Ch. Rivermist King Arthur, she has produced Chs. Rivermist Butler Boy, R. Flying Dutchman, R. Royal Jester, R. Bluebell, R. John O'Groats, R. King Richard, and R. Peppermint among others.

Hornblower, owned by Dr. and Mrs. Ray Snider of Independence, Missouri, finished his championship at the age of eight months and 13 days, a breed record. In subsequent exhibitions Hornblower won more than 50 Bests of Breed, a number of Group placements and a first, handled by Keith Waite. Hornblower has also sired several champions and winners including Harriclown's Sallyforth (bred by Connie and John H. Harrington—among the first OES fanciers in Kansas; he a former OESCA director), and Bobtail Acres Sno-Cone and her litter brothers Bobtail Acres Frosty Knight and Int. Ch. Bobtail Acres Shaggy Wonder Snowman. They were whelped April 7, 1968, out of Ginger Herlihy's imported champion Shaggy Wonder Main Attraction.

Bobtail Acres SW Snowman was returned to Mrs. Yvonne Mewis De Ryck's Shaggy Wonder Kennels where he quickly finished an International championship and has sired several European litters. Horatio and Wildflower have also produced champion offspring. Wildflower, in a litter by Unnesta Pim, produced the dog Ch. Rivermist Roundhouse Punch, who has sired several recent winning Bobtails bearing the Tumbleweed and Blind Bluff prefixes of his co-owners, Marge Leeper and Ken Kopin.

The most widely known son of Miss Muffit and Dan Patch was Ch. Rivermist Dan Tatters, who was co-owned by Bob and Sheila Ziccardi and Jim McTernan. Tatters finished his championship at one year, with four majors and undefeated in the classes, handled by Barry Goodman. After a year and a half retirement he was brought out with Jim McTernan handling and compiled an impressive total of Bests of Breed and Group placements, including a Canadian championship and Working Group first. During his show career Tatters defeated every top-winning professional handled Bobtail.

Tatters was attaining wide popularity as a stud when he died in the spring of 1972, at little more than six years of age. Some of his get are still appearing at the shows in 1975, and his total of 35 champions puts him in third place on the all-time list of OES producers.

134

Am. & Can. Ch. Rivermist Dan Tatters winning Group under judge James Trullinger. Co-owned by Bob and Sheila Ziccardi and Jim McTernan, and handled by the latter.

Dan Tatters, third in all-time rank of sires (35 champions at this printing) pictured with some of his get in win of the Stud Dog class at 1972 OESCA match.

William and Jocelyn Garvey of Connecticut were the breeders of the last litter produced by Tatters. From this litter came Ch. Barrelroll Blues in the Night, co-owned by Sherman Katz and the Garveys. Handled by his owner and Jim McTernan, Blues in the Night was the top winning Sheepdog in the Northeast from the end of 1974 through 1975.

Returning to the Baroness of Duroya-Ceiling Zero litter. Mr. and Mrs. Louis Loeb, then living in the East and now of Missoula, Montana, owned Marco Polo and Bellflower. Marco Polo was widely admired. Shown intermittently he won four Groups, and was used at stud by several breeders before his early death. Among his champion get are Rivermist Lilac and three littermates bred by Pat and Sandi Baker of Shawnee Mission, Kansas (out of Ch. Silvershag Donnemerry): Droverdale Double Trouble, D. Yogi Bear and D. Image of Polo, who won several Groups, a national OESCA specialty, and a Best in Show.

Bellflower became the basis of the Loebs' Ivyridge Kennel. She has produced the champions Ivyridge Lady Isabel, I. Barbrey Allen, I. Elf Knight, and I. Travelin' Man and Rivermist Pennyroyal from a litter by Unnesta Pim. Several Ivyridge OES, sired by Caj Haakansson's Prospect Shaggy Boy received favorable comment. Sedgwyck Squire Chutney owned by Elfriede O'Neill (by Prospect Shaggy Boy out of Ch. Ivyridge Barbrey Allen) was Best of Breed from the classes at Philadelphia in December 1970 over specials, and Winners Dog at Westminster in 1971.

Ch. Rivermist Gentian is now the all time top producing OES bitch with 14 champion get (as of end of 1974). Owned by Captain and Mrs. F. E. Rich of Herndon, Virginia, Gentian has been the foundation bitch of their Jendower Kennels. She was Best of Opposite Sex at the 1965 OESCA specialty held at Westbury, Long Island on October 3rd, when 17 months old. As a producer, five of the six pups in her first litter by Unnesta Pim, whelped July 9, 1966, finished championships: Rivermist Forgetmenot, Jendower's Queen Victoria, Jendower's Rivermist Tobi, Jendower's Rivermist Storm, and Jendower's Rivermist Smoke. Storm and Smoke are both owned by the Riches and have appeared as a winning brace, including a Group third at Westminster in 1970. Smoke finished his championship in seven shows in two months in the spring of 1968, including Winners Dog at the OESCA specialty at Greenwich on June 8th.

Gentian has produced nine more champions in subsequent litters by Ch. Prospect Shaggy Boy and Ch. Rivermist Dan Tatters. Gentian's get have been the basis of the Riches' breeding program which has produced more than 25 champions. Jendower is one of the principal breeding-exhibiting kennels active in the mid-1970's.

136

Ch. Rivermist Hollyhock (Ceilie-Baroness), top winning bitch of her showtime. Owned by Mr. and Mrs. Barry Goodman.

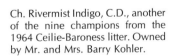

Ch. Rivermist Bellflower (Ceilie-Baroness), foundation bitch of Mr. and Mrs. Louis Loeb's Ivyridge Kennels.

Ch. Rivermist Indigo, C.D., another of the nine champions from the 1964 Ceilie-Baroness litter. Owned by Mr. and Mrs. Barry Kohler.

Two of the most famous in the Ceiling Zero-Baroness litter were retained by the Goodmans, Hollyhock (owned outright) and Nosegay (co-owned with Nancie Miller). Hollyhock became the top winning Bobtail bitch during the period she was shown, winning at one time or another over every top OES male, including Fezziwig Raggedy Andy at Boston in December, 1966, and over Prince Andrew of Sherline on several occasions after he came to the fore in 1968. She was Best of Opposite Sex at OESCA specialties in 1967 and 1968, and at Westminster in 1966, '67 and '68. From litters by Unnesta Pim, Hollyhock produced several champions, including Ch. Rivermist Juniper, Winners Bitch at the OESCA specialty in Atlantic City on November 30, 1969. Nosegay, after a nearly fatal start in life, not only finished her championship but (with several litters by Unnesta Pim) became the second greatest producing dam of champion get in breed history. Included in her 12 champion offspring are R. Pied Piper, R. Sweetbrier, R. King Arthur, R. Big Ben, R. March Flower, R. Blue Iris, R. Blue Chip, R. Bold Ruler, R. Pimson, and R. Feather Merchant.

The overwhelming success of the Ceiling Zero-Baroness of Duroya litter as winners and producers is a perfect example of how success can obscure the difficulties and disappointments of breeding. The early history of the litter is excellent testimony to the importance of perserverance and the willingness to put in hours of work and care essential to assuring pups a good start in life. Baroness' litter of 11 came into life relatively easily, but as is frequently the case in large litters, the pups were small, two of them being so small and lacking in vigor that they were not expected to make it. Baroness was not an enthusiastic mother. The pups had to be supplementary fed every three hours from birth. At first they were too weak to even eliminate for themselves. After each feeding they had to be massaged with a cotton wad dipped in warm baby oil. Combined with some help from Baroness, the round-the-clock feeding and cleaning went on for a few days, when within hours the entire litter became deathly ill. The vet diagnosed the problem as toxic milk, administered gamma globulin shots to all, and recommended, in an effort to strengthen the pups, that they be fed tiny rolled pellets of lean ground beef. These steps, combined with makeshift individual incubators using heating pads, brought the pups around. Now the entire responsibility of feeding, cleaning and caring for the pups fell on the Goodmans. Two days later, Ann Penn offered her bitch, Rivermist Frostflower, as a wet nurse. Frostie had just weaned a litter and was heavy with milk. Her availability in no small part accounts for all the pups surviving their early harrowing experience.

All went well in the following weeks, despite the fact that an inexperienced vet's tail-docking operation had to be redone. At four

138

Ch. Jendower's True Grit, home-bred of Capt. and Mrs. F. E. Rich's Jendower Kennels.

Ch. Sunnybrae Jack Frost, Group-winning son of Dan Patch, owned by Bob and Louise Lopina.

Ch. Jendower's Sugar Bear, owned by Capt. and Mrs. Rich.

weeks, the smallest pup, Nosegay, came up lame. The vet found a broken hind leg, and put it in a cast. Two days later her other hind leg broke. Returning from the vet's, the second smallest pup was found lame. The entire litter was taken back to the veterinarian, who treated the pups with massive calcium injections to counteract a presumed imbalance that was producing brittle bones. The problem was corrected, but a week later the pups developed major abcesses on their shoulders, where the calcium injections had been given. The wounds had to be treated and cleaned several times a day. Mrs. Goodman devised special turtleneck bandages to keep the sores covered and clean. In two weeks the abcesses closed and healed and everyone was fine, except for Nosegay, who it appeared would be permanently crippled. All the pups went to their intended homes, except Hollyhock, who was kept after the original buyer cancelled. Nosegay was kept until she was four months, when she was sturdy enough to go to a home that wanted a good pet, despite having one bad leg. At seven months Nosegay's believed permanent deformity had completely corrected itself, and she went on to finish her championship and become a great producer.

Unnesta Pim

The greatest producing OES stud in the late sixties was the Swedish-bred, International and American Ch. Unnesta Pim. Pim produced more champions in a shorter period of time than any stud in the breed's history. He stands as the second all-time OES producer with 46 champion get at end of 1974.

Pim, bred by Merte Korfitzen of the Unnesta Kennels in Sweden, was whelped June 20, 1960, and was by Ch. Reeuwijks Cupid out of Ch. Shepton Sally Ann. Sally Ann was sired by Ch. Shepton Wonder, while Cupid was a grandson of Wonder through his sire Ch. Shepton Grey Idol. (Wonder was sired by Ch. Shepton Home Guard, who had been imported to the United States in 1947 by Mrs. D. Mather Briggs of the Cartref Kennels, and can be found in the background of many American bred dogs.)

Pim's worth has been demonstrated many times over in Europe and the United States through his get, but as a youngster he was overlooked because of his dark markings. He had a white bib and collar, but a dark head, legs and body. Caj Haakansson acquired Pim when he was a year old, showed him to several European championships, made him top winning Bobtail in Europe, and a television personality in Sweden. Moving to England, Haakansson took Pim with him, registering him there as Bahlambs Unnesta Pim, Bahlambs being Caj's kennel prefix.

In 1965, Haakansson sold Pim to the Goodmans through Art Donahue. Coming to the United States at five years of age, Pim immediately began making a reputation at stud. His first American litter was
whelped December 13, 1965 out of Rivermist Nosegay. His total of 46
champions since then builds out of a succession of winners at the
most important all-breed shows across the United States and at
OESCA specialty shows and matches. At the 1968 OESCA specialty
shows at Greenwich, his daughter Lun Dee's Mersey CD, owned by
Jean Thorkilksen and handled by Barry Goodman, was Winners Bitch
and Best of Winners. Later that summer, at the specialty at Chagrin,
Ohio, a grandson, Rivermist Feather Merchant was Winners Dog
while Rivermist Juniper was Winners Bitch, both being handled by
Barry Goodman. Again in 1970 at the specialty at Greyslake, Illinois,
the dog Carnival Barry Goodboy, owned and bred by Marion Woelbing, at his first show ever went from the senior puppy class to
Winners Dog, also handled by Goodman. Many of Pim's get have
produced champion offspring themselves.

The Continuing Fezziwig Impact

Accurately gauging the impact of the Fezziwig on contemporary
OES is difficult. A given dog because of inherent worth and quality
can have a profound impact on the breed for a time. In the long run
the preservation of the breed lies in the hands of all breeders. In many
respects the important developments in Old English Sheepdogs, particularly in the East, have been the history of Ceiling Zero's ability to
combine with almost innumerable bitches of widely varying backgrounds and produce outstanding get.

The no longer active Happytown Kennels of Madeline and Leon
Shrank of Colonia, New Jersey, represent one starting point for
tracing the direct impact of Fezziwig on the breed in the sixties. The
Shranks obtained their first Bobtail, the bitch Patchwork Plush, from
the Achesons. Plush was very closely related to the Van Rensselaers'
Patchwork Gillian of Van R. Both Gill and Plush were out of Patchwork Phoebe. Their sires, Patchwork Bluebirds and Patchwork Blue-
boy respectively, were half brothers, having the same dam. Subsequently, the Shranks acquired the bitches Fezziwig Isle of Wight Vici
and Fezziwig Madcap Maggie from the Van Ransselaers. Both of
these bitches were out of the Barty and Gillian breeding that had
produced Ceiling Zero. They also acquired the imported stud Shepton
Lord Tom Noddy. Plush was bred to the Van Rensselaers' imported
stud Farleydene Bartholomew, in one of the few litters he sired
outside the Fezziwig Kennel. The Van Rensselaers took the pick

Ch. Shagbourne's Monarch, a Best in Show winner of the early '50s. Owned by Hazel B. Liptak.

Ch. Shagbourne's Messenger, a BIS winner from the classes. Owned originally by Julius and Agnes Kraft (later acquired by Art Field).

bitch from this litter, Happytown Panda, as their stud fee, and gave Panda to the Kraft family of Cleveland, Ohio.

The Krafts had been out of Sheepdogs for several years, but now, in the late 1950s, wanted to get back in. This is the same family that had owned and bred Ch. King's Messenger and his California-owned litter-brother Black Baron in 1940, the top winning Bobtails of their day. Mrs. Kraft baby-sat for the Van Rensselaers on the benches at a Westminster show, and in return for this favor, they gave her Panda.

In December 1960, the Krafts bred Panda to Fezziwig Ceiling Zero. The pups produced (on February 1, 1961) had Farleydene Bartholomew as their grandsire on both the sire and dam sides of their pedigree. This breeding pattern has been a favorite for setting type in purebred dogs since records have been kept. The celebrated turn of the century stud Ch. Stylish Boy, credited in large part with incorporating all-white heads and fronts into the breed, was bred in this same pattern. The Krafts' litter was the first ever produced by Ceiling Zero. From it came two OES who were to play a significant role in the breed's development—Chs. Shagbourne's Messenger and Shagbourne's Pansy.

Shagbourne's Messenger was named in memory of Krafts' earlier great King's Messenger. Shagbourne's Messenger, or Teddy, and King's Messenger were marked alike, although Teddy was a bigger dog. Teddy was conditioned and groomed for the ring by Julius and his wife Agnes, and shown by Julius. Teddy and the shows were no doubt a great pleasure to the Kraft family during an otherwise tragic time, as Julius was incurably ill. He died less than three months after showing Teddy to Best in Show from the classes at the Western Reserve Kennel Club event in 1963. Because of personal circumstances, Teddy was never shown as extensively or used as widely at stud as his quality merited.

After Julius' death, Teddy was acquired by Art Field, who showed him infrequently and used him at stud. Field was the owner and importer of the champion bitch Sunbonnet of Tansley, who in litters by Fezziwig Ceiling Zero and Teddy produced several champions, including Princess Jayne of Flitwick, Flitwick Blue Sue, and Tamara's Patches of Perse, the foundation bitches of Marvin and Tammy Smith's Tamara Kennels. In very few breedings Teddy produced six other champions in addition to Jayne and Blue Sue: Snomore Crazy Quilt, Bramshed's Lady Guinevere, Shepherd's Pride, Guinevere of Tewellyn. Sherlock's Shamus Bobby, and Prince Andrew of Sherline. All but Crazy Quilt are out of the imported bitch, Shepton Mistress Mary. Mary, bred by B. Fox, was whelped February 26, 1962, and was by English Ch. Fernville Fernando, (also the sire of the Goodman's Baroness of Duroya), out of Eng. Ch. Princess

Nasimira. Mary was owned by Mrs. Donald Swanson then of Still Meadow Farm, Goodrich, Michigan. Mrs. Swanson is a former director of the OESCA.

Bramshed's Lady Guinevere and Shepherd's Pride came from the first Teddy-Mary litter, whelped August 10, 1964. Lady Guinevere had not earned a point toward her championship when she went from the classes to Best in Show at the Macomb County Kennel Club show on February 13, 1966, under judge Dr. W. E. Shute. She is the only American-bred bitch, and only one of three OES bitches, to win a Best in Show in the United States during the 1960s. From the second Teddy-Mary litter, whelped July 18, 1965, came Chs. Guinevere of Tewellyn, a Canadian OES specialty show Best of Breed winner, Sherlock's Shamus Bobby, a Group winner, and Prince Andrew of· Sherline.

Prince Andrew of Sherline

Prince Andrew was owned by Howard and Rita Sherline of Detroit, Michigan. He began his show career at ten months in May 1966, at the specialty show of the Canadian OES club in Barrie, Ontario by going from the senior puppy class to Best of Breed over five specials under judge Marvin Kucker. In the United States, Andrew compiled an amazing string of victories, always handled by Bob Forsyth. He completed his American championship in the spring of 1967 with wins that included a Best of Opposite Sex from the classes at the New England OES specialty show under Mona Berkowitz. Following a year's wait to mature, Prince Andrew began his show career in earnest in the spring of 1968. Despite being shown only nine months, and a summer vacation, Andrew ended the year as top Working dog in the nation by the Phillips System, with eight Bests in Show, 27 Group wins, and 30 other group placements. He continued on top in 1969, winning the Group at Westminster, and finishing No. 3 of all Working breeds for the year, with one Best in Show, 23 Group firsts and 37 other places. He again led the breed in 1970, and was the Ken-L-Award winner in the Working group, for having won more Groups, 26, than any other Working dog through the year. In all, Prince Andrew won 76 Groups, making him the winner of more Working Groups than any other Old English, and 11 Bests in Show. In speculating on Andrew's total achievements as a show dog, it must be mentioned that during 1969 he was shown week in and week out against the Boxer bitch, Arriba's Prima Donna, the top winning Working dog in the nation and Best in Show at Westminster in 1970, who was handled by Jane Forsyth.

144

Ch. Prince Andrew of Sherline, top winning Bobtail of 1968–70 period. Pictured winning 1968 OESCA Specialty under Heywood Hartley, handled by Bob Forsyth. Owned by Howard and Rita Sherline.

Winners Dog at the same 1968 Specialty was Jendower's Rivermist Storm (later Ch.), out of Ch. Rivermist Gentian's first litter. Owned by Capt. and Mrs. F. E. Rich and handled by Vernelle Hartman.

The other important Bobtail from the Ceiling Zero-Happytown Panda litter was Ch. Shagbourne's Pansy. Before following this bitch's impact on the breed let us conclude the account of the Shranks' activities.

The Shranks' two Fezziwig-bred bitches, Isle of Wight Vici and Madcap Maggie, produced a succession of winners and producers for them and many fanciers. Among champions with the Happytown prefix have been H. Bopeep, H. Winnie the Pooh, H. Lord Tareyton, H. Barnacle Bill, and H. Ragamuffin of Card. Many other Happytown dogs appear in back of OES throughout the United States today, including H. Shaggy Aggie, H. Samantha, and H. Miss Quickly. Barnacle Bill, Ragamuffin of Card and Lord Tareyton were all sired by Kathryn Perlmutter's Ch. Ticklebee's Archibald. Mrs. Perlmutter of Rumson, New Jersey, owned and bred several champions and producers with her Ticklebee's prefix in the late '60s.

Happytown Miss Quickly by Shepton Lord Tom Noddy out of Fezziwig Madcap Maggie, whelped April 7, 1962, was the foundation bitch of George and Joan Demko's Knightcap Kennels. The Demkos have served the OESCA in a variety of capacities since the middle-sixties. Joan was the club's secretary for several years, and is currently the Old English columnist for the *American Kennel Gazette,* in which role she is following in the footsteps of some of the breed's most distinguished fanciers. George has served as director of the Eastern region and vice-president of the club. He has also judged at match shows. The Demkos bred Miss Quickly to Fezziwig Zero in early 1965. The litter, whelped March 6, 1965, contained among others, Chs. Knightcap's Gimlet, who the Demkos kept, and Knightcap Moody Blue. Moody Blue is owned by Joseph and Douglas Caroli of Elmsford, New York. He was Winners Dog at the 1967 OESCA specialty show at Westchester in September. In August 1968 at the specialty at Chagrin he was Best of Breed, handled by Jack Funk. He also won and placed in several Groups during his show career. Moody Blue's win of Best of Breed at Chagrin was part of a Knightcap sweep of the top three spots. Gimlet, who earlier in the year had won Best of Opposite Sex at the New England OES specialty, was again Best of Opposite Sex, handled by Joan Demko. The Winners Bitch and Best of Winners was the eight month old puppy from the American-bred class, Knightcap Fabulous Fanny, owned and handled by Anna Jacobson, then from Cleveland and now from Peoria, Illinois.

Earl and Anna Jacobson have been very active in Old English since the late sixties. Both have served the Old English Sheepdog Club of America in numerous capacities, and at this writing Earl is president. Anna co-owns with Serena Van Rensselaer Ch. Fezziwig Hidden Assets (Ch. Fezziwig Fringe Benefits ex Aisby Ladybelle) who has

146

Ch. Fezziwig Masquerade, bitch, Best of Winners at OESCA Specialty. Owned by Fezziwig Kennels.

Ch. Fezziwig Daisy Mae, Best Opposite at the 1969 OESCA Specialty. Owned by Joseph and Milly McCabe.

Ch. Fezziwig Melissa, Best Opposite at the 1971 OESCA Specialty. Owned by John and Linda Keck.

produced numerous champions, many of them carrying the Jacobson's Knottingham prefix.

Fabulous Fanny was Best of Opposite Sex at Westminster in 1969, handled by Jack Funk, only a few weeks before her unfortunate early death. Fabulous Fanny, Top Banana, Ch. K. White Rose, Ch. Banbury Muffin of Shaggyrock, Ch. Elizabeth's Silver Shadow, and Ch. Cresida of Mumbly-Peg, among others were all sired by the Demkos' Ch. Silvershag Snowbright. Snowbright was bred by Louise Forest, whelped July 15, 1965. Snowtatters was sired by Ch. Fezziwig Fainthart Falstaff, a full brother to Ceiling Zero, owned by Dr. and Mrs. Donald Pace, then living in Omaha, Nebraska and among the five Midwestern OES fanciers in the early sixties.

Ch. Happytown Winnie the Pooh by Shepton Lord Tom Noddy out of Fezziwig Madcap Maggie went to Cora Marshall, who also owned Ch. Shagbourne's Pansy. Both of these bitches have played a significant part in the breed's development in the upper central Midwest. Pansy finished her championship, and from a litter by Ch. Downeylane Donnybrook, produced the champions Shandy Kip Pansy, Shandy Kip Hathaway, and Shandy Kip London. London finished his championship with widespread favorable comments, was a Group winner and had other Group placements, but because of personal difficulties was placed with Hollis Hedlund of Loretto, Minnesota, who has used him widely at stud. London can be found in the immediate backgrounds of many Midwestern Bobtails today, and is still actively being used at stud. Among his champion get are Tonkawood Cholly Gee and Tonkawood Modesty Moppet out of Happytown Winnie the Pooh, Moppet of Brunswick, Duke Karl of Brunswick, Sir Hugo Chadsworth Goldman III, Greyfriars Grey Dawn, Double JJ's Princess Astarte, and Double JJ's Lady Slipper. All of these dogs have in turn produced winners. Sir Hugo and Duke Karl have already sired champions with numerous other get pointed. Duke Karl has won three Groups and placed in several others for his owners Mr. and Mrs. G. Geiger of Chicago, Illinois, handled by Jack Funk.

Ambelon Kennels

The Shranks' Shepton Lord Tom Noddy figures prominently in the background of the leading contemporary OES breeder in New England, Anne Raker of Amberlon Kennels in Lincoln, Massachusetts. Anne has the distinction of being one of the few people ever to train and handle an Old English Sheepdog to a Utility Obedience title. This was her bitch Driftwood's Little Bo Peep bred by Hazel Foster Collins by Driftwood's Billie Barton out of Matilda Mia of Driftwood.

Ch. Knightcap's Moody Blue, 1968 Specialty winner. Pictured in win under Heywood Hartley, handled by Bert Tormey. Moody Blue was bred by George and Joan Demko, and owned by Joseph and Douglas Caroli.

Am. & Can. Ch. Ambelon Fireworks, winner of 3 Groups and BIS in Canada in one weekend, at 9 months of age. Winner of the New England Specialty in 1970, he returned to win it again from the Veterans Class in 1975. (Pictured in 1970 win under Melbourne Downing, with Bob Forsyth handling.) Bred and owned by Anne Raker.

During her Obedience career, Bo Peep earned 17 class firsts, was three times the highest scoring dog in trial, and twice had perfect 200 scores. Quite a feat, given the breed's tendency to be easy going and too casual when working in Obedience. Bo Peep was also the dam of four champions, Ambelon's Ole King Cole, A. Miss Dickens, A. Flying Cloud, and A. Fogbound, the last three named all from the same litter sired by Fezziwig Ceiling Zero.

Two other Ambelon owned and shown bitches, Chs. Pami-Woods Holiday and Fellscove Jezebel have produced Ambelon champions, both by Shep Crescent. Shep Crescent, whelped June 25, 1962, by Shepton Lord Tom Noddy out of Raggmopp, was acquired as an older dog and used extensively at stud. Among his get are Chs. Ambelon's Lord Plushbuttom, A. Secret Agent, and A. Fireworks. Fireworks, whelped August 2, 1967, out of Pami-Woods Holiday, is the youngest OES Best in Show winner, going to Canada at nine months of age and winning three Groups and a Best in Show in one weekend, handled by Barbara Partridge. In the spring of 1968, while still a puppy, he finished his American championship with a string of wins including Winners Dog at the New England OES club's specialty show on June 1st, and a week later Reserve Winners Dog at the OESCA specialty show at Greenwich. Fireworks has since gone Best of Breed at the New England Specialty in 1970 and again in 1975, the last just a week prior to his winning the Veterans' Class at the Old English Sheepdog Club of America specialty.

Bahlambs Kennels

One of the most interesting developments in American Old English Sheepdogs was the immigration of Caj Haakansson and his Bahlambs Kennels to the United States in mid-1968. Haakasson, a Swede, has traveled widely in Europe and the British Isles. His Bahlambs Kennel prefix is registered in England and Sweden. Three years prior to his arrival in the United States, Haakansson's Int. Ch. Bahlamb's Unnesta Pim had been sold to Barry Goodman, and of course had already made a major impact on the breed here. Pim is in the background of Haakansson's imported Bobtails, through his European get. Mona Berkowitz's English-American Ch. Prospectblue Rodger, a top winning Working dog following his arrival in the United States in June 1967, was sired by Haakansson's Eng. Ch. Prospect Shaggy Boy, then owned by his breeder Mrs. Isobel Lawson. Haakasson, located in Silver Spring, Maryland—a suburb of Washington, D.C., is continuing in this country the breeding program he had begun in England and Sweden. The basis is stock imported in 1968 and 1969, including the

150

Int. Eng. Swed. Norw. Finn. & Am. Ch. (Bahlamb's) Prospect Shaggy Boy, sire of 14 champions. Pictured finishing Am. title at 10 years of age. Bred by Mrs. Isobel Lawson (England) and brought to America in 1961 by his owner Caj Haakansson.

Ch. Millie (handled by Lorraine Donahue) going BOB, and kennelmate Bahlamb's Bleak Blue Blackguard scoring BOS (from WD, handled by owner Caj Haakansson) in 1970 showing under Mrs. Augustus Riggs IV. Millie is a Shaggy Boy daughter.

studs Ch. Prospect Shaggy Boy, Ch. Bahlambs Bleakblue Black-
guard, Ch. Bahlambs Brilliant Blue Barrister, and Bahlambs Brilliant
Blue Best Brand, as well as the bitches Ch. (Bahlambs) Prospectblue
Fair Lady, Ch. Millie, Kandi, Bahlambs Bright 'n Bountiful, Bah-
lambs Blue Buggie Burgoyne (now owned by the Riches of Jendower
Kennels.)

Shaggy Boy was the most significant stud at Bahlambs. Bred by
Isobel Lawson he was whelped May 10, 1961 and was by Eng. Ch.
Blue Brigand of Tansley out of Eng. Ch. Blue Glamour Girl. Both of
Shaggy Boy's parents were top winning Bobtails in England in their
day. Shaggy Boy was the pick of his litter and kept by Mrs. Lawson
until sold to Haakansson just prior to Crufts in February 1966, where
he won his third Challenge Certificate and finished his English championship. While Mrs. Lawson owned him, Shaggy Boy had been used
widely at stud producing many winners including Chs. Prospectblue
Rodger, P. Bulk, P. Cindy, and Bahlambs P. Fair Lady, all out of
Farleydene Peggotty. Fair Lady known as Sally, is one of the major
broods in Haakansson's breeding program. She attracted widespread
favorable comment in a brief American show career that included
Winners Bitch and Best of Winners at Westminster in 1969. In
addition to Fair Lady and Rodger, Shaggy Boy's American champions include Haakansson Millie, Jendower's Cloud Nine, and Jendower's Blue Max. With a total of fourteen champion get Shaggy Boy
ranks tenth on the all time list.

American and Swedish Ch. Bahlambs Bleak Blue Blackguard and
his litter brother, Swedish Ch. Bahlambs Brilliant Blue Barrister,
represent a bloodline distinct from Shaggy Boy. To a large extent
Haakansson's breeding program is based on a combination of these
two lines. Bahlambs Brass Band, finished in December 1970, represents this combination. He is one of the earlier American Bahlambs
breedings, whelped August 1, 1969, by Bahlambs Brilliant Blue Best
Band out of Millie. Brilliant Blue Best Band was sired by Barrister out
of Fair Lady. (Barrister and Blackguard are both grandsons of
Unnesta Pim through Int. Ch. Teddy Bear Bobo. Millie is by Shaggy
Boy out of Ch. Teddy Bear Angela, a littermate to Teddy Bear Bobo.)

In the Midwest

Moving away from the East Coast, there are a number of Old
English breeders in the Midwest, including Double JJ Downeylane,
Droverdale, Silvershag, and Tamara, among others that must be
mentioned in an account of American Old English Sheepdogs in the
1960s.

Ch. Shepton Bobbibingo, English import, foundation stud of Dr. Louise Forest's Silvershag Kennels. (Pictured at approximately one year of age.)

Ch. Silvershag Snowtatters (at about 20 months), owned by Dr. Forest.

Ch. Silvershag Madcap Margot, winner and producer c. 1968, owned by Dr. Forest.

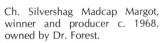

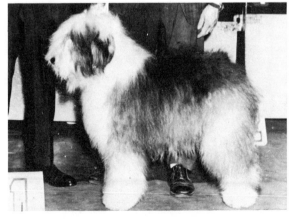

Even in the Middle West the impact of Fezziwig breeding remains significant. All of the kennels mentioned above trace parts of their stock to Fezziwig breeding.

The Silvershag Kennels of Dr. Louise Forest in New Hartford, Iowa, may have produced more champions than any other kennel in the 1960s. More than 35 Bobtails completed championships with the Silvershag prefix.

Silvershag produced champions out of more studs from more different bloodlines than any other American kennel: Champions Shepton Bobbibingo, Downeylane Donnybrook, Fezziwig Fainthart Falstaff, Lillbrad Sir Lancelot, Rivermist Robber Baron, Rivermist Dan Patch, Silvershag Snowtatters, S. Wyndham, S. Snowbab, S. Darcindingo, S. Snowtatters Dirk, S. Snowtatters Echo, and S. Pembroke, all produced Silvershag champions (as well as having sired winners and producers for others).

The list of bitches that have produced Silvershag champions and champions for others is even longer, and includes among others: Greyfriars Jennie, Chs. Silvershag Ruffles, S. Donnemerry, S. Miss Debonaire, S. Snowruffles, S. Frolic, S. Madcap Margot, S. Snowlace, S. Boadicea, S. Snowfrills, S. High Top Boots, Lady Nana of Newton, Shayloran's Candy Cotton, as well as non-champion producers of champions, Silvershag Sweet Sue, S. Small Patience, S. Bar-Maid, S. Darcine, S. Jaquenetta, S. Maida and Susin Dora. It is not possible at this early date to accurately assess the impact of all these various winners and producers, although it is evident that the total impact of the Silvershag breedings on the breed in the United States and the Middle West in particular has been enormous.

The basis of the Silvershag breeding is interesting, because it combines a bitch from the Rocky Mountains with an English imported stud—Greyfriar's Jennie and Shepton Bobbibingo. These two are in back of virtually all OES that have had the Silvershag prefix.

In the West

Although until the sixties Sheepdogs were virtually unknown and almost never seen outside the Northeast, one of the breed's most dedicated fanciers has been continuously active in the Far West through the fifties and sixties, and into the seventies. This is Harriet Poreda of Greyfriar Kennels in Colorado. Through Silvershag breeding in the Midwest and Shaggybar breeding in California, among others, Greyfriar stock can be found in the back of many contemporary American Bobtails. Forest's Jennie was by Greyfriar's Woody out of Greyfriar's Bar-Maid. Woody was sired by Ch. Norval Pride

Ch. Silvershag Snowbright, one of the all-time top Old English sires (16 champions). Bred by Louise Forest, and owned by George and Joan Demko.

Ch. Silvershag Ruffles, main early producer for Dr. Forest's Silvershag Kennels.

Ch. Silvershag Donnemerry, foundation brood of Pat and Sandi Baker's Droverdale Kennels.

Ch. Silvershag Boadicea, dam of champions. Owned by Jim and Dee Mattern.

Ch. Silvershag Cut-Up, Group winning bitch, owned by Marion Woelbing.

Ch. Silvershag Carnival Candy, late '60s winner, owned by Dr. and Mrs. Sheldon Rennert.

156

King and through him can be traced back to Mrs. Lyndley's famous imports of the late thirties.

Bobbibingo was whelped March 19, 1959 and is by Beau Geste out of Burford Belle, bred by Miss Florence Tilley and Mrs. S. Wiggin. Through his dam Bobbibingo is a grandson of Ch. Shepton Wonder. From the Bobbinbingo-Jennie litter, whelped April 28, 1960, came the bitch Ch. Silvershag Ruffles who was to be the main early producer for Silvershag. Among her nine champion get are Silvershag Miss Bustle 'N Bows, S. Snowdrifting, S. Snowfrills, S. Snowlace and S. Snowtatters. The last three named were sired by Ch. Fezziwig Fainthart Falstaff, whelped July 12, 1963. This litter was one of the only two Falstaff, a younger full brother of Fezziwig Ceiling Zero, sired before his death. Snowtatters was beaten to death in his run on June 21, 1966. At the time of his death he was beginning what appeared to have the makings of an important career in the show ring. From his few litters have come Chs. Jolly Old Nick, Silvershag Wyndham, S. Little Prudence (all out of Ch. Silvershag Frolic), S. Diggory, S. Dobbins, S. Delia (all out of Ch. Lady Nana of Newton) S. Snowtatters Echo, S. Snowtatters Dirk, S. Snowblaze, S. Snowbright and S. Snowpatter (all out of Ch. Silvershag Madcap Margot.) The bitch Ch. Shayloran's Candy Cotton, out of Rosmoore Pink Lady by Beckington Reprint and a full sister to Shayloran's Billy Hayseed, has produced several champions for Silvershag, including S. Sugarsparkle, S. Spun Sugar, S. Carnival Candy, and S. Carnival Cut-Up.

Carnival Candy and Cut-Up were sired by Ch. Silvershag Snowtatters Dirk. Cut-Up went to Marion Woelbing of Franklin, Wisconsin, who had her shown by Jack Funk to a championship and two Group wins in 1968 and '69, making her one of the few bitches to win a Group in the United States in the last twenty years. As a dam Cut-Up produced the specialty show Winners Dog, from the puppy class, Carnival Barry Goodboy. Carnival Candy eventually went to Dr. and Mrs. Sheldon Rennert of Scarsdale, New York. They had her shown to an undefeated championship by Bob and Jane Forsyth in the summer of 1969, and as a special with Jack Funk handling, she compiled a record of ten Bests of Breed and several Group placements, as well as producing a litter by Ch. Silvershag Pembroke before an unfortunate early death in 1970. The Rennerts were among the organizers of the Greater New York Old English Sheepdog Club in late 1968 and early 1969, and Sheldon was the club's first president.

Among the many Silvershag dogs that have done to other homes and subsequently played a major role in the breed's development are the bitches Chs. Silvershag Boadicea and Silvershag Donnemerry. Boadicea was owned by Jim and Dee Mattern, then of Dayton, Ohio. Jim served the OESCA as treasurer for several years. In two breedings to Fezziwig Ceiling Zero, Boadicea produced several champions including Bear Creek Polar Zero, Blue Knight, B.C. Blue Bruin, B.C. Ocita, and Honey Bear, among others. Ocita and Honey Bear have in turn become the basic broods of Mrs. John Albert's Sugar Creek and of Pat Miller's Blandford Kennels respectively. Silvershag Donnemerry has been the foundation brood of one of the most successful recent Midwestern breeders, the Drover Kennels of Pat and Sandi Baker, of Shawnee Mission, Kansas. Donnemerry has produced champions by Chs. Fezziwig Bartholomew, Rivermist Dan Patch and Rivermist Marco Polo. Among her champion get are Droverdale Derby, D. Tattered Patches, D.BB Derry Air, D. Yogi Bear, D. Double Trouble, D. Image of Polo, and Shasta's Daisy.

Image of Polo by Rivermist Marco Polo, whelped October 15, 1967 had a distinguished show career and is making a mark as a producer. Included in his show wins was Winners Dog at Westminster in 1969, followed by championships later that year in the United States and Canada, including several Group wins and a Best in Show under Percy Roberts in Canada. In 1970 Polo was Best of Breed at the OESCA specialty show at Greyslake, Illinois in June, and subsequently won several Groups, as well as a Best in Show under Alva Rosenberg late in the fall. He was handled to all his wins by his breeder-owner Sandi Baker. The Bakers were among those responsible for organizing the OES club in the Kansas City area in the late '60s and have served it in a variety of capacities. Pat Baker was also a director of the OESCA.

Silvershag Donnemerry was sired by Ch. Downeylane Donnybrook CD. Donny was the basic stud of Deedy and Bob Abrams' Downeylane Kennels in Chesterfield, Missouri, outside St. Louis. The Abrams were among the first Bobtail fanciers in the Midwest in the late fifties. They had had 20 years experience in Collies before acquiring their first Bobtail. Over the years Deedy served the OESCA in many offices, eventually as vice-president. For several years in the mid-'60s, she wrote the OES column for the *American Kennel Gazette*. The Abrams were responsible for getting the first OESCA supported show west of the Mississippi, at Des Moines, Iowa on September 8, 1963. The veterans of the breed's development in the Midwest (including the Abrams, Louise Forest, Lillian Lovejoy, Harriet Poreda, and the James Andersons of Double JJ in Minnesota) tell of going months and even years in the 1950s and early '60s without ever seeing another Bobtail besides their own, at a show. Five hundred mile journeys in one direction were common for these exhibitors in hopes of finding a major. Downeylane Donnybrook had a number of Group placements before he met another OES in breed competition and earned his first championship point. Donny was

Am. & Can. Ch. Droverdale Image of Polo, Best in Show and Specialty winner, bred and owned by Pat and Sandi Baker (handler).

Ch. Loyalblu Billy Moon, home-bred champion, owned by Dr. and Mrs. Hugh Jordan; shown by Mrs. Jordan.

Ch. Fezziwig Hidden Assets, and ROM sire, co-owned by Serena Van Rensselaer and Anna Jacobson (Knottingham Kennels).

whelped January 1, 1959, by Raj Timmy out of Lizabell of Oakwood. Raj Timmy, owned by Ernest and Chris Volger of Moscow Mills, Missouri represents one of the few Midwestern lines of descendants from Mrs. Lyndley's Lynnhaven dogs of the 1940s.

Donny has the distinction of siring more Old English champions from fewer breedings than any other stud. His champion get include Silvershag Donnemerry, Beowulf Wiglaf, Beckington Beau Brummel, Normandon Princess Anne, Downeylane Gay Edward, D. Delightful, D. Dagmar, D. Daisy Mae, Shandy Kip Pansy, Shandy Kip Hathaway.

Ch. Downeylane Dreamboat, bred by the Volgers whelped June 20, 1961, by Raj Timmy out of Marcris Gwen of Aquataine, Lizabell (Donny's dam) and Gwen were litter sisters by Cartref Pied Piper out of Alzacons Pride of Balfour, also representing one of the lines of descent of the important American Bobtails of the '40s. In an earlier breeding by Fezziwig Fainthart Falstaff, Dreamboat had produced among others, Ch. Downeylane Double D of Hobar, or Boo, co-owned by Barbara Bournstein and Deedy Abrams. In a breeding designed to double up on the Fezziwig line, Boo was bred to the Ceiling Zero son, Rivermist Dan Patch. From this litter came Downeylane Drummerboy, whelped January 10, 1966. In September 1966, at eight months of age from the junior puppy class, Drummerboy was Winners Dog and Best of Winners at the first national OESCA specialty held in the Midwest, at Kansas City. The Reserve Winners Dog at that specialty came from the senior puppy class—Rivermist Pied Piper, from the first litter ever sired by Unnesta Pim in the United States, whelped December 10, 1965. Downeylane breeding appears in the background of many contemporary OES; in addition to the previously mentioned Droverdale dogs, Ivy of Greenberrie Hill whelped December 7, 1963, was by Donny out of the Goldmans' Shepton imported Fair Lady of Lake Forest. Ivy has become the basic brood of Irene Stahl's Hermitage Kennels in Flanders, New Jersey. From two litters by Fezziwig Ceiling Zero, including the next to last one sired by him, whelped in January 1969, Ivy has produced a number of winners and producers.

Double JJ Kennels

Mr. & Mrs. James E. Anderson of Bigelow, Minnesota got the foundation brood of their Double JJ Kennel from Harriet Poreda. This was Ch. Greyfriar Double JJ's Penny, C.D., whelped March 3, 1958, by Greyfriar's Woody out of Greyfriar's Bar-Maid, a full sister to Louise Forest's basic brood Greyfriar's Jennie. The Andersons were the earliest contemporary OES fanciers in Minnesota, one site, among many, where the breed has attracted a dedicated following, and that has founded its own local breed club (in Minneapolis-St. Paul) in the late sixties. Penny in a litter by Snowpatch, whelped June 3, 1959, produced the dog Friar Tuck of Sherwood, owned by Mr. & Mrs. Henry Abramowicz of St. Paul, who was handled by Hollis Wilson to the first Minnesota OES championship as well as numerous Bests of Breed and a Best in Show at the Land O' Lakes Kennel Club on June 10, 1962.

In another breeding, whelped October 16, 1961, Snowpatch and Penny produced the champions Sherwood's Robin Hood and Sherwood's Lady Marian among others. Snowpatch was by Patchwork Bluebirds out of Patchwork Sugarplum. His get represent a main line of descent from the Achesons' imported OES of the late forties and early fifties. Lady Marian has played an important part in the ongoing Double JJ breeding program, while Robin Hood went to Vickie Johnson and Mildred Winkels of Lombard, Illinois. He was the main stud in the founding of their Win-Son Kennels. He produced the champions Win-Son's Visibility A OK and W.S. Yes I Can See out of the bitch Tonkawood's Panda Bear. Among other Double JJ champions are Double JJ's Lady Slipper, D. Princess Astarte, D. Magic Dragon, D. Leach's Tausha, and D. Jeeves Cricket. Magic Dragon and Tausha were both sired by Ch. Fezziwig Peeko Hannaford, who the Andersons acquired from the Van Rensselaers in the mid-sixties. Peeko Hannaford was the last of the Barty-Gillian offspring to complete an AKC championship. He was bred to Rivermist Heather among others. Heather has produced seven champion get, placing her in a tie for tenth place among all-time top producing OES dams as of the end of 1974. Heather was leased by the Andersons for breeding purposes. She was the major pointed, but unfinished, sister to the famous winners and producers by Ceiling Zero and Baroness of Duroya.

During the sixties there were several imported dogs in the Midwest that made important contributions to the breed's development. The most significant of these was the dog. Ch. Tempest of Dalcroy, or Harvey, bred by Ann Lloyd by Fairacres Ben out of Bluemist of Dalcroy, whelped September 3, 1962. Harvey was obtained for Marvin and Tammy Smith of the Tamara Kennels in Brighton, Michigan by Eric Minett of the Daphnis Kennel. Harvey has Ch. Fairacres Commander as his grandsire on both sides of his pedigree. He produced 20 champions, in few breedings, with more than half of his total of champion get having been bred by the Smiths out of two bitches, Ch. Tamara's Patches of Perse and Greyfriar's Old Lace. Harvey is the sixth all time top producing Sheepdog Stud.

Ch. Tempest of Dalcroy (wh. 1962), one of the all-time top sires (20 champions). Bred by Ann Lloyd (England) and owned by Marvin and Tammy Smith's Tamara Kennels.

Ch. Tamara's Patches of Perse, foundation bitch of Tamara Kennels, dam of 8 champions. Patches is a Ceiling Zero daughter.

Patches of Perse was the first Tamara Bobtail. She was whelped June 22, 1962 by Ch. Fezziwig Ceiling Zero out of Ch. Sunbonnet of Tansley. In several litters by Tempest of Dalcroy she produced the champions, Tamara's Pyewacket, T. Royal Biggsbee, T. Memory of Dawn, T. Wendy Morrow, T. Oliver of Dalcroy, T. Pollyanna, and T. Smokey of Bishop. Most of these have in turn produced winners and producers of their own. Tamara's Smokey of Bishop in addition to being a Group winner sired several champions, including the multiple Group winner, Best of Breed at Westminster in 1971, Brooks Blue Boy owned by Florence Pangborn of Northville, Michigan and handled by George Carlton. The Best of Opposite Sex at Westminster 1971, Lady Bufferton of Latham, was also sired by Smokey of Bishop. Greyfriar's Old Lace by Ch. Tarawood's Flannel Pants out of Gloria's Own Callistopee, has produced four champions by Tempest of Dalcroy, Tamara's Sparkle Plenty, T. Snow Cloud, T. Memory of Suzanne, and T. Shaggy Shoes MacDuff.

Among Harvey's other champion get are: Tamara's Talisman, T. Belvadeare, Lyndon Meadows Lady Patience, Belvadeare's Trafalga, Chatsworth Mister Higgins, and Nestledown's Mr. Tough Guy. Tough Guy whelped March 19, 1967, bred by E. G. Ford, out of Shepton Great Charm, a full sister to Louise Forest's Ch. Shepton Bobbibingo, did extensive winning in a three month period from May to August 1968, including several Group wins handled by Jack Funk. Tough Guy died of heat prostration at 17 months just prior to the OESCA national specialty at Chagrin, Ohio in August.

A double-up breeding on Tempest of Dalcroy has been the basis of a number of champions produced under the Morrow prefix. In this case, Ch. Tamara's Snow Cloud out of Tempest of Dalcroy and Greyfriar's Old Lace was bred to Ch. Tamara's Wendy Morrow by Tempest of Dalcroy out of Tamara's Patches of Perse and produced Chs. Morrow's Mr. Peepers and M. Lady Wendemere, Mr. Peepers has in turn produced a number of champions including Aab's Delia Daisy Wonder Girl, Moria's Johnny Rebel, Mr. London, and Morrow's Duke of FuzzBuzz. FuzzBuzz, owned by Mr. & Mrs. Ivan Forbes of Birmingham, Michigan, was a multiple Best in Show winner in 1969.

In the late sixties the Smiths imported from Europe, Shaggy Wonder Prince Charming. Prince Charming is one of many OES with the Shaggy Wonder prefix of Mrs. Yvonne Mewis De Ryck of Belgium that have been imported to the United States, including the champions SW Lord, SW Meteorbright, SW Main Attraction, SW Old Fashion, SW Pretty Baby and SW Once Again. Prince Charming in addition to being a Group winner has produced champions Sir Charles'Iggle Iggle and Warden's Bonnie Blue Bonnet from his first

Int. and Am. Ch. Shaggy Wonder Lord, wh. 1962. Lord was winner of 13 CCs in 8 countries, and his championships included Germany, Luxembourg, Belgium, Switzerland and Czechoslovakia. Pictured with his Belgian breeder, Mrs. Yvonne Mewis De Ryck.

Int. and Am. Ch. Shaggy Wonder Meteorbright, owned by Harv Schmid and Bob Beckert.

Ch. Shaggy Wonder Main Attraction, owned by Jack and Ginger Herlihy's Bob Tail Acres Kennels in California.

American litters, as well as Ch. Tamara's Henry Higgins Havoc, Winners Dog at the record OESCA specialty show held at Anaheim, California in September 1970.

Other Shaggy Wonder OES, all of whom are related to each other, are scattered around the United States. All the Shaggy Wonder dogs descended from Mrs. Backx-Bennik's Dutch Reeuwijk's Kennels. Mrs. Backx-Bennik was one of the first post-World War II European Bobtail fanciers. In the United States, Reeuwijk's breeding, aside from its Shaggy Wonder descendants is found in the St. Trinian Kennels of Dr. and Mrs. Erly P. Gallo of Winsted, Connecticut, who finished Reeuwijk's Kinky (Reeuwijk's Charming Masterpeice-Reeuwijk's Film Star) in 1967. Reeuwijk OES are descended from Mrs. Backx-Bennik's Ch. Shepton Grey Idol, sired by Ch. Shepton Wonder, and hence to the famous Bobtails of the pre-World War II era in England.

Shaggy Wonder Prince Charming and SW Once Again owned by Harv Schmid and Bob Beckert of the Armorblu Kennel in Park Ridge, Illinois were full brother and sister. They were sired by Ch. SW Meteorbright out of Ch. Shaggy Wonder Listliss I Am. SW Listless I Am's brother, Ch. Shaggy Wonder Lord had a distinguished career as a show dog and producer in Europe before arriving in the United States. He was sired by Chang-Shi Comedy Starlight, a son of Ch. Shepton Grey Idol, out of Reeuwijk's Fusby Farmgirl, a daughter of Ch. Reeuwijk's Cupid, the sire of Unnesta Pim. He has produced two American-bred champions, both out of the bitch Heather Blu, Sir Christabaer Blu and Shaggy Blu Beard, as well as the European bred imported Chs. Shaggy Wonder Pretty Baby and SW Old Fashion. Old Fashion and SW Main Attraction are both owned by Jack and Ginger Herlihy of California. Main Attraction was a full sister of SW Meteorbright. She was bred to Ch. Rivermist Hornblower and produced the Chs. Bobtail Acres Sno-Cone and B.A. Frosty Knight.

Elsewhere in the Midwest there were a number of '60s Bobtails that should be mentioned. Millicent and Conrad Ott, Jr. from Grosse Pointe Park, Michigan exhibited a pair of Bobtails to championships—the bitch Ragmuffin Bo Peep, and her son by American and Canadian Ch. Boswell Biff of Yorkville, Ragmuffin Thunderhead. Thunderhead has in turn produced several champions, including Lady Billie Jo of Lucas Lair and Morrow's Calamity Jane. Boswell Biff of Yorkville whelped May 27, 1961, by Am.-Can. Ch. Blue Admiral of Box out of Ch. Saltbox Granny Bee, was owned by Carl Noylander of Toronto, Canada. Biff came from a litter that included the other champions, Bonny Blue of Saltbox and Salt Box Lady Deborah. Bonny Blue was owned by Mr. & Mrs. Louis Baer of West Boxford, Massachusetts. Handled by William Trainor, she compiled

Am. & Can. Ch. Blue Admiral of Box, English import, top winner of the breed in 1961. Onwed by Roger E. Richards.

Ch. Wood's Canyon Showman, 1955 Best in Show winner at Golden Gate. Owned by Marjorie Woods.

Ch. Driftwood's Monte, a top Northwest winner of the mid-60s. Bred by Hazel Foster Collins, and owned by A. J. McDonald.

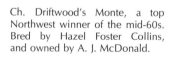

a record of 10 Bests of Breed, including victories over Chs. Fezziwig Raggedy Andy and Tarawood's Blue Baron, and 16 Best of Opposite Sex wins, including the OESCA specialty show at Detroit on March 7, 1965. Louis Baer was an officer of the OESCA for many years in the late sixties. Biff was the top winning OES in Canada in 1964, with two Bests in Show, three Groups and 10 placements. In the United States he was Winners Dog and Best of Winners at the OESCA specialty at Westbury in October 1965. Biff and his littermates as well as champions Perri Winkle of Beau Cheval, Mrs. Minniver of Beau Cheval, and Patchwork Morning Glory, Winners Bitch at the OESCA specialty in 1964, were all sired by Ch. Blue Admiral of Box, an imported stud, and one of only three specials ever to defeat Fezziwig Ceiling Zero. Blue Admiral was the top winning Bobtail in the United States in 1961, handled by E. J. Carver, placing eighth of all Working dogs.

Another OES fancier from the central part of the country, and one of the new Southern fanciers during the early sixties is Mrs. Maud Mowell from Knoxville, Tennessee. A number of Dogpatch Bobtails finished to championships in the sixties, including Dogpatch's Mopsie Marie, D. Silver Monarch, D. Silver Dutchess, D. Beau Brandy Shag, D. Monette, D. Blue Velvet, D. Blue Knight, and Sir Oliver Michael. The last four named are all out of Fezziwig Mona Lisa, a daughter of Fezziwig Ceiling Zero.

In the Rockies

Old English Sheepdogs were virtually unknown in the Rocky Mountain area until the mid-sixties. However, two of the breed's longest continually active fanciers were breeding in the Far West throughout the fifties and sixties. These are Lillian Lovejoy of the Lillibrad Kennels in Denver, Colorado and Harriet Poreda of Greyfriar Kennels, originally from Washington and now in Lakewood, Colorado. Lillian and her late husband Brad Lovejoy were involved with Sheepdogs before World War II. Their active contribution to the breed's development began in the early fifties with the acquisition of Ch. Norval Pride King, bred by Norval G. Smith by Ch. Lynnhaven Great Son out of Cheyenne Blue Moon whelped July 11, 1952. Pride King was directly descended on both sides of his pedigree from the famous OES of the pre-World War II period. His sire, Lynnhaven Great Son, was by Mrs. Lyndley's imported Best in Show winner Ch. Shepton Noble King, Great Son was out of Lynnhaven Raggedy Ann II: she was sired by the imported Ch. Shepton Commander, out of the imported Ch. Hillgarth Blue Blossom. Through these dogs, Pride

King was directly descended from Ch. Southridge Roger and the other important English OES of the thirties and twenties. King's dam, Cheyenne Blue Moon, was descended from the Cartref, Rosmoore, and Merriedip breeding of the pre-World War II period. King finished his championship in 1955. During his show career, handled by Mrs. Lovejoy, he compiled a record of 45 Bests of Breed in 46 times shown, beginning at eight months of age, with 36 Group placements and wins, and seven Bests in Show. His show career was abbreviated by a nearly fatal illness. Subsequently he left a major impact on the breed as a producer. He sired nine champions: Sidicky of Harbour Cross CD, Silver Snow, and the first "Lillibrad" champion, Lillibrad Lindy Lou CDX all out of the Lovejoys' Sheba's Arabella: Woodruff, L. Happy Holligan and L. Fancy of Hop-Pet-Hos, out of Ch. Beckington Aristocrat; L. Blue Boy and L. Prince Charming out of Lillibrad Lindy Lou; and L. Mischievious, Beckington Aristocrat was bred by Mrs. M. K. Givson in England by Shepton Celebrity out of Lady Winnie, whelped March 28, 1956. Celebrity was sired by Ch. Shepton Home Guard. In addition to the three champions by Norval Pride King, Aristocrat produced Chs. L. Christopher Sam, L. Shaggy Sue, and L. Fluff Bucket all by Lillibrad Sammy's Shadow; Calico Lady of Lillibrad and L. Sir Lancelot by Ch. Lillibrad Prince Charming, Prince Charming, Blue Boy and a non-champion full brother Lillibrad Sammy's Shadow were a product of a father to daughter breeding (Ch. Norval Pride King to a Ch. Lillibrad Lindy Lou CDX) whelped March 9, 1956 and October 21, 1956.

Prince Charming went to Mr. & Mrs. Arthur V. Gustafson of Chicago, Illinois, who had him shown to an impressive series of wins by Jack Funk, before his sudden death. In all he won 17 Bests of Breed, six Group firsts, and three placings, and four Bests in Show. He was Winners Dog, Best of Winners and Best of Breed at the OESCA specialty show in 1960, and Best of Breed and second in the Group at Westminster in 1961. Prince Charming is the only instance of four generations of father to son Best in Show winners in the United States as of 1975 (Prince Charming-Norval Pride King-Lynnhaven Great Son-Shepton Noble King.)

Lillibrad Blue Boy was owned by Mrs. Herbert E. Bennett, who had owned the famous winners of the twenties and thirties—Chs. Kinnelon Scally Wag and his son, Sunny Boy. Blue Boy did all the swimming scenes in Walt Disney's "The Shaggy Dog," standing in for Lillibrad Sammy's Shadow, the shaggy dog in the rest of the film.

Lillian Lovejoy became the first president of the Old English Sheepdog Club of America from west of the Mississippi in the fall of 1966, succeeding Hendrik Van Rensselaer. Throughout the sixties a succession of Lillibrad champions were shown, including Chs. L.

168

Hotshot Harry, L. Denver Dan, L. Snow Bunny, L. Huck Fin, L. Lady Meg, and L. Sheriff Tubs. Lady Meg was sired by the Fezziwig Ceiling Zero, grandson Ch. Rivermist Horatio. Various Lillibrad studs and bitches have contributed to the development of the breed outside the Lillibrad kennel. For example, Lillibrad Sir Lancelot was bred to the Ch. Shepton Bobbibingo-Greyfriar's Jennie daughter Ch. Silvershag Frolic, and produced Ch. Silvershag Madcap Margot. Margot in two litters by Ch. Silvershag Snowtatters produced a succession of champions, including the Demkos' Ch. Silvershag Snowbright, widely used at stud in the East in the late sixties. Snowbright, with 16 champion get, ranks as the seventh all-time producer as of the end of 1974.

Although Harriet Poreda of Greyfriar Kennels in Lakewood, Colorado has been involved with Bobtails for 20 years, the first Greyfriar OES did not finish an AKC championship until 1962. Since then at least 50 OES have completed championships with the Greyfriar prefix, as well as 15 others that were either not named Greyfriar, or were by a Greyfriar stud or out of a Greyfriar bred bitch. Through such dogs as Louise Forest's Greyfriar's Jennie, the James Andersons' Ch. Greyfriar Double JJ's Penny, the Marvin Smiths' Greyfriar's Old Lace, and Stan Goldberg's Greyfriar's Angel Feathers, among others, the Greyfriar prefix can be found in back of many contemporary Sheepdogs with the Silvershag, Double JJ, Tamara, and Shaggybar names, and in turn behind dogs bred from these kennels. For example, the Van Rensselaers of Fezziwig fame have produced a number of champions and producers by Fezziwig Ceiling Zero and his younger brother Fezziwig Sir Basil out of the bitch Silvershag Sweet Sue. Sweet Sue is out of Greyfriar's Jennie. Greyfriar has produced more champions out of more different studs than any other American kennel. Only three of these have not been Greyfriar-bred studs; Chs. Smokey Bob of Dalcroy, Tarawood's Flannel Pants, and Shandy Kip London. Champions from Greyfriar studs include; Little John of Greyfriar, Greyfriar's Woody, G. Pickwick Patches, G. Blue Hickory, G. Alfie, and the Chs. G. Jolly Roger, G. Admiral Hilton, G. Sir Fang, G. Little John, G. Monroe, and G. Fancy Pants. Among the bitches that have produced champions for Greyfriar are Miss Angel Feathers, Gloria's Own Callistopee, Greyfriar Happy Anniversary, G. Royal Showoff II, G. Shy Shady Lady, G. Misty of Arran, G. Heidi, and the Chs. Moppet of Brunswick, G. Royal Peggy, G. Miss Meticulous, G. Matilda, G. Missy Bevan, G. Maggie, and G. Maid of Cotton. Maid of Cotton, in addition to being a Group winning bitch is the dam of four champions by Ch. Greyfriar Little John; G. Bo Peep of Belmore, G. Queen of Hearts, G. Heather and Bar-Don's Tammy. Tammy is owned by Dr. & Mrs. Oren Bush of Oklahoma City,

Oklahoma, among the first bobtail fanciers in the Great Plains. In addition to Tammy, the Bushes have also owned and finished Professor of Greyfriar (Ch. Greyfriar Sir Fang UD—Greyfriar Shy Shady Lady) the Winners Dog at Westminster in 1970. In the middle sixties the Bushes owned and campaigned the OESCA specialty Best of Breed (at Kansas City in 1966) and Best in Show winner, Fezziwig Bartholomew, whelped June 27, 1963 by Ch. Farleydene Bartholomew out of Raretree Tine. Barty was the first Bobtail many contemporary Great Plains and Southwestern OES fanciers saw in the show rings. Dr. Bush succeeded Lillian Lovejoy as president of the OESCA in the fall of 1968.

The basis of Greyfriar breeding has been certain combinations of their early fifties Bobtails, Ch. Towser W. Black and the bitch Favour's Lady in Ermine. These two produced the dog Little John of Greyfriar, who in a breeding to the imported Shepton Blue Bonnet, owned by Hazel Foster Collins of Driftwood kennels, produced the bitch Greyfriar's Bar-Maid. It is interesting to note that Blue Bonnet was a daughter of English Ch. Shepton Surf King, a grandsire of the Van Rensselaers imported stud Ch. Farleydene Bartholomew, Favour's Lady in Ermine, in a breeding to the Lovejoys' Ch. Norval Pride King, produced the dog Greyfriar's Woody. The mating of Woody and Bar-Maid in the late fifties produced the basis of contemporary Greyfriar stock. The original line has been added to principally through the bitch Gloria's Own Callistopee, and the use of the studs Chs. Smokey Bob of Dalcroy and Tarawood's Flannel Pants. Gloria's Own Callistopee, by Ch. Friar Tuck of Sherwood (the Double JJ bred Best in Show winning stud out of Ch. Greyfriar Double JJ's Penny) out of Hilpisch's Little Miss Muffet was an amazing bitch. She lost a front leg in an accident, but in three litters by Greyfriar Blue Hickory, Smokey Bob of Dalcroy and Tarawood's Flannel Pants produced among others the Chs. G. Maggie, G. Little John, G. Admiral Hilton, G. Summer Smoke, and G. Fancy Pants, all of whom have in turn made a marked contribution to the breed as producers. Fancy Pants, by Tarawood's Flannel Pants, has produced the Greyfriar champions: G. Tareyton of Majon, G. Unsinkable Molly B., G. Sir Fang, G. Missy Beven, G. Tiffany of Ronanjo, G. Maid of Cotton, and G. Miss Meticulous.

Among the many fanciers who acquired Bobtails from Greyfriar was Anne Weisse of King's Row Kennels in La Crosse. Anne had owned OES since the end of World War II, including experience with them in Germany and Europe when the breed was virtually unknown. She was a director of the OESCA for several terms. Her Greyfriar bred or derived OES were American and Canadian Chs. Greyfriar's Rollicking Rogue, G. Lord Fauntleroy, King's Row Bonny Suzanne

Ch. Fezziwig Bartholomew going Best in Show at Kansas City 1966 under Mrs. W. C. Edmiston in follow-up to win of the first Old English Sheepdog Specialty held west of the Mississippi. Owned by Dr. and Mrs. Oren D. Bush's Mitepa Kennels.

Ch. Professor of Greyfriar, early '70s winner. Bred by Harriet Poreda; owned and handled by Dr. Bush.

(by Lord Fauntleroy out of Ch. Silvershag Sally Snow Boots), and more recently Tamara's Memory of Suzanne out of Tempest of Dalcroy and Greyfriar's Old Lace.

West Coast

There have been Old English Sheepdog fanciers in California and on the West Coast since the first World War. Mrs. Walter Colverd, Chris Shuttleworth, Mrs. Herbert Bennett, and even Mrs. Lewis Roesler of Merriedip fame owned and showed a number of Bobtails in California in the 1920s and '30s. During the second World War, Mrs. Howard J. Hickingbotham's Ch. Black Baron was almost undefeated in Working Group competition. After the War and through the '50s, a number of California and West Coast OES were shown, finished championships and placed in or won an occasional Group, and even a few Bests in Show: Chs. Wood's Canyon Guardian, a son of Black Baron; Jolly Darby of Delemere and Merriedip Mistress Monnie, both owned by D. C. Phillips (Monnie was for a time the greatest winning OES bitch); Mr. Chips of Driftwood; Woods Woolley Blue Buttons; Lord Beaverbrook of Waverly; Wood's Woolley Darling Scamp; Blue Baron Jr.; Babette of Hungjao CDX, a Group winning bitch; Marwood's Starlight Heather; Wood's Canyon Showman, Best in Show at Golden Gate in 1955; White Baron and Mr. Zip of Delemere; Delemere How Now; and Marwood's Toddie, who finished just before Mona Berkowitz's Shepton Surprise in late 1961. Toddie, and the other Marwood and Wood's Canyon Bobtails were either bred or owned by Mrs. Marjorie Woods of La Honda, California, virtually the only active breeder anywhere on the West Coast in the fifties, except for Hazel Foster Collins in Washington.

However, except for these Bobtails, there were no other West Coast OES to make championships between the early 1940s and early '60s. There were only a few more total Old English on the entire coast in those years. There are now more Bobtails exhibited in California than in any other state in the Union. It requires more dogs and bitches competing in the classes in California than in any other part of the country to earn a major. The largest Old English Sheepdog specialty show ever held until then was the first independent specialty since 1929 of the Old English Sheepdog Club of America at Anaheim, California on September 19, 1970, with more than 150 entries. The success of this show was in large part due to Hugh Jordan of Loyalblu Kennels, who in October 1970 was elected president of the OESCA, the first Californian to hold the position.

The Anaheim OESCA specialty results in many respects reflect the various developments within the breed during the sixties. Fittingly

172

Best of Breed went to the longest continuing exhibitor of Sheepdogs today in the United States, Mona Berkowitz, with her imported Ch. Prospectblue Rodger. Her activities in California since the early sixties helped to introduce the breed to the West Coast. Best of Opposite Sex went to the Jordans' imported Prospectblue Elizabeth. The Winners Dog came from the Michigan kennel of the Smiths', Tamara's Henry Higgins Havoc, while the Winners Bitch, Fezziwig Melissa, came from the Van Rensselaers' East Coast kennel and was sired by Fezziwig Ceiling Zero from his last litter. At the all-breed show following the OESCA specialty, the American-Canadian Ch. Rivermist Feather Merchant was Best of Breed, over the other top specials, thus bringing into the picture another major name in contemporary American Old English.

Because the breed on the West Coast has gone from virtually no registrations, no breeders, and no exhibitors, to thousands of registrations and many breeders and exhibitors in less than ten years time, it is impossible to accurately assess recent developments. A few trends are evident, and there are a number of exhibitors and breeders that have made their mark. Perhaps the most significant trend in West Coast OES is the very large numbers of single litter breeders that have emerged. The other major trend is the willingness of California Bobtail owners to exhibit their dogs. Large and even huge entries are the order of the day in California. Reflecting the proliferation of breeders and breedings within the state, it is possible to see more Bobtails of more different backgrounds and bloodlines in California than anywhere else in the country. It is possible to see imported English and European OES, others from the major kennels in the East, Midwest and Far West, as well as various combinations and permutations of these bloodlines all in the ring simultaneously. The results of the combinations of older American and imported stock taking place in California and elsewhere in the North and Southwest cannot as yet be evaluated. For certain, from some of these efforts will come the champions of tomorrow, and top winning all breed specials.

One of the first West Coast breeders was Stan Goldberg (no longer active) of the Shaggybar Kennels in Sausalito, California. He had Old English from the late fifties. His principal contribution to the breed was through the get produced by his champion stud Woodruff. Woodruff was bred by Lillbrad Kennels by Ch. Norval Pride King out of Ch. Beckington Aristrocrat. Woodruff sired the Chs. Cabin Boy of Lake Shore, Mumbly Peg of Lake Shore, Blue Panda's Darling Duchess, Blue Panda Shaggybar Tiny Tim, Shaggy B'ar Lady Chelsea, Shady Lady of Shaggybar, Nobility's Cotton Candy, Nobility Shaggybar Lottablu, Hill's Sir Oliver of Shaggybar, and Shaggybar

Bottomsup. Sir Oliver and Bottomsup were both bred by Goldberg out of Greyfriar Angel Feathers, whelped February 12, 1963. Angel Feathers was a full sister to the foundation brood at Silvershag, Greyfriar's Jennie and the Double JJ foundation brood. Ch. Greyfriar Double JJ's Penny, by Greyfriar's Woody out of Greyfriar's Bar-Maid. Bottomsup was kept by Goldberg who had him shown to two Bests in Show among other wins, before his unexpected death at three years of age. Hill's Sir Oliver of Shaggybar went to Patricia Hill of Los Altos, California, who finished him and used him at stud. Among his champion get are Sir Andrew of Bitterroot, Fabulous Fred of Mistihills, Mistihills Squire Andrew, Gladrag's Sebastion, Mistihills Halmor Gillian, and Mistihills Bit of Heather.

The last five named were all bred by Mrs. Carol Elliot of Mistihills Kennel of Woodland, California, out of Mistihills Bonnie Belinda. Bonnie Belinda was bred by Deedy Abrams out of her Ch. Downey-lane Dreamboat by Ch. Fezziwig Fainthart Falstaff. Mrs. Elliot succeeded Mrs. Abrams as the writer of the OES column in the *American Kennel Gazette* in the mid-sixties.

Elsewhere in California into the 1960s were a number of Old English Sheepdog breeders of note including: Mrs. Winifred Barnes of Bridewell Kennels in southern California; the previously mentioned Bob Tail Acres Kennels of Mr. and Mrs. John Herlihy in Walnut Creek; the Tipton Brier Kennels of Mr. and Mrs. Leon Nilsen in Sunland; the Nobility Kennels of Beverly Thode in Stockton; the Loyalblu Kennels of Dr. and Mrs. Hugh Jordan in Whittier; the Bobmar Bobtails of Dr. and Mrs. R. S. Porter in Chatsworth; and the transplanted Momarv Kennels of Mona Berkowitz in Thousand Oaks, among others.

Winnie Barnes established her Bridewell Kennels in England, where she was acquainted with Henry Tilley of Shepton fame, before relocating in southern California. Among others, the Bridewell name was associated with Chs. W. C. Charlie Bridewell, Adam of Bridewell, Bridewell Fair Lady and Tommy Atkins, all sired by Cheyenne Sam out of Tessa II of Bridewell. Adam of Bridewell has sired Chs. Pepsi of Tara and Bridewell Polly Flinders. (Polly, out of Lady Lucifer, was bred by Mrs. Hugh Jordan.) Mayflower of Bridewell has produced Chs. Archibald of Bridewell and Sir Reginald of Bridewell.

The most famous Bridewell Bobtail was Bridewell Lord Nelson, owned by the celebrated animal trainer, Hal Driscoll. Lord Nelson played "Lad" in the television show "Please Don't Eat the Daisies" which ran for several years in the mid-1960s, and in that role probably gave more Americans their first glimpse of an Old English Sheepdog than any other Bobtail. He was by Cheyenne Sam out of

Ch. Shepton Surprise, English import bitch, foremost winner of 1962 (at only three years of age). Shown winning Group at Santa Barbara under judge Len Carey, Surprise was owner-handled by Mrs. Mona (Kucker) Berkowitz, whose Momarv Kennels is the longest in continuous operation in the breed and has been at the top in both East and West.

Ch. Shaggy Bar Bottoms Up, a repeat Best in Show winner of the mid-60s, bred and owned by Stan Goldberg's Shaggybar Kennels (California) and handled by Jim Mc-Manus. Like Ch. Shepton Surprise above, Bottoms Up died at very young age.

Tessa II of Bridewell, and among others sired Captain Kid Boots, Ch. Bomar's Christmas Dawn (bred by Dr. and Mrs. Porter, and co-owned by them with the Hoovers of Riverside, California, until she was finished as a champion), and Ch. Taralane's Beauregard Blue CD. Beauregard, whelped June 12, 1966, out of Lady Lucifer, was owned, bred and exhibited by Mrs. Hugh Jordan.

The Jordans exhibited a number of imported Bobtails with considerable success, including Champions Two Trees Black Eyed Susan, Prospectblue Elizabeth (BOS at the OES Specialty, September 1970) and Prospectblue Samuel. In the mid-1970s, under their Loyalblu prefix, the Jordans have emerged among the most prominent breeder-exhibitors of Old English in the United States.

Mr. and Mrs. Leon Nilsen of Tipton Brier Kennels in Sunland, were among the first active Old English breeders and exhibitors in southern California in the early sixties. The Nilsens organized the first OES club supported match in California. Following the OESCA's reorganization and the creating of a Western region in the mid-sixties, Leon was the second Western region director, succeeding Hazel Foster Collins in October 1966. An early Tipton Brier litter by Sonny Boy of Tansley out of Ch. Shepton Pride and Joy included the bitches Tipton Wall-Eyed Bo Peekaboo and Ch. Tipton Brier Bonnie Kate. Wall-Eyed Bo Peekaboo went to Stan Goldberg. In a litter by his Ch. Woodruff, whelped October 30, 1962, she produced Chs. Shady Lady of Shaggybar and Shaggy B'ar Lady Chelsea. Lady Chelsea was owned by Mrs. Grace Irvine of Fair Oaks, California, and was shown to her championship undefeated in the classes with two Group placements, five Bests of Breed and seven Best of Opposite Sex wins.

One of the longest continuously active contemporary American OES breeders is Hazel Foster Collins of the Driftwood Kennels in Woodinville, Washington. Mrs. Collins has had Bobtails since the early thirties. She was virtually the only Bobtail fancier within a thousand miles for thirty years. The result of her isolation from the mainstream of the breed's development has been almost no impact of Driftwood breeding outside the Pacific Northwest and almost no Driftwood champions until the 1960s. The first OES champion with the Driftwood prefix, Mr. Chips of Driftwood, finished in 1952. The next Driftwood champion did not finish until 1962. Since then a succession of Driftwood champion OES have finished in the Northwest, including Driftwood Cavalier Blue Mist, D. Monte, D. Shasta Blue, D. Barton Boy, D. Oliver Twist, D. Peeping Tom and D. Azure Empress. Cavalier Blue Mist, a bitch owned by Mrs. Louis Cragin, whelped June 12, 1957, by Driftwood Cavalier out of Shepton Blue Bonnet, won the Group at the Seattle Kennel Club show from the

Am. & Can. Ch. Rivermist Feather Merchant, Can. CD, top winning Old English in Canada in early '70s. A Unnesta Pim-Nosegay offspring, co-owned by Dr. and Mrs. Gary Carter and Jim McTernan.

Ch. Rivermist Blue Iris, CD, another conformation and Obedience winning Pim-Nosegay offspring, owned by Jean S. Thorkildsen.

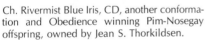

Ch. Aragorn's Irresistible, CD, scoring Best Adult at 1971 OESCA match, handled by owner Jean Thorkildsen. Irresistible is a dam of champions.

open Class on July 30, 1961, a feat accomplished 20 years before by her great-grandsire Shepton Sea Rover. Blue Bonnet in a breeding to Harriet Poreda's Little John of Greyfriar produced the bitch Greyfriar's Bar-Maid, who is back of much of the Greyfriar breeding of the sixties. Driftwood's Oliver Twist, owned by John and Rosemary Murphy of Seattle, was the number 10 ranked Old English for 1967, according to the Phillips System, with one Best in Show, two Group firsts, and a Group second. In 1968, he was number five ranked Bobtail with five Group wins and six Group placements, while in 1969 he was sixth ranked in the breed with two Group wins and four placements. The Driftwood stock, through such dogs as Driftwood Laughing Cavalier can be traced back through the Lynnhaven and Merriedip breeding of the thirties and forties, and also includes many of the famous English names of the post World War II period, such as Ch. Shepton Surf King and Boldwood breedings, through the imported bitch Shepton Blue Bonnet.

The most known and influential Old English kennel on the West Coast, if not in the entire country, is the Momarv Kennel of Mona Berkowitz, established in the East and relocated in Southern California in the early sixties. As indicated in an earlier chapter, Mrs. Berkowitz is one of the most important figures in the history of American Old English Sheepdogs. The impact of Momarv Bobtails in the East mainly through the show winnings and get of Ch. Merriedip Duke George, was tremendous. The impact of Mrs. Berkowtiz's OES since relocating in Southern California has been even more extensive. There have been three main contributions of Momarv to OES, beyond the fact that more than any other individual Mrs. Berkowitz can be credited with introducing the breed to the West Coast: First, Mrs. Berkowitz has owned a succession of top-winning all-breed Old English Sheepdog specials throughout the sixties. Second, she has bred, for herself and numerous others, a succession of winners and producers. Third, her important studs have made a permanent mark on the breed as producers through being bred to bitches other than Mrs. Berkowitz's.

Since moving to California, Mrs. Berkowitz has bred more than 16 champions with the Momarv prefix, owned several imported champions and had her studs produce more than 20 other champions. The major Momarv show Bobtails have been Chs. Shepton Surprise, Shayloran's Billy Hayseed and Prospectblue Rodger. Surprise was an imported bitch, who was the top winning OES and No. 5 of all Working breeds in 1962, and the *Kennel Review* award winner as Best Western Working Dog for the year. Billy Hayseed was bred in Canada by Mr. and Mrs. Harold Riches, whelped May 6, 1962 by

Beckington Reprint out of Rosmoore Pink Lady. He was originally owned by Reprint's importer, Mrs. Claude Crafts of Rosmoore Kennels in New Hampshire. At the 1964 OESCA specialty show, judged by Mrs. Berkowitz, he was Best of Winners. Under Mrs. Berkowitz's handling, Billy Hayseed finished the year as the No. 3 winning Bobtail. Throughout 1965, '66, and into '67, he continued to give an impressive account of himself in California show rings, going Best of Breed at the first supported show of the OESCA on the West Coast and then Best of Breed at the first OESCA specialty in California. He sired at least 11 champions, (before a prostrate condition forced his premature retirement from active stud duties) including the Momarv champions: M. Mighty Like A Rose, M. Fancy Free, M. Gentle Johnny (all out of Momarv's Burning Bright); M. Horatio, M. Harry Hayride, and M. Reginald Hathaway—all out of the imported Group winning bitch, Ch. Shepton Rollingsea Morning Glory. Mighty Like A Rose and Bruno Boy Hayseed, owned and handled by Mrs. Berkowitz were ranked respectively fifth and sixth among the top winning OES for 1967. Mighty had five Group placements, while Bruno went from the open class to Best in Show at the San Gabriel Valley Kennel Club show, over 1,825 dogs, on April 23, 1967. Later that year, at the Santa Barbara Kennel Club show, he was Best of Winners at the first OESCA specialty held in California.

The 1970s

Breed trends begun in the 1960s continued at an accelerated pace in the 1970s. The most significant of these trends were: increasing popularity, many small but serious breeder-exhibitors, and an increasing difficulty in pointing to particular individuals as having wide-spread significant impact on the breed's development. Registration statistics and the results of the Old English Sheepdog Club of America's specialties point up these trends.

The yearly registrations of Old English Sheepdogs in the 1970-1975 period show:

Year	Total Registrations	Popularity Ranking
1970	6785	31
1971	10511	25
1972	13321	23
1973	14751	24
1974	16050	23
1975	15623	21

Old English increased well more than double in the period. At mid-point of the decade, the breed—along with most other AKC breeds—appears to have reached something of a population plateau, being currently established at about twentieth place in popularity with annual registrations well past 15,000.

The top winners at the national specialties held in this period were:

9-19-70   OESCA, Anaheim, California—Judge: John Cassevoy

WD: BW   Tamara's Henry Higgins Havoc, C.D.—Dr. Robert C. and Anita D. Hulse, owners; (Thomasina Smith, breeder).

WB   Fezziwig Melissa—John & Linda Keck, owners; (Hendrick & Serena Van Rensselaer, breeders).

BOS   Ch. Prospectblue Elizabeth—Dr. & Mrs. Hugh Jordan, owners; (Mrs. Isobel Lawson, breeder).

BOB   Ch. Prospect Blue Rodger—Mrs. Mona Berkowitz, owner; (Mrs. Isobel Lawson, breeder).

3-28-71   Classes at Texas K.C.—Judge: J. Lynn Welsh

WD.   Misty's Sea Wolf of Haystack—Virgil C. and Rose M. Williams, breeders and owners.

WB, BW   Hester of the Emberges—Linder B. and Walker L. Wright III, owners; (Miss D. A. Malins, breeder).

BOS   Ch. Fezziwig Melissa—John and Linda Keck, owners; (Serena and Hendrick Van Rensselaer, breeders).

6-21-71   Class at Greenwich KC—Judges: H. Anthony Hodges, dogs, Mona Berkowitz, bitches and intersex

WD   Knightcap's Devilish Dobie—Mercia & Sidney Moosnick, owners; (George & Joan Demko, breeders).

WB, BW   Nana Patchwork Panda—David C. Breslin, owner; (Marlene Anderson, breeder).

BOS   Ch. Tamara's Carole's Folly—Carole Phillips, owner; (Thomasina Smith, breeder).

BOB   Ch. Gweheloy Blue Valley Boy—Norma J. Rockwell, owner; (Mrs. Betty Tidhey, breeder).

8-25-72   OESCA, Ravenna, Ohio—Judges: Mona Berkowitz, Dogs and intersex, Mrs. James W. Mattern, bitches.

WD, BW   Moppimore's Little Giant—Judy Parker, owner; (Vikki Strickland, breeder).

180

Ch. Rivermist Blue Bell, a Pym daughter, owned by Jim McTernan.

Ch. Kotton Kandy Misty Muffet, a Dan Tatters daughter, BOS at the 1972 OESCA Specialty. Co-owned by Arnold Kamens and Jim Mc-Ternan.

Ch. Tatters Rivermist Tom Fool, a Dan Tatters son, co-owned by Bob and Sheila Ziccardi and Jim McTernan.

WB	Wedgewood's Blind Faith—Nancy L. Olson, owner; (Clifford and Caryl Green, breeders).
BOS	Ch. Kotton Kandy's Misty Muffet—Arnold Kamens and James McTernan, owners; (A. & E. Mirman, breeders).
BOB	Ch. Stonebarrow's Friar Tuck—Dr. L. E. Jones and B. Wendall Raky, owners; (B. Wendall Raky, Jr., breeder).

10-27-73   OESCA, New Orleans—Judge: Mr. Larry Downey

WD	Double "JJ's" Foursquare George—Mrs. Joyce M. Anderson, owner and breeder
WB, BW	Bonnie Annie Lie of Towzie Tyke—Mr. and Mrs. W. A. Pound, owners and breeders.
BOS	Ch. Langley Snowmaiden—Kathy & Ben Bedford, Jr., owners; (Joan & Roy Butler, breeders).
BOB	Ch. Fezziwig Vice Versa—Mr. and Mrs. Van Rensselaer owners and breeders.

9-21-74   OESCA, Buena Park, California—Judge: David C. Parker

WD, BW	Some Buddy's Friendly Pippin—Sandra Haeseker, owner; (Dr. J. G. and Mrs. T. B. Carter, breeders).
WB	Some Buddy for Me—Dr. and Mrs. J. G. and Mrs. T. B. Carter, owner-breeders.
BOS	Ch. Rivermist Feather Merchant—Dr. & Mrs. J. G. Carter and J. McTernan, owners; (B. Goodman and N. Miller, breeders).
BOB	Cheerio Ragged Pacesetter—Bruce & Donna Samuelson, owners; (Kenneth & Pauls Leach, breeders).

6-6-75   OESCA, New Canaan, Ct.—Judge: Mrs. Ramona Van Court Jones, dogs. Dr. Hugh Jordan, bitches & intersex

WD	Bahlamb's Blue Billy Boy—Arthur Donahue, owner; (Caj Haakansson, breeder).
WB, BW	Wagsend Wind Song—Russel & Jane Shaw (owners).
BOS	Ch. Jendower's Cloud Nine—Capt. & Mrs. F. R. Rich, owners and breeders.
BOB	Ch. V. D. Mar's Visibility Zero—R. Arble, C. Moulton and D. Shephard, owners; (David & Mary Shephard, breeders).

Wins at Westminster Kennel Club's annual show in New York City in February have traditionally been among the most coveted awards in dogs. The Old English Best of Breed winners in 1970, '71, and '72, Ch. Prince Andrew of Sherline, Ch. Brooks Blue Boy, and Ch. Fezziwig Vice Versa respectively, failed to place in the Working Group. Vice Versa's win in 1972, handled by his owner-breeder, Hendrick Van Rensselaer, made him the first amateur handled OES to win a Westminster Best of Breed since Mona Berkowitz had handled Duke George to victory in 1959.

In 1973, Terry and Kathy Crow from Vermillion, South Dakota, came East with their Ch. Dustmop's St. Nicholas to take the breed, also owner-handled by Terry. St. Nicholas went on to place fourth in the Working Group. St. Nicholas was owner-handled to many wins, including several Bests in Show, and was beginning to make an account of himself as a producer before his unfortunate accidental early death in 1974.

Fezziwig Vice Versa won his second Westminster Best of Breed in 1974 and went on to place second in the Working Group.

Nineteen seventy-five was a historic one for the breed at Westminster—Ch. Lancelot of Barvan (Ch. Tarawoods Beau Billy D— Tarawoods Mistee Weather), bred and owned by Mr. and Mrs. Ronald Vanword of Newmarket, Ontario, Canada, and handled by Malcolm Fellows, went all the way to Best in Show! The judge was Harry T. Peters, Jr., whose father had been so strongly indentified with the breed in its early days in America. Sir Lancelot thus became but the second Old English to win the ultimate prize at Westminster— the first having been Mrs. Tyler Morse's Ch. Slumber in 1914.

Ch. Sir Lancelot was retired from competition following his Garden win, but others were quick to take center stage. The strongest winning of these was Ch. Loyalblu Hendihap. Whelped October 1971, Hendihap is by Loyalblu Right Time ex Ch. Mistress Mary of Taralane. He is co-owned by his breeders, Loyalblu Kennels (Dr. and Mrs. Hugh Jordan) and by Dick and Lorry Boerner. His wins for the year (which not only made him top breed winner in the Phillips ratings, but No. 2 of all Working as well) included 4 all-breed Bests in Show, 3 independent Specialties and 19 Group Firsts. He has been handled by breeder/co-owner Linda Jordan.

The Old English Sheepdog Club of America salutes as Register of Merit sires the dogs that have sired 5 or more champions, and as Register of Merit dams those that have produced 3 or more champions. At end of 1974, the all-time totals of Register of Merit awards won by owners read as follows:

	Number awards
Mr. and Mrs. Hendrik Van Rensselaer (Fezziwig)	11 (1 co-owned)
Dr. Louise Forrest (Silvershag)	9 (2 co-owned)

Mona Berkowitz (Momarv)	7
Mr. and Mrs. Barry Goodman (Rivermist)	5 (1 co-owned)
Anne Raker (Ambelon)	5
Lillian Lovejoy (Lillibrad)	4
Mr. and Mrs. Marvin Smith (Tamara)	4
Mr. and Mrs. James E. Anderson (Double JJ)	3 (1 co-owned)
Sandi Baker (Droverdale)	3 (2 co-owned)
Joan Demko (Knightcap)	3
Mr. and Mrs. Robert Abrams (Downeylane)	2
Mr. and Mrs. Terrance Crow (Shaggiluv)	2

A compilation at end of 1974 shows the following to have been the all-time leading producers of champions in the breed:

		TOP SIRES	Champions sired:
*	1.	Ch. Fezziwig Ceiling Zero	63
*	2.	Ch. Unesta Pim	46
*	3.	Ch. Rivermist Dan Tatters	35
	4.	Ch. Fezziwig Vice Versa	27
	5.	Ch. Rivermist Dan Patch	22
*	6.	Ch. Tempest of Delcroy	21
	7.	Ch. Silvershag Snowbright	16
*	8.	Ch. Shandy Kip London	15
*		Ch. Farleydene Bartholomew	15
*	10.	Ch. Prospect Shaggy Boy	14

* = Deceased at time of compilation

		TOP DAMS	Champions produced:
*	1.	Ch. Rivermist Gentian	14
	2.	Ch. Rivermist Nosegay	12
	3.	Miss Muffet of Tatters	11
*		Ch. Patchwork Gillian of Van R	11
*	5.	Ch. Baroness of Duroya	9
		Ch. Silvershag Donnamerry	9
		Ch. Silvershag Ruffles	9
*		Ch. Tamara's Patches of Perse	9
*	9.	Ch. Beckington Aristocrat	8
	10.	Ch. Greyfriar's Maggie	7
		Ch. Jendower's Queen Victoria	7
		Ch. Shaggshire's Tiffany Star	7
		Ch. Silvershag Frolic	7
		Ch. Silvershag Sweet Sue	7

Why has the Old English Sheepdog come to prominence in the last decade? Those that know the breed say it has always been the comical clown, easy to get along with, and great with children—a sure candidate for popularity despite the hair and size. Obviously, many factors have contributed to the breed's rise in popularity. Dogs in general have increased tremendously in popularity. As never before, people have the means to acquire dogs, and in the case of the Bobtail the leisure time to devote to caring for them. A succession of great show winners from Duke George to Fezziwig Ceiling Zero, Fezziwig Raggedy Andy, Rivermist Dan Patch, and Prince Andrew of Sherline brought the breed prominent attention in the dog show world. A Walt Disney movie, "The Shaggy Dog," brought the Sheepdog before the public in every town in the United States. In the middle-sixties a long running television series, "Please Don't Eat the Daisies," put an Old English in the homes of millions of Americans every Saturday evening for a half hour. Old English also did their part in promoting everything from gasoline to sofas, and of course, along the way brought the breed widespread national exposure. No doubt all of these factors, and perhaps a new trend towards long hair and a fascination with the Bobtail's unique countenance, contributed to the breed's rise in popularity.

With Hendrik Van Rensselaer of Fezziwig Kennels serving as president and principal driving force, the OESCA reorganized in the mid-sixties in order to best serve the interests of a nationwide fancy. Since then the presidents of the Club have been successively: Lillian Lovejoy of Denver, Colorado, the first OESCA president from west of the Mississippi; Dr. Oren Bush from Oklahoma City, Oklahoma; Dr. Hugh Jordan from Whittier, California; Mr. Van Rensselaer again; Dr. Bush again; and currently Earl Jacobson of Peoria, Ill. In the late sixties a series of local Old English Sheepdog clubs began to spring up across the country. Most of these have already had matches, and are meeting regularly, although still too young to have gone through the official process of becoming affiliated with the OESCA and the American Kennel Club. It is in the hands of these local organizations and the thousands and thousands of individual fanciers from Maine to Florida to Arizona and Alaska that the future history of the breed lies.

APPEARANCE: Body short, muscular, compact; great symmetry; elastic gallop; ambling or pacing characteristic of trot or walk

EARS medium-sized; carried flat to head; moderately arched

NECK fairly long; arched gracefully; well-coated with hair

LOIN stout; gently arched

TAIL preferably none; should never exceed 1½-2" in adults; puppies' tails docked at first joint if born with tails

HINDQUARTERS round, muscular; hams densely coated

HOCKS well-let-down

COAT profuse; good hard texture,not straight; shaggy, free from curl; undercoat waterproof

SIZE: Height, males 22" and up; females, slightly less; measurement from shoulder to stern practically same as height. Type, soundness, balance, character more important than size

SKULL capacious, squarely formed; well-covered with hair; well-arched parts over eyes

EYES vary with color; very dark preferred

NOSE black, large; capacious

TEETH strong, large; evenly placed; level

JAW fairly long; strong; square; cut off;stop well-defined

SHOULDERS sloping, narrow at points; lower at shoulder than at loin

FORELEGS straight;good bone; length medium; not leggy; well-coated

FEET small, round; toes well-arched; pads thick, hard

COLOR: Gray, grizzle, blue or blue-merled with or without white markings or in reverse. Shades of brown or fawn objectionable

RIBS well-sprung; brisket deep, capacious

Official Breed Standard of the Old English Sheepdog

AUTHOR'S NOTE: The comments (in the same smaller type of this introductory note) that follow each item of the official standard, were written by Mr. and Mrs. Edward P. Renner, and were first published in the *Old English Sheepdog Club of America Yearbook for 1963*. It was explained that they were meant to "help novice fanciers more clearly understand the terminology of the text of the standard, and to appreciate quality in the owning, showing, breeding or judging of 'Bobtails'." Hope was expressed that "this will in no way be construed as advocating any changes in the standard."

Skull—Capacious and rather squarely formed, giving plenty of room for brain power. The parts over the eyes should be well-arched and the whole well covered with hair.

> SKULL—5 points. The skull should give the feeling of being well-chiseled and full-blown with adequate space between the ears, rather than narrow and smoothly tapered. A full-coated head with heavy "fall" (hair falling over the eyes) tends to look well-rounded and hide the chiseling.

Jaw—Fairly long, strong, square and truncated. The stop should be well-defined to avoid a Deerhound face. (The attention of judges is particularly called to the above properties, as a long, narrow head is a deformity.)

JAW—5 points; FOREFACE—5 points. The jaw should continue the well-sculptured line of the skull, with the "stop" (area between the eyes) forming a near vertical line in profile, as opposed to the near horizontal line of the skull dome. While the jaw should be fairly long and full, it should give the appearance of being cut off abruptly rather than continuing on to a narrow point.

Eyes—Vary according to the color of the dog. Very dark preferred, but in the glaucous or blue dogs a pearl, walleye or china eye is considered typical. (A light eye is most objectionable.)

EYES—5 points. Walleyes will vary in color from milky white to a medium blue. The objectionable colors of hazel, yellow or amber have commonly been called light eyes, but this in no way refers to the china or walleyes.

It is also preferable that the skin around the eye socket be black, rather than pink. (English definition of walleye: one brown and one blue eye.)

Nose—Always black, large and capacious.

NOSE—5 points. Referring to the explanation above of the jaw, "giving the appearance of being cut off abruptly", it follows that the nose is larger than it would be if the jaw continued on to a point which would make for a small button nose.

Teeth—Strong and large, evenly placed and level in opposition.

TEETH—5 points. Recession of the lower jaw (overshot), or a protruding lower jaw (undershot), is most objectionable. Crooked teeth are not desirable.

Ears—Medium sized, and carried flat to side of head, coated moderately.

EARS—5 points. The ears should be well-placed on the skull and carried perfectly flat, showing no signs of being pricked or carried alert at the base.

Legs—The forelegs should be dead straight, with plenty of bone, removing the body a medium height from the ground, without approaching legginess, and well-coated all around.

Feet—Small, round: toes well-arched, and pads thick and hard.

LEGS—10 points. FEET—points included in Legs. Legs and feet have been combined, assuming that ten points alloted to legs also cover any faults to be found in the feet. Feet should show no sign of being splayed, meaning the toes have lost their arch and are spreading. Dog should appear well up on its toes. Legs should be parallel when viewed from front or back.

Tail—It is preferable that there should be none. Should never, however, exceed 1½ or 2 inches in grown dogs. When not natural-born bobtails however, puppies should be docked at the first joint from the body and the operation performed when they are three to four days old.

> —Natural-born bobtails seem to have passed into extinction as most current breeders have never encountered any.

Neck and Shoulders—The neck should be fairly long, arched gracefully and well-coated with hair. The shoulders sloping and narrow at the points, the dog standing lower at the shoulder than at the loin.

> NECK and SHOULDERS—5 points. The words "arched gracefully" are worthy of note, as many dogs detract from their appearance by carrying their heads quite low while moving. Shoulder faults are encountered when the bone lacks the required forward slope, or in separation at the points. A standing Sheepdog should give the appearance of being high behind, rather than sloping downward from the shoulder to the loin as does the German Shepherd.

Body—Rather short and very compact, ribs well-sprung and brisket deep and capacious. *Slabsidedness highly undesirable.* The loin should be very stout and gently arched, while the hindquarters should be round and muscular and with well-let-down hocks, and the hams densely coated with a thick, long jacket in excess of any other part.

> BODY and LOINS—10 points; HINDQUARTERS—10 points. Faults to be found in this area include a long back, giving the dog the appearance of being longer than it is tall, rather than the desired square look. Also, a shallow brisket, or one that is not well-let-down in the area between the elbows. The area from the loin through the hips and hams should not be narrow or pinched looking. In the hindquarters, there should be some bend of stifle and hock joints, with the foot appearing forward of the hock joint, rather than the bones following a near straight line from the hip joint to the foot. A major fault in this area is cowhocks, which means that the hock joints appear much closer together than the stifle joints or feet when viewed from the rear; this condition causing very faulty movement.

Coat—Profuse, but not so excessive as to give the impression of the dog being overfat, and of a good hard texture; not straight, but shaggy and free from curl. *Quality and texture of coat to be considered above mere profuseness.* Softness or flatness of coat to be considered a fault. The undercoat should be a waterproof pile, when not removed by grooming or season.

COAT (Texture, Quality and Condition)—15 points. JUDGES ATTENTION! It must be remembered that our breed is a working dog. Too often the dog with a coat trailing the ground has been put over the dog of superior soundness with less but nevertheless the desired working coat. Points are specified for "Texture, Quality and Condition", which means also that some could be lost for inadequate grooming.

Color—Any shade of gray, grizzle, blue or blue-merled with or without white markings or in reverse. *Any shade of brown or fawn to be considered distinctly objectionable and not to be encouraged.*

—Although puppies are born a near-black-and-white, when they come into adult coat it should have cleared to the lighter shading, making an adult coat of near-black objectionable. While marking patterns are not dealt with, any complete mismarking should be discouraged. The brown coat referred to is not meant to apply to stained or sunburned coat.

Sizes—Twenty-two inches and upwards for dogs and slightly less for bitches. Type, character and symmetry are of the greatest importance and are on no account to be sacrificed to size alone.

—While the size limit of 26 inches at the shoulder has been removed from the standard, it should be remembered—especially by breeders—that extreme oversize can be undesirable and lead to other faults.

General Appearance and Characteristics—A strong, compact-looking dog of great symmetry, practically the same in measurement from shoulder to stern as in height, absolutely free from legginess or weaselness, very elastic in his gallop, but in walking or trotting he has a characteristic ambling or pacing movement, and his bark should be loud, with a peculiar "pot-casse" ring in it. Taking him all round, he is profusely, but not *excessively* coated, thick-set, muscular, able-bodied dog with a most intelligent expression, free from all Poodle or Deerhound character. *Soundness should be considered of greatest importance.*

GENERAL APPEARANCE and MOVEMENT—15 points. The scale of points has been listed with the descriptive material to point up the relative values. Note again the number allotted to areas of soundness to emphasize its importance. Judges should take care not to fault the "roll" or pacing movement. While temperament is not mentioned in the standard, the traits of clownishness, friendliness, intelligence and loyalty that are so pronounced in the breed should be highly valued, and their perpetuation ever strived for by those breeding Old English Sheepdogs.

190

Scale of Points

Skull.	5
Eyes.	5
Ears.	5
Teeth.	5
Nose.	5
Jaw.	5
Foreface	5
Neck and shoulders.	5
Body and loins.	10
Hindquarters.	10
Legs.	10
Coat (Texture, quality and condition).	15
General appearance and movement.	15
	100

Approved October 13, 1953

The Walt Disney movie, "The Shaggy Dog", did much to put the Old English Sheepdog in the public eye. Here its canine star, Lillibrad Sammy's Shadow (bred by Mrs. Lillian Lovejoy of Colorado and owned by Mrs. Billye Anderson of Rialto, California), poses with his trainer, Bill Koehler and Roy Disney, Jr. "Sam" received the Patsy Award honoring him as the top animal motion picture star of 1959.

- Photo by Mary Eleanor Browning.

192

Acquiring Your Own
Old English Sheepdog

<hr>

THERE is a reason this chapter is buried inside the book. Hopefully by the time you turn to these pages you will have some idea what you are letting yourself in for if you are considering buying an Old English. Sheepdogs, or any dog for that matter, should not be casually acquired with the intention of seeing "whether it'll work out," with thought that if it does not, the dog can be as casually discarded as it was obtained. This is too frequently the case in these days of affluence and overindulged children. The purchase of *any pet* should be viewed as an addition to the household. The needs of a particular breed and the responsibilities to all pets should be clearly known and recognized *before an animal is ever brought home.*

Old English Sheepdogs are large, robust animals. For all their adaptability, *Bobtails are much too large and much too hairy for most people.* Even if you intend to keep your Sheepdog strictly as a pet, his coat requires a great deal of attention. This is above and beyond the daily attention any dog requires. Unless you are prepared to give a dog the necessary care and affection it needs day in and day out, you will be far better off never buying one in the first place. In addition to the daily feeding, minor cleaning, and grooming that all dogs require, Sheepdogs need be extensively exercised. Take these few sentences as an inadequate warning of the continuing concern a Bobtail will be throughout his life.

If despite having been forewarned you are convinced the Old English Sheepdog is the breed for you, the following discussion is intended to help you get the best dog possible. In a sense, this entire book is meant to help the novice get a Sheepdog he will be happy with. This chapter is merely a reminder of some things to consider and some suggestions to help.

There are two overriding considerations to keep in mind when you set out to buy your Old English. First, *take your time*. The more you investigate, the more you familiarize youself with the breed, the better your chances of getting the dog you want. It is better to wait weeks or months to get a dog you know something about and can reasonably expect to develop into what you want, than to regret a hasty decision. Second, you must *trust and have confidence in the people from whom you are buying your dog.* If you have any reservations at all about the integrity or intentions of someone trying to sell you a dog, long and careful second thought is in order.

There are certain basic questions every would-be Sheepdog purchaser must answer for himself. Do you want a pet, or are you thinking of breeding or showing? This is an important question to decide before you look for your dog. A pet should not cost as much as a potential breeding or show dog. When a dog is classified as a pet only, this does not define the animal's potential as a household companion. A Sheepdog with known poor temperament cannot even be classified as a pet. From the standpoint of living with a dog, the difference between an animal with show or breeding potential and a pet means nothing. For example, a male with one or no descended testicles is disqualified from the show ring. A bilateral cryptochrid (an animal with no testicles) is incapable of producing live sperm, while a unilateral cryptochrid (usually referred to as a monorchid) is not recommended for breeding purposes. Yet these dogs can make excellent pets, and may be handsomer in appearance than many show winners. They will not cost as much as a show or breeding quality animal.

There are a variety of other conditions that may make a dog a poor risk as breeding stock, but perfectly acceptable as a pet. A badly undershot mouth and bad cowhocks are two such conditions. A pup that is accidently blinded in one eye can still be an excellent pet Sometimes a breeder will have a dog he feels is of questionable worth as breeding stock. Such pups are ordinarily sold for less than other pups of apparent breeding quality, with the provision that if they fail to mature into worthy breeding stock they will not be bred.

Hereditary abnormalities that bar a dog from the show ring may or may not prevent the dog from being a good pet. Hereditary deafness or blindness are such problems. A puppy that is blind should be destroyed. Blindness and deafness do occur in Old English puppies. Some breeders feel that a known deaf dog should be destroyed, but a deaf dog can be raised and live a useful life as a companion in the right home. This usually means a home without children, where the

194

dog will get proper attention. Certainly the foremost consideration in placing a deaf dog is the home it goes to. A deaf dog should be given away. Several deaf Sheepdogs have been placed in homes with retired people and done extremely well.

Although you may definitely know that you want a pet and have no intention of breeding or showing, you are still better off buying from someone trying to breed dogs of show quality. A pet quality dog from a conscientious breeder is likely to be a better animal than a dog from a casual backyard breeder who is more interested in making a few extra dollars than producing quality Old English Sheepdogs. Random, haphazard breeding very quickly results in dogs that for all practical purposes are purebred, registered mutts. A Sheepdog can be purebred, and when mature look almost nothing like the shaggy bear you think you are buying. Unless care is taken in every generation of breeding to produce dogs that closely resemble the standard, there is no reason to expect any dog to resemble the breed ideal.

If the mother of the puppies you are considering does not look like the Old English Sheepdog you want, you had better check carefully what the sire of the pups looks like. There are two chances for a puppy to develop into the Sheepdog you want if his parents do not appeal to you: *little and none.*

For the most part, you are better advised to spend the extra money and buy an Old English with show and breeding potential. This is especially true if you feel that a bitch is for you. Most owners of registered purebred bitches breed them, even if it is only once for practical sex education for the kids. If you are *certain* you do not intend to breed or show, a male is highly recommended. You are less likely to do the breed a disservice by breeding a poor quality male.

If you are interested in a Sheepdog as a pet and companion, with the possibility of showing it, but are not interested in breeding, you should buy the best animal you can — regardless of sex. As an individual you may have a preference for a dog or bitch based on your experience in other breeds. In Old English Sheepdogs many of the secondary sexual differences between dog and bitch are not as apparent as in other breeds. Male Old English are not more given to wandering than bitches. Males tend to be as sweet and affectionate as bitches. This is especially true of dogs that are not used regularly at stud. Both male and female Old English tend to get along with other dogs.

The basic difference between male and female Old English Sheepdogs is size. The breed varies greatly in size as a whole. There are large dogs and large bitches. There are small dogs and small bitches. However, given a litter to choose from, the dogs will ordinarily be noticeably larger than their sisters when full grown. If you want a larger dog you are better off buying a male. Again, the best indication of a pup's mature size are his parents. A small bitch and a small dog will most likely produce small offspring. A large dog and bitch can be expected to produce large offspring.

Beyond the questions of pet or breeding quality and sex is the consideration of age in buying a dog. Most people want a puppy. But you do not want too young a dog. No puppy should be removed from his littermates before seven weeks of age. Many breeders feel nine to ten weeks is young enough to let a puppy go to a new home. If you want a show quality dog, the older the animal is the better. This is also true if you want to avoid, if possible, the jobs of housebreaking and training. In either case, an older dog is more expensive.

Old English Sheepdogs as adolescents, regrettably, change hands far too frequently. People are convinced the breed is for them, acquire a puppy and then when the dog is six months to a year or so of age, find out that Old English Sheepdogs are too much for them. Local papers are filled with ads for young Sheepdogs that are being sold because they are too much work or too boisterous, or what have you. These animals, unless they have been abused, often make ideal pets and are frequently easier to evaluate for show potential than very young puppies. Very often someone who parts with an adolescent feels a definite attachment to the dog and is first and foremost interested in placing the dog in a good home. Occasionally established breeders will have older dogs they want to place in good homes.

In buying a dog, young or old, you must be certain it is in good health. You want a thorough history of a puppy's development. The more the breeder appears to know about Sheepdogs, the greater the lengths he or she has gone to breed healthy animals, the more confidence you should place in the pups.

A purchaser of a puppy should understand the nature of hip dysplasia, and exactly what guarantees the seller makes. It is best for all concerned that the exact terms of agreement be in writing. A would-be Sheepdog owner should not feel he is offending anyone by asking for written understandings. Specified arrangements can avoid a great deal of heartbreak and ill-feeling. The chances of acquiring or breeding normal puppies are greatly diminished if the parents of the litter are not X-rayed. If both parents have been X-rayed clear, probabilities are low that resulting puppies will be so dysplastic they will be cripples, although this can occur.

Under all circumstances puppies, whether purchased for showing and breeding or as a pet, should be fully guaranteed for either replacement or full refund of money if dysplasia develops so severely that the animal has to be destroyed. Also, some refund should be provided for if the animal is dysplastic to the extent that it needs treatment by a veterinarian to alleviate dysplasia pain.

The person who wants a dog or bitch for breeding should be very explicit when buying. An animal purchased with the intention to breed should be fully guaranteed in writing against dysplasia *no matter how slight*. For practical purposes, hip dysplasia guarantees are governed by a time limit, usually set at a year.

To begin your search for the best possible Old English Sheepdog, you should have some idea what type of dog you want. This is not as strange as it may sound. It is obvious that you want an Old English Sheepdog, but there can be a great deal of difference between Old English Sheepdogs from one bloodline and another. The only way to get a definite idea what type you want is by seeing as many adult dogs as possible. This will also help in determining whether you prefer a large or smaller one, a dog or bitch, and so forth. The best place to see adult dogs is at an all-breed dog show. At a dog show you can see and talk with owners of Old English Sheepdogs, and a variety of other breeds, if you are still uncertain about Bobtails. There are convenient-to-get-to dog shows in every section of the country at which you can expect to see a large entry of Old English Sheepdogs. The Old English Sheepdog Club of America supports the entries at several shows in each region of the country during the year. As local clubs develop, they are putting on their own specialty matches and supporting the entry at all-breed shows in their vicinities.

By writing the American Kennel Club at 51 Madison Avenue, New York, N.Y., 10010, you can obtain the name and address of the corresponding secretary of the Old English Sheepdog Club of America. From her you can obtain a wide variety of information that will be useful in helping you find an Old English Sheepdog. She can tell you the dates and locations of Old English Sheepdog Club of America specialty and supported shows and matches. More importantly, she can give you the name and address of an officer of a local Old English Sheepdog Club, as well as the names and addresses of various other people in your area who may be of help.

At a dog show a catalogue is an invaluable information source. A catalogue is the equivalent of a program for some other sporting event. In it you will find the names and addresses of all people who have a dog entered at the show. Under each breed you will find the name of the dog, its whelping date, the name of its breeder, and its sire and dam. This information can be invaluable in helping you obtain the Sheepdog you want quickly. If you like a dog at a show you have its breeder's name. The dog's owner should be able to tell you where the breeder lives and provide a lot of other information. Few

Old English Sheepdog owners are not flattered to have someone approach them and say, "I like your dog. Where can I get one like it?"

When you have decided what type of dog and where you can obtain it, you will probably have to go and look at a litter and make a choice. However, you should not hesitate to deal with people by phone and mail at long distance, provided you feel you are dealing with reliable individuals. If you are buying from an established breeder, the best course is to tell him exactly what you want and let him select the puppy for you.

Markings should have no bearing on a decision when selecting a potential breeding or show dog. You can, of course, let markings and individual mannerisms sway your decision in selecting a pet.

Because of the demanding nature of the Old English Sheepdogs as a breed, there is at present no reputable breeder that has Old English Sheepdog puppies for sale at all times. The most successful Old English breeders in the last decade have seldom had more than three litters, if that many, in a year. It cannot be emphasized too strongly how important it is to take your time in trying to obtain an Old English Sheepdog. The Old English Sheepdog Club of America compiles and distributes an active membership list in January of every year. If you have difficulty getting to a dog show or contacting a knowledgeable Bobtail person get in touch with the corresponding secretary of the Old English Sheepdog Club of America through the American Kennel Club and request a membership list. There will be a member near you. Contact him in order to begin your search for a Sheepdog. Do not haphazardly buy the first Old English Sheepdog puppy you happen on that is for sale.

8 months old puppy, owned by H. Hedlund, Minn.

Puppy Care

RAISING A LITTER of puppies is great fun. Old English pups are not the prettiest of new borns. Typical birth weight is between 12 ounces and a pound. Whelps as small as six and eight ounces are regularly saved with adequate care. Any pup whelped at less than ten ounces should be considered a borderline case and a careful eye kept on it. Small whelps that are normally vigorous and capable of sucking usually survive.

A Sheepdog whelped at one pound is a large whelp. Whelps up to 26 ounces have been recorded. These giants are usually one or two puppy litters and delivered by Caesarian. Pups of 20 ounces can be delivered normally by a bitch, although there will no doubt be more than the usual discomfort and strain.

Tail Docking

Assuming your litter is healthy, the bitch is doing fine, and the pups are regularly nursing, the first thing that must be attended to is tail docking and the removal of the dewclaws. *Under no circumstances should you attempt to dock your litter's tails.* Sheepdogs must have the tail completely removed. This is a major operation, even on extremely young pups, and should only be performed by a veterinarian. Correct tail docking is most important. If your vet has never docked Sheepdog tails he should be advised to speak with a vet who has and learn the basic technique. An incorrectly docked tail can be unsightly and even disqualifying in an adult. Having an older puppy or adult's tail redocked is a major operation which is not recommended.

Puppies should have their tails docked when very young. Three days is usually given as the right age. In small litters, where the pups are larger at birth, docking may be performed at two days. Conversely, in small whelps a week may be soon enough. A healthy, vigorously nursing pup of 14 ounces is more than large enough to have its tail docked, whether it is two days or a week old.

The individual technique used in tail docking varies widely from veterinarian to veterinarian. Some use a local anesthesia, others do not. Some tie the tail off at the base, others do not. (Old English Sheepdogs are allowed one joint. Some breeders believe this to be less painful, less prone to infection, and that it enables the adult to stay clean, and to enjoy "wagging the button".) Some put a stitch or two in the wounds, others do not. The basic procedure in all cases is two-fold: first the tail is snipped-off close to the base, and then the skin at the base of the tail is peeled back and an additional piece of tail bone removed. Puppies must be held securely throughout this operation, and you may be called on to do the holding. The pup will squeal a good deal. This is more because he is being held than because he is in pain.

Beyond having the tails docked and keeping a weather eye on them there is little that need be done for young pups that are being adequately nursed by their mother. The most important consideration for the young puppy is good food, plenty of rest, and warmth and freedom from drafts.

Weaning

Sheepdogs are large animals at maturity. Their rate of growth during the first year is amazing. Human children ordinarily triple their birth weight in a year. A Sheepdog puppy may easily weigh sixty to eighty times its birth weight at a year. The basis for developing a healthy, potential show winner is good nutrition. Most breeders recommend supplemental feeding long before a litter is ready for weaning. It has been suggested that by ten days, when the eyes are open and the pups moving around on all fours, albeit somewhat unsteadily, is not too early to start supplemental feeding.

At first a shallow tray with a thin combination of one of the powdered bitch's milk substitutes, condensed milk, and one of the powdered baby cereals is recommended. This mixture is gradually thickened. It is also an excellent supplement for the bitch. Many breeders mix up the supplement, put it in a large shallow tray, allow the pups to lick at it until bored, and then give the remainder to the dam.

A litter will usually make quite a mess of itself in the process of learning to take food other than from the mother's breast. This is to be expected and a supply of soft towels and some patience will be

200

needed to keep the pups clean. The mother will do a reasonably good job of this initially. By time the pups have their eyes open their nails will be growing rapidly. They should be trimmed and checked regularly. If they are not, the bitch will end up with a thoroughly scratched gut, which in addition to being painful is a possible source of infection.

There are two points of view expressed by Old English breeders on weaning and supplemental feeding. Some feel that it is best to begin weaning a litter as early as possible. Others feel the pups should be kept with the dam as long as possible. In either case it is agreed that individual circumstances dictate decisions, and that supplemental feeding from an early age is desired. Those who want to wean their pups young, recommend starting at about three weeks of age. By this time they point out the pups should be drinking easily at the supplemental feedings they have been getting for a week to ten days.

The principle of weaning is simple, less nursing and more supplemental feeding. Many breeders establish an alternating pattern of meals from a pan or weaning tray and one from the dam, six or eight times a day. For example the pups might be allowed to nurse from the mother early in the morning. They would then be removed from the dam and fed from a tray at mid-morning. Two hours later or thereabouts, they would be allowed to nurse from the dam again. Early in the afternoon, they would be given a supplemental feeding, followed by a nursing session late in the afternoon. In the early evening they would again receive a supplemental feeding, and late at night the dam would be put back with them for the night. Two of the supplemental feedings will usually be thicker and include some lean ground beef and crumbled puppy kibble. Gradually the puppies should be allowed to nurse fewer times a day for shorter periods, at the same time that their feedings are increased in size and the content of it includes more meat and kibble.

Occasionally a bitch will dry up, unexpectedly, relatively early. If the pups are two and a half weeks old or so, that is if it is possible to feel the first milk teeth with a finger, you need not be overly concerned. This is especially true if the litter is large and has been feeding greedily. In any case, for safety check with your veterinarian and follow any specific recommendations he makes.

In very young pups, continued squealing and whimpering may be an indication they are not getting enough to eat. *Your vet should be consulted and his advice followed.* Eye droppers and bottles can be used to feed pups. In very young or weak pups a tube can be inserted directly down the gullet and into the stomach and the food pumped into them. But it is best for them to suck and work their paws naturally to bottlefeed. Care must be taken to prevent their getting milk into their lungs. Pups that must be reared entirely by hand are usually fed every two hours around the clock for the first four days to a week. This is exhausting at best, but if carefully done the pups will come through in perfect shape.

Many Sheepdog breeders feel the first solid food a puppy should receive is finely scrapped ground beef beginning at about two weeks of age. This need be no more than finely ground beef by three weeks, at which time the first kibble is introduced to the diet. If your bitch is nursing the pups and you are supplementing this with several feedings a day, the feedings should be increased in size and frequency as soon as the bitch gives any indication she is ready for the pups to be weaned. This may happen as early as three weeks. It is seldom later than six weeks. The larger the litter, the sooner the bitch will wean them of her own accord. At six weeks most Old English litters will be almost completely weaned. At this time they should be getting five or six feedings a day.

It is considered wise to feed the pups a lot, frequently. Some breeders feed the same basic mixture, a combination of puppy kibble, ground beef, milk, and water, at every feeding. Others feed mostly beef and liver at one feeding, and mainly kibble and evaporated milk at the others. Most breeders also recommend frequent supplements of cottage cheese, scrambled eggs, wheat germ, cooking oils and fat, and whatever multiple-purpose vitamin and mineral supplement the veterinarian recommends. Cod-liver oil, bone meal, and a variety of other supplements are also used by breeders. It is best to follow the advice of your vet in giving supplements.

At around two months to ten weeks of age, a puppy's daily ration can be reduced to four feedings a day. At three to six months of age the number of feedings can be reduced to three times a day. Between six months and a year the number of feedings can be reduced to twice a day. Sometime between a year and 18 months it is usual to reduce a Sheepdog to one meal a day.

When the pups begin eating solid food regularly most bitches will stop cleaning up after them. At this point, you will have your hands full. Many breeders use towels or blankets, often tacked in place, in their whelping boxes as long as the pups are being looked after by their dam. Newspapers are ordinarily recommended, but they are messy at best, and towels or blanketing are neater and cleaner. They can be changed once a day, and washed out for reuse.

Once the pups begin eating solid food it is necessary to use newspaper, and constantly change it. The pups now have to be checked and cleaned after every feeding and bowel movement, fore and aft. The anus should be checked to be sure there is no blockage, gently washed and a dab of vaseline applied. The mouth, legs, chest, and

202

A 12-puppy litter at 15 days old.

often the whole body will have to be washed and wiped after feeding. You may find the fat fellow who waddles into the middle of the feeding tray and lies down in the meal very funny, but once his mother stops cleaning up after him, such a mess will be your responsibility. A puppy who is not cleaned will turn into something very much like a paint brush that is not cleaned. The coat, wherever it has gotten the food mixture of evaporated milk, cereal, and meat on it, will cake and clot. This is not only unsightly and uncomfortable for the pup, but if not removed, unhealthy.

Many of the problems of keeping after a litter are mitigated if they are born in warm weather, and can be outside from an early age. By the same token, a winter litter is going to be more work. It is virtually impossible to raise a litter of puppies without their being infected by one or more of the common intestinal parasites or worms. Roundworms are routinely found in almost all pups. If the bitch whelping the litter has *ever* had worms, it can be assumed the pups will have them. *Your veterinarian* will advise you when he wants to check for worms and then prescribe the proper medication in the proper dosages for the pups. The type of medicine used to expel the parasite is extremely important, as is the dosage. Basically all anthelmintic agents (de-wormers) are poisons. They should only be used when recommended by your veterinarian. *The directions he gives should be followed exactly.*

Inoculations

Pups should receive temporary inoculations against the dog killers distemper, hepatitis, and leptospirosis regularly from the time they are six weeks old, if not as early as four weeks. When to begin these temporary shots will be decided by your veterinarian. If for some reason the pups are not nursed by their mother from the time they are born, they will not receive her natural immunities, which are transmitted to them in the first milk she produces. In this case they would have to receive temporary inoculations continuously at two week intervals from the time they are whelped. Temporary shots are protective for two weeks at the most. Many breeders shade the spacing between inoculations toward ten days to be confident the immunity is not exhausted before the next shot. Puppies should be regularly immunized until they are old enough to receive their permanent inoculations.

There are several varieties of permanent inoculations. Your veterinarian will have a preference and will administer the shot or series of shots to the pups at about three months of age. Permanent shots should be given to the pups that are in good health, free of intestinal parasites, and also free of temporary protection of earlier shots. This means that when the permanent, or first permanent shot, is to be given, somewhat more than the full two week period of temporary immunity protection must be passed. Obviously, at this time extra care should be taken to prevent the pups from being infected.

All pups should be wormed before they are sold. Worming is ordinarily not performed before the pups are six weeks old, unless absolutely necessary. Youngsters are continually prone to reinfestation and must be constantly checked.

Evaluating Puppies

At some point pups must be evaluated and decisions made as to which seem to have the most potential and which the least. Six weeks is certainly young enough to make a preliminary *guesstimate* of which pups are potentially better animals. The older the pups are before any final decision, the better.

Puppies that still have their milk teeth are basically too young to be critically evaluated. Obviously, all the dogs in a litter are not going to be equally good. In Old English a relatively poor specimen with maturity and good grooming and presentation can be made into a champion. This does not make the dog a first rate specimen. More importantly, even in litters of striking uniformity and obvious worth certain pups are going to be to some degree dysplastic. The dysplastic pups may well be those with the best potential as show animals.

Grading a litter depends on a number of things. First of all it is important to know whether the pups have had a normal puppyhood. Sickness or health problems out of the ordinary can seriously retard, if not permanently affect a puppy's development. Many breeders like to feel the basic worth of a pup can be determined when it is whelped. At that time it is possible to tell about head structure, neck length, shoulder lay back and basic conformation. But this is dubious at best, and there are too many intangibles. Much of a pup's size and weight at birth is determined by prenatal environment and not hereditary. It is well known that smaller pups develop into robust adults.

Many breeders divide their litters according to sex and evaluate the males and females separately. When they have decided which puppy dog and which puppy bitch are the best, they compare the two. After deciding which of these two is better, they compare the number two dog or bitch with the pick of the opposite sex and so on. Other breeders simply evaluate the whole litter and decide which of the pups are the best and rank them. One reason for comparing dogs and bitches separately is that bitches, particularly as the pups get older, may be smaller than dogs. This can be misleading in making a decision.

How do you grade a litter? This depends on what you want. The purchaser of an animal as a pet and household companion need be concerned only about the pup's record of good health, apparent good temperament, and beyond that, individual mannerisms or markings that have direct personal appeal.

Someone interested in show prospects has considerably more to worry about in trying to evaluate a litter. There are several areas where definite comparisons can be made *between* the pups in the litter. It is important to realize that in grading a litter you are only comparing the given pups. Some will be better than others. This in no way means the best dog will be a great one. In some instances a fourth, fifth, or even last choice in one litter will be much better than the pick of another breeding. No matter how annoying it may be to some breeders, when a litter is an outcross you cannot be as confident what the pups will develop into as you can if the breeding is between two related individuals, unless the breeding is a repeat of a successful match. It is true that if the parents of a litter are good dogs, and they complement each other, the possibility of the pups being good dogs is definite. Nevertheless it sometimes happens that outcrosses of apparently perfect complements do not work out. Two dogs may be mated, both of whom have good bites, but all the pups may have bad mouths and so on. The fault that occurs in this case

A Bobtail Acres Kennels litter.

is a product of the breeding combination not because the sire or dam was dramatically faulty in this respect. It is also true that every intensely bred bloodline will have its own inherent faults. In a successful bloodline such faults are not going to be major—the bloodline would never be successful if they were—but there will be family faults that must be considered.

There are certain obvious points that can be evaluated on young puppies. The mouth and bite can be checked. It is ordinarily felt if a dog's mouth is undershot when the puppy teeth are still present, the final bite will be badly undershot. This is a guide in Sheepdogs, but there are definite instances of Old English with undershot mouths as pups, having level or scissors bites as adults. If a puppy does have an undershot mouth and you want a show dog, eliminate it unless it is so outstanding in all other respects as to demand additional consideration.

The head is one area where definite comparisons can be made in puppies. In a young Sheepdog the head should be very blocky. There should be a pronounced stop. The muzzle should be shorter than the skull in a young puppy. A pup that has a long or snipy muzzle will probably be very faulty in this area as an adult. Eye coloration can also be determined, if you have definite preferences one way or another. The color of the eyes should be considered a minor extra, once the basic decision about the litter's worth have been made. Most breeders indicate that while the standard allots five points to both the eyes and the bite, they are very concerned about a good mouth, but only secondarily concerned about the eye coloration when it comes to selecting pups.

There are several points of view about the running gear on Sheepdogs as youngsters. One point of view holds that it is possible to determine which of the pups are going to be sounder than the others, both in the front and the rear. Others feel that it is almost impossible to tell about ultimate soundness on any pup younger than six months. An obviously cowhocked pup can usually be detected, but this does not mean the uncowhocked littermate will remain that way.

Most breeders indicate that neck length is one area that can be determined with reasonable confidence in Old English puppies. The neck should look ample, if not almost thin. A bullish necked puppy will in all probability develop into a short or no-necked adult. In general, grading youngsters is a very subjective business. A weathered eye, trained to see structural variations that may be very slight, as opposed to simple differences in size, is needed. It is a mistake to see the largest pup as the pick, simply because he is the largest pup. The animal that is to be the pick must look right, is the feeling of most breeders.

If you want a dog as a pet you can allow markings to influence your decision. In trying to spot a potential show animal breeding markings should have no bearing on your decision. A stylish dog may occasionally do better in the ring but for the most part markings should be disregarded.

Social Development of the Puppy

For all the work and concern raising a litter is, it is definitely a great pleasure. Old English Sheepdog puppies are not particularly attractive when they are born. They are small, lacking in pigment, and surprisingly slick coated with rather ratty looking tails. From this meager beginning, they grow into furry balls of shuffling, animated fun.

To a very large extent the most important aspect of any Old English Sheepdog is its temperament. This is hopefully given the best potential by breeding only animals with the most reliable temperaments. The future reliability and temperament of any dog is determined long before it leaves its breeders. One of the major responsibilities of a breeder is to give his pups the proper socialization to people at a very young age. The latest scientific research reveals how important the earliest months of a dog's life are. Research designed primarily to increase the percentage of pups from any breeding that can successfully be trained as guide dogs indicates that there are five critical periods in a pup's development, all of them occuring *before a dog is four months old.* This means if the breeder neglects his pup's social development the best chance to create a worthwhile pet and companion may have been ruined. It is important for a breeder to know the stages in a pup's early socialization, so that his animals receive both the necessary physical attention and the necessary accustoming to people. Anyone purchasing a Sheepdog should realize, beyond considerations of health and nutrition, how important a pup's first four months of life are. If you have reason to feel the pups have not received adequate personal attention, you may want to look elsewhere. This is absolutely true if the puppies exhibit any antisocial behavior.

It has been conclusively demonstrated that the five critical periods in a puppy's social development are: from birth to 21 days, from 21 to 28 days, from 28 to 49 days, from 49 to 84 days, and from 84 to 112 days.

During its first three weeks, a puppy reacts only to the simplest stimuli: warmth, cold, wetness, hunger, and its mother.

In all breeds an amazing change occurs at the beginning of the fourth week. The second critical stage is one week long, the fourth week. The pup is beginning to critically react to the outside world at this time. He needs his mother. *Removal from the dam at this time can have drastic subsequent effects.*

The third critical period in the developing puppy is from 28 to 49 days. At the end of this period the pup will have developed his nervous system to an adult's capacity. He now needs experience. It is at this point that the role of human contact becomes critical in a puppy's development. Prior to the beginning of the eighth week of life the puppy needs to remain initially with his mother and with his littermates throughout the period. As peculiar as it sounds a dog must learn that it is a dog. The first seven weeks of life and the association with the dam and his littermates are vital in this respect. Puppies removed from the litter too early have been demonstrated to have difficulty breeding later, a product of their lack of self identity as dogs. During this period the socialization of the pups toward one another begins. This is good to a certain extent. If allowed to develop too much it can have adverse effects later. A pecking order will emerge among the pups. Aggressiveness and shyness can be too easily stamped in the pups if allowed to continue beyond the seventh week. Aggressive pups will develop into troublemakers, while shy ones can become unreliable deadheads. It is most important that a puppy live with his brothers and sisters long enough to develop competitive spirit and to realize he is a dog.

The critical period for developing a puppy's relations to humans is between the eighth and twelfth weeks of life. Research has demonstrated down to the day, that the 49th day is the ideal time for a puppy's relationship with his mother to be replaced by a relation with a human. Through feeding, playing, and general care in this critical period the bond between dog and man can be firmly and correctly established. Human contact in this period is almost the entire key to the dog's future potential as a household companion. Puppies that under experimental conditions were isolated from human contacts through the first four months were incapable of being trained. Research in training Seeing Eye dogs has demonstrated that the fundamentals of training must begin during this surprisingly early period. A puppy between 12 and 16 weeks can be taught the basic commands of sit, stay, come, and heel. With proper attention a puppy will enter the eighth week of life an undisciplined clown and emerge from the twelfth week as a reasonable household companion, willingly obeying the basic commands that make owning a dog a pleasure.

The word willingly is perhaps the key to training. As in so many things dogs can be *compelled* to obey. It is true dogs understand violence, the principal training aid of too many. However, there is a world of difference between the dog that willingly obeys his master and the animal that is cowed into obedience through dire threats. Old English Sheepdogs, as puppies and adults, do not adapt to being cowed. They resent it. In all likelihood Old English are destined to be clowns. They can and do learn just about anything dogs can learn. They never seem to learn with the same precision characteristic of a Doberman or a German Shepherd Dog.

In any case, it is *absolutely essential* in Sheepdogs that they receive abundant human attention. Since most Old English are going to treat you as though they are the human, and you are some sort of tolerated companion, it is important that they be permitted to remain in the companionship of their littermates through the first seven weeks of life. Experience indicates that from the seventh week on, given plenty of individual daily attention, Old English do best if separated into pairs or threesomes and allowed to remain together an additional two to four weeks. Some breeders separate dogs and bitches, and subdivide the sexes according to their aggressiveness. The aggressive boys are put together, the shy boys together, and similar divisions made with the girls. Other breeders separate the pups strictly according to aggressiveness-shyness. It is important to keep a close watch on the overly aggressive and the shy. These fellows will need a full dose of individual attention and then some. Aggressive individuals should be kept in pairs, while the quieter littermates seem to benefit from being in threesomes or more when possible.

Fortunately, with adequate attention early temperament problems of excessive aggressiveness and excessive shyness are minimal in

Old English. In a litter of six or seven you may see one individual who is more aggressive than the others. You do not want noticeably shy ones. A typical litter at seven weeks should be bounding over one another to get attention when *any* human walks into the room. A puppy who hangs back *should be suspect* from the very beginning. There is no point in fooling yourself because the animal's conformation potential seems as good or better than anything else in the litter. Shyness for no apparent reason in a young Old English is a major problem. It should be very carefully watched and everything possible in the way of personal attention be done to overcome it. A puppy who is readily recognizable as shy at seven weeks is a candidate for getting out of the breeder's house and into a home where he can receive constant *correct* attention.

For the most part Old English are better left with Sheepdog companions through nine or ten weeks of age. This gives them additional time to develop their digestive systems and mature. *At any rate, there is no reason to take a puppy away from its littermates before it is a full seven weeks of age.*

The fifth critical period in the developing pup's socialization is between 84 and 112 days. It is in this period that responsive, disciplined behavior can be taught. The period from 49 to 84 days gets the pup ready for the training in this period. During this final critical period the dog must learn that his human companions are the boss and he is the obeyer. A Sheepdog will learn this basic fact of life, but basically he is only showing his superiority to humans by tolerating such presumptiousness.

Old English are not a breed that serve readily as servants. Only to a limited degree can they be rigidly disciplined to behave in a precise manner all the time. A good Old English will exhibit an uncanny sense of what is important, and what is good behavior but not particularly important. The same Old English that can be unfailingly taught to walk on a city street off-lead with no fear that the dog will step off the curb without permission, will time and again drag out a favorite slipper that his master is still getting use from, to play with. Old English learn almost instinctively not to drink away from home, and yet around the house any unclosed toilet bowel is a perfectly acceptable watering trough.

The inherent character of Sheepdogs continually amaze even the most experienced breeders. Nevertheless the Old English Sheepdog is still a member of the common species of dog. The critical periods in a puppy's development are the same. As a breeder or buyer of an Old English you should be aware of them and see to it the puppies receive adequate individual attention. If anything,

210

Old English Sheepdogs require more human companionship in the early critical stages of their personality development, at the same time that they should be kept together first as a litter, then in pairs or threesomes for eight to ten weeks or longer.

Selling Your Puppies

Inevitably, if you have been fortunate and have a litter, you must part with them. It is at this point that you must remember your fundamental responsibilities to your puppies *both* as individuals and as Old English Sheepdogs. If you have been careful and selective in choosing the sire, and put in the hours of work required, you are only shortchanging yourself if you unload your puppies cheaply in order to get rid of them. You should not have a litter unless you are prepared to keep any or all the puppies until they can be placed in good homes.

Pricing pups and grading a litter is largely a personal matter. Certain things should be kept in mind by both sellers and purchasers of pups. First of all, it is pointless to sell a good pup for less than it is worth. By the same token it is foolish to sell a pup that is not particularly good as a potential show animal when it is not. Only under the rarest of circumstances will the majority of pups in a litter merit consideration as genuine first class show potential. In all candor, unless a breeding is a repeat or one similar to another successful one, or the pup is coming from one of the very few longstanding successful breeders, there is no point in considering any youngster as a true first class show specimen. This is so even if both parents are champions. The fact is that in Old English too many people are claiming their pups are show potential; as often as not the potential is as much as these pups will realize when it comes to the show ring.

If you are starting out as a breeder with definite plans to continue, you cannot be too careful in placing your pups. Even if you have a litter for the fun and experience, you owe it to the pups and the breed to be as selective as possible in placing them. You should be quite frank in any guarantees about hip dysplasia. If you are a novice or are confused, the best policy is to try and place all your puppies in homes that first of all want a good pet, and perhaps secondarily a potential show animal. If hip dysplasia develops these people will want to keep their pet and some accomodation can be made by way of refund. If you sell or plan to sell any of the pups as show and breeding stock, you had better be prepared to make rather extensive promises about the hips, or send the buyers elsewhere. You should be especially concerned about who acquires the puppy bitches you produce. The future of the breed depends on what is done with *every* bitch. You should explain why a particular bitch is not in your opinion breeding potential and should be spayed, or if it is potentially breeding quality, what the buyer is letting himself in for.

Many breeders sell puppies on a co-ownership basis to protect themselves in the future. This is well and good, except that any co-owner by AKC rules can do as it pleases with the animal. You will need clearly understood assurances and agreements when any "deal" is worked out with a young puppy. With patience and care all pups can be placed in homes that will do right by them as individuals and as members of the distinctive breed, Old English Sheepdog.

Bob and Jay Lamb with three generations of Bobtail bitches. At right, grandmother Ch. Fezziwig Andrea (a Raggedy Andy daughter, owned by Mr. and Mrs. Van Rensselaer); at left, mother Ch. Fezziwig Andorra (co-owned by Mrs. Van Rensselaer and Mrs. Lamb); center, daughter Fezziwig Ann Dee, owned by the Lambs.

Day to Day Care

THE day to day problems and considerations of living on peaceful terms with any large dog are similar. They must be fed, sheltered, exercised, and their health attended to. As with children you must be prepared for minor accidents and major mishaps. This chapter is an outline of the common problems, and their solutions, that all dog owners deal with from time to time. Wherever possible special advice particularly applicable to Old English Sheepdogs is included.

For the most part good dog maintenance is a matter of regularly performing a few simple tasks, and knowing when an unexpected accident or illness is beyond your abilities to deal with it. There are many books and articles available that deal exclusively with such topics as feeding, kenneling, and first aid, among hundreds of pertinent subjects. By all means read and acquire these more detailed works whenever possible. *But do not under any circumstances attempt to become your own veterinarian.*

Old English Sheepdogs are hardy, robust dogs. If treated properly they live long, trouble free lives. The breed is prone to no major hereditary abnormalities. Sheepdogs are not sickly. They almost never have skin problems. The most important aspects to assuring your dog a long life and health are good nutrition and adequate exercise.

Feeding Your Sheepdog

Feeding your Sheepdog correctly can be as simple or as complicated as you choose to make it. There are many books on the market of the pampered pet variety that will detail for you recipes to suit your dog's palate. This is not necessary. It is a waste of time and money, and will in all likelihood not make your dog better nourished than his unpampered neighbor. Understanding the nutritional requirements of dogs is an advantage in correctly feeding yours, but today this is largely superfluous knowledge. The major manufacturers of dog food, a multi-million dollar industry in the United States, have invested thousands upon thousands of dollars in research to find out exactly what a dog's food requirements are and how to provide them cheaply and conveniently. It is safe to say, that a dog fed on the products of any name brand manufacturer according to directions will be better and more correctly nourished than nine out of ten dog owners.

The dog is a meat eating animal. His entire digestive apparatus, from fangs to intestines, are designed to make him an efficient meat eater. In the wild state the dog feeds for the most part on grass eating animals. The dog's teeth are designed to kill and shred flesh. The digestive system is designed to utilize flesh. These basic facts have not been greatly altered by the dog's long association with man or by the highly differentiated special purpose breeds that have been artificially created. The dog together with all other animals must consume adequate amounts of water, minerals, vitamins, carbohydrates, fats, and above all else proteins, to be healthy.

Rather than become involved in long accounts of what vitamins, minerals, proteins, are, and what foods contain them, and how much of each per pound of body weight your dog requires, it is easier to detail the basic precepts of experienced Old English breeders in feeding their adult dogs. This is not to say that all experienced Sheepdog people have the same ideas on feeding. If anything there are as many different diets as there are feeders. However, on two accounts there is a striking uniformity about feeding adults. First, your Old English's basic diet should be a name brand kibble. This is the opinion of the overwhelming percentage of active Sheepdog breeders. There is good reason for this. Kibble prepared by the major dog food companies represents a complete, balanced diet for a dog. The second point of agreement among experienced breeders in feeding recommendations is that the kibble be supplemented. The amount and types of supplements are endless.

Kibble is available in a variety of styles, from a gritty powder to large blocks. These products are available in small quantities from five pounds, at local supermarkets, up to forty or fifty pound sacks. The largest sizes are most easily obtained through a dealer in pet and dog supplies or a feed and grain outlet. The larger the quantity, the cheaper the price per pound. Anyone with an Old English Sheepdog should buy the largest size available. Many companies have coupons or other savings plans when you purchase the largest sizes. Currently a 50 pound bag of dog food (depending on the manufacturer and your location) costs between under five dollars and over seven dollars, or between 10 and 15 cents a pound. The same kibble purchased in four or five pound bags at the supermarket will cost nearly twice as much per pound. No one seems to be able to explain adequately why certain reputable brands cost almost a third more than others. The least expensive and the most expensive reliable products are both complete, balanced diets. Old English breeders say that the costlier brands are more palatable to their dogs. It is also noted that some of these brands are "richer" than the less expensive brands. This translates that these brands produce looser stools than the cheaper ones. Whatever, the differences between brands, it is apparent you can experiment until you hit upon one that you like. Some Sheepdogs will wolf down a particular brand and ignore another. You might accommodate a fussy eater to the extent of trying another brand, but it is not necessary. Rather than taste, consistency, hardness, and texture seem to have the most to do in determining which kibble a given dog will relish, and which he will ignore as long as possible.

Before discussing how much, how often, and what to supplement the basic kibble ration with, reference to the other varieties of commonly available and specially prepared dog foods should be made. No breeder recommends as the basic food for an Old English Sheepdog any product except kibble. Canned dogs foods and the imitation meat products should not be the basis of a Sheepdog's diet. Either or both these items can be used as a supplement to kibble. Some breeders recommend them highly for this purpose, but they should not constitute the basic diet. Canned dog food comes in two basic varieties, the all meat and the complete meal types. All meat products are inadequate because they will not provide your dog with a balanced diet. Canned foods are too bulky, containing too much water for an active adult Sheepdog to be able to eat enough to nourish himself. A mature Sheepdog, by manufacturers' directions, would require 4 to 10 cans a day. Since a can usually weighs nearly a pound this means an 80 pound dog has to eat at least 4 pounds a day. Your dog does not have enough stomach to accomodate this much bulk. Additionally, canned food and the other special products are relatively expensive. Canned food runs between ten and thirty cents a can, although it can be purchased by the case for less.

There are two basic views on how to feed kibble. One is to feed it dry. The other is to moisten it with water or a variety of other supplements. Most dry kibble is not particularly palatable. Breeders usually moisten their feed. On the other hand dry kibble is simple, clean, and has the added advantage of not going bad. Any meat or meat product added to a kibble preparation will go bad if not eaten promptly. This is particularly true in hot weather. Of course, it has been pointed out that what a human might consider spoiled, is not in the least offensive or dangerous for a dog's somewhat less sensitive esthetic considerations and much stronger stomach.

Dry feed is less messy for the dog. This can be an important consideration in maintaining face coat in top shape. Food particles under the best of conditions tend to stick to and accumulate in a Sheepdog's beard. A messy eater combined with a sticky meal can ruin many hours of grooming in a few minutes.

Dry feeding is also good for self-maintenance in a dog. This means a bowl is kept available at all times with kibble in it. Many owners find this is a more compassionate way to feed their household companions, inasmuch as they do not feel the dog is starving from one day's meal to the next. This is entirely a matter of an owner's psychology, not the dog's welfare.

One of the best reasons for dry feeding is that it helps keep teeth clean. A hard chunk or block kibble will have a natural cleaning action on the teeth. Breeders who dry feed their dogs recommend dry supplements be thrown in with the kibble. Wheat germ and a multipurpose vitamin are most commonly mentioned, as well as an occasional helping of beef suet. Liver or other meat supplements are given separately a couple of times a week.

Most breeders feed their dogs a moistened kibble. The variety of moisteners is endless. Warm water is recommended by manufacturers. Many breeders use a can of dog food and a slight amount of warm water with kibble. A can of dog food when thoroughly mixed will moisten and coat a large amount of kibble. Other breeders use a portion of raw ground meat in the same way as a can of dog food. Still others prefer a broth. Broths are the basic gimmick in getting a finicky eater eating, and to put flesh on a dog. Virtually any meat or meat product can be thrown into a pot with water and slowly simmered to produce an appealing broth. Any cut of beef makes an excellent stock. Beef hearts, kidneys, liver, brains and tripe can all be cooked in this way. Kidneys may be strong and brains bland, but they are perfectly useful. The same parts of lamb or sheep are equally useful. Most breeders recommend avoiding pork and pork products, with the exception of bacon drippings.

Many breeders find that their dogs will eat anything covered with a broth made from chicken or chicken gizzards. Old English Sheepdogs seem to have a particular affinity for chicken. As it happens, chicken is the least expensive meat supplement you can buy. No one says they feed chicken raw, as is commonly recommended for beef. There is no reason it could not be given fresh, *stripped from the bones.* Chicken gizzards and hearts can be purchased in quantity in most parts of the country. They cook into an excellent stock. There is probably a chicken wholesaler within driving distance of every Old English Sheepdog owner in the United States. At the wholesaler, it is possible to buy gizzards and hearts in large quantities inexpensively, often at less than 25 cents a pound. A few whole birds can be purchased cheaper at the dealer's as well. Some breeders say they stew chicken necks and cut-up whole birds in a pressure cooker. In this way the bones disintegrate to the point of being no concern. Chicken bones, and all other bones as well, can be very dangerous.

Those breeders who have access to horsemeat recommend it. Fresh horsemeat can be ground and fed raw as with beef, or thrown in the pot with some water and a stock cooked.

How much, when to, and out of what to feed your dog are all problems the new dog owner must work out for his particular Old English. Some consideration on what to put the dog's food and water in may save work and money in the long run. There are an endless variety of specially made bowls. Feeding and watering dishes are made of plastic, stainless steel, pottery, and enamel. Pottery bowls may look nice, but they break too easily. They are not worth buying for an Old English Sheepdog. Sheepdogs frequently knock over or otherwise intentionally throw their bowls around. One fussy bitch would not tolerate any particles in her water bowl. Whenever she found something in her water she would spill the bowl on the spot and carry the bowl off and loudly dump it in the back hallway. Plastic bowls are both durable and cheap. However, plastic bowls crack or chip. Over a period of time they stain and become impossible to completely clean. This is because the plastic is porous and dirt particles become imbedded. Enamel finished products are more expensive, extremely durable, but subject to chipping. Stainless steel products are the most expensive. They are virtually indestructible. With a little effort stainless steel remains spotlessly clean indefinitely. Stainless steel bowls or trays the same size as plastic or pottery may cost five to ten times as much. Over the course of a dog's lifetime stainless steel products are worthwhile. Some breeders in cold northern areas say metal products in general are not as safe in the winter particularly for water. At least one Old English has had the unfortunate experience of trying to get a drink when his metal bucket was frozen and gotten his tongue stuck to the metal.

The shape of a feeding dish or water bowl can make a difference for the Old English Sheepdog owner. This has nothing to do with how well the dog is nourished, rather how much of a mess the dog makes of himself when eating or drinking. Trying to maintain your dog's face coat in the pink of condition can be very discouraging if he eats like a pig or drinks by trying to submerge his entire head in his water. Food particles cemented into the face and beard by water are the bane of the determined groomer. One way to cut down this problem is to feed from a shallow rather than a deep dish. You are not going to make your dog's face food particle free and dry under any conditions. The true slob will make a mess of himself no matter how you feed him. However, a square or rectangular tray, no more than two inches deep with the food spread evenly over it can do a surprisingly effective job of preventing food from accumulating in the face coat.

Baking or roasting trays make effective feeding dishes of this sort. Water can also be provided in a shallow tray. For the house-dog a large bowl, only slightly filled, is more practical. A dog drinking from a tray with no sides above the water level will slop water in a wide area around the tray. This is all right outside, but troublesome in the house.

When to feed your dog is almost entirely a matter of personal choice. The most logical time is when it is most convenient for you. In the typical family, the wife seems to be the dog feeder as often as not. Some find it easiest to get the dog's food at dinner time. Others find it simplest to feed the dog as soon as the husband and kids are out of the house in the mornings.

In general, a dog is less active after it has been fed. This is because the dog should get his day's ration in one serving, and he must digest it. Guard dogs on night duty are ordinarily fed in the morning after coming off duty. Some people have found that their Sheepdogs are more restless at night if they are fed in the morning. This may be desirable or not, depending on your point of view. Whatever your decision on the time to feed your Sheepdog, it is highly recommended that you feed him as near as possible to the same time every day and in the same place.

Occasionally a dog does better on two smaller feedings a day, rather than on one large one. This is often the case with a Sheepdog prone to loose stools. Some breeders recommend not feeding normal, healthly adult dogs at all one day a week. This tends to make a dog a more vigorous eater the rest of the week. Others, rather than completely starving a dog one day a week, will feed very lightly, perhaps only a cup or so of dry kibble. It is worth experimenting to see if this technique or a modification of it works with your animal.

The list of special supplements certain individuals swear by for their Old English Sheepdogs is endless and amazing. Some claim that carrots are the greatest supplement for the coat yet discovered.

218

Others feel that coconut oil is the best thing for putting coat on an Old English Sheepdog. No one has ever been able to prove that anything beyond a good, well-balanced diet will grow coat on an Old English Sheepdog. Here are some sample diets of adult Old English Sheepdogs:

(1) Five year old bitch, weight 55 lbs. fed once a day between five and six in the evening, fed very lightly on Sundays: 2 to 4 cups of kibble, 3 to 6 Milkbones, 2 heaping tablespoons of wheat germ, all purpose vitamin tablets, two to three times a week some meat (either chicken or beef), occasionally a part can of dog food in kibble, infrequently beef liver cooked, in the winter more fat in the form of vegetable oil.

(2) Three year old dog, weight about 100 pounds, fed once a day late in the afternoon, dog actively used at stud: 5 cups of kibble, one pound of raw ground beef, 6 tablespoons of cooking oil, multi-purpose vitamin powder.

(3) Ten year old dog, weight 75 pounds: 4 cups of kibble, one can of dog food.

(4) Two year old bitch, weight 80 pounds: 5 cups of kibble, one to one and a half pounds of cooked meat (chicken gizzards or ground beef) two or three times a week.

From these sample diets it is obvious that the amount of food manufacturers usually recommend and the amount Old English Sheepdogs actually eat are quite different. For the most part, an Old English Sheepdog requires far less food than manufacturers recommend.

Many novice Sheepdog owners complain that their young dogs, usually between a year and two years of age, are poor eaters and underweight. If the dog is in good health and has been checked by a veterinarian, he is not suffering from what the owner may think is lack of nourishment, provided his diet is reasonable.

A fussy eater can be made to eat his food in two ways: starve him or force feed him. Force feeding is messy, annoying and seldom worth the trouble. To do it, and it is common to force show dogs to eat to keep them in flesh, the dog's food is rolled in balls the size of golf balls and shoved down his throat. Starving is not cruel, and if the dog is in good health, will not hurt him. The dog is given his food at the usual time and place. He is given twenty minutes to eat. If he does not eat the food is removed, and the dog is given nothing to eat until the same time the next day. Few fussy eaters go as many as three days without eating.

Exercising Your Sheepdog

All Old English Sheepdogs require a sufficient amount of exercise. Not enough exercise, combined with too much food, is probably the chief killer of Sheepdogs at relatively early ages, of which we hear so much today. The question of proper exercise and how to provide it goes hand in hand with the question of living quarters for the dog, and brings up an important related consideration. Namely, is the Old English Sheepdog an animal for city or apartment living?

Without question Old English Sheepdogs adapt readily to life in the city and in confined apartments. The problem is whether or not it is in the best interests of the animal to expect him to live his life under these unnatural conditions. No matter how pretty and fluffy, the Old English Sheepdog is an outdoor breed. Some breeders will not sell a puppy to anyone who lives in an apartment under any circumstances. Others will sell to apartment dwellers only after careful investigation. It is doubtful whether any Old English Sheepdog living in an apartment gets enough exercise.

This is not to say Old English Sheepdogs living in the suburbs are any better exercised. There are many conscientious city dwellers who walk their Sheepdogs two or three times a day for several miles in total, something their suburban living counterparts may never do. Beyond the problem of limited fresh air and exercise that the city dog faces, is the question of whether or not an Old English Sheepdog really tolerates living indoors, especially in climates that require heat for several months of the year. Some city dwellers claim their Sheepdogs are perfectly at ease in their apartments in the dead of winter. This may be so, but most experienced Old English fanciers feel that the breed is not basically a house dog. Continued living inside, especially in the winter, may ultimately shorten the dog's life.

It is important to remember that when it is said the Old English Sheepdog is not a house dog, this only refers to what owners think. The overwhelming percentage of Old English would much prefer to spend all their time under your feet in the house. A large majority of experienced Old English Sheepdog owners do not think apartment or city dwellers should get an Old English Sheepdog. There are many other breeds better adapted to thrive in apartments. For the most part these are small breeds. Their small size also eliminates the problem one has in coping with the bulk of an Old English in an apartment.

Determining how much exercise your dog needs is not as easy as you might think. Some dogs need considerably more than others. Your dog should feel well-muscled and in lean hard condition. If there are any loose rolls of flab on the ribs or chest, your dog is

getting too much to eat and not enough exercise. Unless you are a jogger or a determined walker, it is extremely difficult to exercise an Old English as thoroughly as is necessary by merely walking. A full grown Old English would not be adequately exercised with two or even three 20 minute walks a day. However, a brisk walker can do a mile in less than nine minutes, and three miles or thereabouts in a day would be ample exercise for the typical Sheepdog. The solution is thus relatively simple. Your Sheepdog should be walked as often and as much as possible every day. If it is at all possible, you should provide him with some sort of exercise pen or yard, in which he can be left safely to exercise.

For walking a Sheepdog, a leather or cloth lead six feet or longer is recommended. Chains can be dangerous to you. More than one Old English owner has been caught unaware, and had his hand lacerated by a chain lead when his dog jumped at a squirrel.

Surprisingly few Old English Sheepdog owners keep any sort of collar on their dogs, unless it is needed, as when walking him. Collars can wreck the coat on an Old English's neck in short order. This is disastrous on a potential show dog. On a pet it can make him look peculiar with a band of hair worn off around the neck.

When collars *are* needed, two types are recommended. Most Old English people find it easiest to use a choke collar. A choke is the usual training device for all dogs, and is inexpensive and effective for controlling even the most robust male. Chokes are usually chain link, but most Sheepdog owners report a little searching will uncover a nylon cord choke large enough for a Sheepdog. The nylon choke is not as effective for training, but will not shred or break off the neck coat as fast as a chain choke. For those who feel choke collars are offensive and prefer an adjustable collar, rolled leather ones are the best. This type is durable, strong, and will do the least damage to neck coat.

Common sense applies to anyone walking a Sheepdog. *Always curb your dog.* This means you walk the dog in the street, and under no conditions do you let him relieve himself on the sidewalk or someone's lawn. You do all dog owners a disservice when you permit your dog to foul someone else's yard. If you know that a neighbor down the block is a dog hater, walk your dog in a different direction. It is only reasonable to go to all lengths to avoid difficulties of any sort with your neighbors. Among the most unpleasant problems the dog owner faces is that of nasty neighbors. Complaints to local authorities may be annoying. There is no way you can replace a dog that has been poisoned by a vicious, disturbed neighbor. It may sound unduly alarming to warn against such a possibility, but the number of incidents of this sort reported every year is staggering. Better safe than sorry.

Fencing and Runs

"Good fences make good neighbors," might well serve as a guide for all Old English Sheepdog owners. Fencing can also solve the problem of providing an exercise space for your dog. Any owner of a Sheepdog is better off fencing his entire yard. This is especially true of the back yard, which can usually be fenced completely and be almost unnoticed from the front of the house. A fenced yard is like an insurance policy on your Old English Sheepdog. Too many Sheepdogs are killed every year by automobiles. The dog that is in a fenced yard is a lot less likely to be run down. Fences will also prevent your dog from running through neighbors' flowers, knocking over garbage cans, and causing various other disturbances, all calculated to make you extremely unpopular.

Fencing can be as elaborate or simple as you want. It can also be expensive. Almost any material three feet high will make an effective Old English barrier. This is because the breed is not given to wandering, and if the limits of his private world are defined, he will ordinarily not try to get out. Almost nothing short of a seven or eight foot stockade barricade will stop a determined full grown Sheepdog. Before you build or have any fencing installed, it is best to check local ordinances. Some areas prohibit chain link, while others allow nothing but chain link. Some communities do not allow any permanent construction, so that supports cannot be set in concrete and so forth. Beyond having your yard fenced or perhaps in lieu of, many Old English Sheepdog owners build a special exercise yard or pen for their dog(s).

Many suburbanites think they have no space on their lots for an adequate exercise run for their Old English. This is usually not the case. Owners have put runs along the sides of garages, down the side of the house, along a fence in the yard, and in other convenient, but out of the way spots on a suburban lot. It is surprising how much space you can find for a good exercise area with a little looking and thought. The exercise run for the owner of one or two Old English is meant to be a modification of the kennel run at any large breeding or boarding establishment. The idea and intention is the same — to provide the dog with a clean, comfortable place to be out of doors and exercise.

The trick is to build the run so that the rest of the yard and property still looks normal. A deluxe run of ten by forty feet might accomodate three large dogs readily, while a five by fifteen area would be adequate for a dog that received additional exercise regularly. A mature Sheepdog that is given free access to roam a backyard can make a mess of lawn and landscaping in a few days. This is another good reason for providing some sort of exercise run.

Most runs should be surfaced with some material other than grass or dirt, which when wet are going to make a Sheepdog a mess. A properly surfaced run can be used in almost any weather with the dog hardly getting wet. Some owners have roofed their exercise runs with plastic laminate sheets or similar materials and report they are able to keep their dogs outside in the worst of weather for extended periods of exercise. Exactly what to surface a run in varies greatly according to locale and experience. If you are going to put in an exercise yard the best thing to do is see what other Old English owners in your area have done, or if there are none close, see what owners of other large breeds have done. Some Sheepdog people recommend using concrete run surfaces where possible. Many breeders feel concrete is too hard on the dogs' feet, tending to make animals down in the pasterns and splaying the feet. Some professional dog conditioners recommend sand as the best run surface. Most Old English Sheepdog breeders recommend gravel. The type and cost of gravel can vary greatly from one section of the country to another. In most places ten tons can be purchased and delivered for less than fifty dollars. Where possible uniform sized gravel should be used. Crushed stone, as opposed to gravel, is not recommended as it usually casts off a heavy layering of dust. Do not be skimpy in putting in a gravel bed for your run. Six inches is not too much. Some breeders recommend a foot or more.

In building any exercise area the natural lie of the land must be considered for the best possible drainage. Any low or wet spots should be attended to. Novice owners of Old English Sheepdogs report that careful investigation and construction of their own exercise pens has been the greatest aid in maintaining their Sheepdogs, a consideration that had not occurred to them before buying their dog.

Housing Your Sheepdog

Where to house your dog is related to the problem of building an exercise run. Virtually every Old English breeder recommends providing a Sheepdog with some accommodation other than exclusively in the house. An unheated porch is perhaps the best place for a pet to spend his nights. In lieu of this a comfortable dog house sheltered from the wind in the exercise yard is a good choice. Sheepdogs are better off not spending long periods of time in a stuffy, heated house in the winter. They adapt to this treatment, but if at all possible it is better to keep them out with adequate protection from rain or snow and wind. Many experienced breeders report that their older dogs age rapidly during hot summer months, and with the coming of cooler weather regain some of their youth.

Sheepdogs seem as often as not to prefer your bed to any other sleeping quarters. Usually this is more humorous than practical. There are many special dog beds available in sizes big enough to accommodate Old English Sheepdogs. Surprisingly few breeders indicate that they provide any special bedding for their dogs. House animals are allowed to sleep in any convenient spot. The kennel owners, and most breeders who keep several Old English, indicate they allow each dog a chance to be the house dog for a day or so, and then put him back in the kennel and allow another dog to be the house dog. The kennel dogs are provided with a few old blankets or discarded sheets or other cloth or some shredded newspaper. Nothing is provided in the warmer months.

Some Old English owners who have kept a show animal in top shape over an extended period of time, from several months to several years, say that extra care in providing for the dog's bedding can save coat. Most kennel facilities have concrete or other durable, hard flooring. The average owner's kitchen tiles are comparable. A dog that sleeps and lies on this hard surfacing for long periods will wear coat away on the elbows and legs, and may if feeling particularly devilish rub head and face coat off on the floor. To avoid this, an elevated bed with a soft cushion can be a great help. Some breeders have installed all-purpose carpeting in their dog's housing to soften the floor and prevent excessive wear. At least one determined and sympathetic Old English owner purchased a secondhand easy chair and installed it in his dog's kennel to prevent the animal from ruining his coat. The average owner need not be so considerate.

224

Even cold winter concrete will be satisfactory for the hardy Sheepdog, provided it is dry and in a draft free location. When a dog gets older it is no favor to bring him into the house, so long as his quarters are dry, clean, and protected.

OES Hygiene

In addition to the daily chores of feeding and exercising your Old English Sheepdog there are certain other things that should be done *every day.*

The dog's eyes should be checked and any accumulation of dirt and drainage removed. All dogs build up deposits of dirt at the corners of their eyes. If this is not removed, it can cause trouble. Some Old English Sheepdogs have a very wet drainage from the eye. This can be completely normal but troublesome. Some cornstarch or baby powder carefully applied will help to dry out the mess and make it easier to comb clean.

Old English Sheepdogs should have their anuses checked every day for any feces that may have been caught in the coat. This is one messy, distasteful job that is particularly necessary in Old English Sheepdogs as opposed to most breeds. Whether it is because the tail is completely removed, or because of the coat, or because of a combination of these factors together with a tendency toward loose stools

225

or what have you, the Old English is particularly prone to accumulating feces around the anus. This is a problem and can be dangerous. In hot weather the animal can actually be a walking breeding ground for insects that deposit their eggs in fecal matter. The lice and maggots that arrive when the eggs hatch can infect and kill even a healthy dog in short order. Such eggs often hatch in six hours. It is not uncommon for a Sheepdog to actually be unable to pass a bowel movement because the anus is clogged with entangled feces. Every Old English Sheepdog owner is going to have this problem at one time or another. By checking regularly it can be almost avoided. The area immediately around the Old English's anus should be carefully and completely clipped often enough to keep any and all excess hair removed. A scissors and care is all that is necessary for this job. When you check the dog a medium-sized steel comb, made especially for this job, can be used to remove any slight accumulation. When you encounter a major mess you should remove it quickly. The best way to do this is with a pair of gloved hands and disposable paper towels. Rubber gloves made for wearing when doing dishes are excellent for this chore. As much as possible should be wiped and pulled away. If the weather permits, a hose can be a great benefit. The entire rear end area can be thoroughly doused with cornstarch when as much as possible of the feces has been removed by hand and hose. The dog can then be left until the hair has dried. At that time a comb can be used and the dried feces remaining effectively removed. Many Old English Sheepdog owners are faced with this problem in puppies between six and 18 months. The usual cause is excessively loose stool. When the stool is firmed up the problem is eliminated.

The teeth, toenails, and ears of your Old English Sheepdog should be checked regularly, although they do not require daily attention. The teeth should be checked for tartar accumulations. This appears as yellowish-brown caked matter on the teeth. It is a hard shell-like coating. Tartar can be removed with a heavy duty dental scaler available at most supply stores. Scaling a dog's teeth is not particularly difficult. It should and can be done regularly by the average owner. If you have not seen it done, ask your veterinarian or someone who knows how to give you a demonstration. A dog's teeth can and will decay without proper care. Abscessed teeth and other dental problems are extremely serious and require the veterinarian's immediate attention. Old English Sheepdogs do not have numerous teeth problems. Many ten and twelve year Old English Sheepdogs have all their teeth in perfect condition. In addition to regular scaling, as needed, it is a good idea to clean the dog's teeth with baking soda and water, using a brush every couple of weeks. Hard dog biscuits and bones are also good for keeping a dog's teeth clean naturally. In the natural state a dog who lost his teeth would be doomed to slow starvation. The pet can live a long life even without most of his teeth. Regular, careful attention will avoid many problems.

Dogs and Old English Sheepdogs as much as any breed, are prone to bad breath. A particularly foul odor might be reason to see the veterinarian. Most cases of bad breath can be remedied by regular cleaning and scaling. If necessary the use of one of the special products on the market for "doggy breath" usually works. A dog's mouth, cheeks, flews, and lips, can harbor a surprisingly large amount of food and food particles. This debris can itself have a vile odor. Worse, the debris together with the moisture and warmth of the mouth provide a perfect breeding ground for bacteria.

Toenails can be a surprisingly difficult problem. Many unsuspecting owners have been raked across the legs or even face by their boisterous pet's unclipped nails. The problem of long sharp nails can be greatly reduced if the dog is walked regularly on paved surfaces. Many dogs provided with a gravel or concrete surfaced exercise run never require special nail clipping, as they continually wear the nails down to an acceptable level. A puppy should be trained to tolerate a thorough nail trim, so that you will not have to wrestle an unwilling adult in order to get the nails cut.

There are a variety of special dog nail cutters on the market. A heavy duty model is the best. When cutting a dog's nails you should be careful to avoid the quick. If you cut into the quick the nail will bleed, often a surprisingly large amount of blood, and more importantly such a wound is very painful. In cutting and trimming a dog's nails it is also a good idea to file them down once most of the excess has been cut off. A heavy duty bastard file from the shop is well suited to this task.

The ears should be checked regularly. Old English Sheepdogs are not prone to ear infections as are some breeds. However, a neglected Old English can easily develop major ear problems quickly because of the heavy coat. All hair should be removed from the ear. This is not difficult but requires some care. Never pull the hair out. A surgical forceps is an excellent tool to have for this task. Many owners let the veterinarian remove the hair periodically. Your dog's ears should be cleaned regularly to remove any accumulation of wax and dirt. This simple chore is very important, and can save a lot of anguish. It can easily be removed with cotton and baby or mineral oil or one of the special products for the job. Do not use alcohol, as it is too strong. There are many powders and liquids on the market

227

that can be sprayed in the ears every two weeks or so to prevent cankers and infections; your veterinarian may have a product he especially recommends. This simple preventative can save a great deal of anguish.

Ear infections and problems are extremely dangerous and must be treated by the veterinarian as soon as they are discovered. An infected ear will have an especially foul odor that cannot be missed, unless the animal is never approached by a human. Occasionally a Sheepdog will develop a subdermal hematoma in the ear flap. This condition is not seen in Old English as frequently as in breeds like St. Bernards and Newfoundlands, but it does happen. Essentially a small blood vessel in the ear ruptures and blood flows into the space between the skin and cartilage of the ear. The result is a very tender bulb-like swelling on the ear. The best procedure, should your Old English develop this condition, is to have a piece of the skin removed and the wound sewn shut. It is possible to simply drain off the blood, but such a technique is only likely to be temporary and the problem will reoccur.

The Old English Sheepdog should be checked regularly for skin problems and possible cuts or foreign matter entangled in the coat. Fortunately Old English Sheepdogs as a breed are almost completely free of skin problems. The various forms of mange and eczema are seldom seen in Old English Sheepdogs. Because of this any noticeable soreness or infection on the Old English's skin should be immediately treated by a veterinarian.

Hot spots and ringworm are as common in Old English Sheepdogs as in any breed. Hot spots are rough, scaly and in bad cases hairless patches of skin. They are also referred to as summer eczema. Old English seem to get them most frequently on the head and neck areas. They are seldom bigger than a quarter. The veterinarian in your location is the best source of information on how to treat them.

Ringworm is a highly infectious fungus problem. It is more common in the hotter Southern and Southwestern portions of the United States. If your area has ringworm, you should be on the lookout for the signs. The usual sign is a raw or crusty scab about the size of a dime. Ringworm infection can resemble a hot spot. The vet will be able to determine exactly what the problem is by a microscopic culture of the infection. Because of the breed's special coat, which most owners consider the dog's pride and joy, it is highly recommended that any unusual skin condition be checked by a vet immediately.

A dirty Sheepdog looks bad; an Old English with great chunks of coat missing is a doubly sorry sight. It is amazing how few successful breeders have ever had any problem with the bane of so many dogs —fleas.

The various external parasites—fleas, lice, ticks, and flies come in almost an infinite variety. All or most of them are found throughout the United States and all can be major problems. Any excessive scratching or itching should be closely checked. If fleas are present they will usually appear as tiny black hopping specks. A veterinarian should be contacted immediately and the steps he suggests followed exactly. This usually involves dipping or dusting the victim and then attempting to disinfect the places the animal sleeps in. Getting rid of fleas, once they establish themselves, can be next to impossible without a full scale fumigation of house and property. Fortunately Old English do not seem to have the trouble with fleas or lice that many breeds do.

Ticks, on the other hand, seem particularly prone to feasting on Old English. In areas where tick infection has been heavy, it is possible to find old English with ten or even fifty large ticks. The tick burrows into his victim and then sucks up blood, becoming distended as he gorges himself. A tick as large as a dime is common, and some as big as a quarter have been removed from Sheepdogs. Virtually all of this is blood the tick has drained from his host. A tick is a tiny red spider-like insect, usually about an eighth to a quarter of an inch across. You can remove the ticks from a dog that has one or two on him by dabbing the ticks with ammonia or alcohol to make them release their grip on the dog. Ticks should not be plucked from the dog's hide as the head and mouth parts are usually broken off and left in the dog's flesh, providing a ready site for infection. Dogs that are heavily infected should be dipped in a solution recommended or prescribed by your veterinarian. Any and all dipping solutions and powders to remove external parasites such as fleas and ticks are either directly poisonous, or at the very least, not safe for internal consumption by dogs or children. There are innumerable home remedies for external parasites. Where your valuable Old English Sheepdog is concerned you are better advised to get a prescription from the veterinarian, use it as directed, and dispose of any leftover or excess immediately.

Because of the coat it is possible for an Old English Sheepdog to cut himself or get any number of strange objects entangled in the hair that go undetected unless you check the animal regularly. It is presumed that you will be grooming the dog regularly, but it is still a good idea to give the dog a quick once-over between groomings. This is easily done as you play with the dog. There are few Sheepdogs that do not love to have their stomachs rubbed. General horsing around with the dog can be combined with a check for parasites, cuts, and foreign matter.

Health Problems

There are many types of health problems the average dog owner must deal with. These range from the routine treatments for worms to infectious diseases to accidents, and finally to old age and death. The best indication of any health problem is the opposite of the normal indications of good health: routine alertness and activity, clear eyes and nostrils, healthy coat, pink tongue and gums, and usual appetite. The reverse of these indications of good health combined with an elevated temperature is evidence something is wrong and the veterinarian should be called.

A dog's temperature is an accurate indication of his health. The normal temperature for an adult is considered to be 101.7°. This is three degrees *higher* than the temperature ordinarily considered normal for humans. Puppies usually run a slightly higher temperature than adults and 102.5° is considered normal. Normal temperatures in adults and pups are only averages; slight variations are usual. A below normal temperature is virtually never seen in dogs, except in bitches that are about to whelp. A temperature between 102°–103.5° is a borderline elevation depending on whether it is a puppy or adult and individual circumstances. In general any dog, puppy or adult, with a temperature above 103° is a reason to consult the veterinarian. This is especially so in that you will ordinarily not take a dog's temperature until other signs that all is not well have been seen.

A dog's temperature is taken rectally with any clinical thermometer. It should be thoroughly shaken down, dabbed with vaseline or mineral oil and carefully inserted in a dog that is at ease and controlled. With puppies, the best course is to have someone hold him. In an animal that has been accustomed to the grooming table, standing on top of it is an ideal place. An accurate rectal temperature will register in slightly more than one minute. A temperature of 104° is a definite fever and your veterinarian should be contacted immediately. If the temperature is as high as 106° the dog should be gotten to the vet if humanly possible. In an absolute emergency, aspirin given at the dosage of one grain for every seven to ten pounds of body weight every three hours, may break the fever. Aspirin usually comes in five grain tablets. A 90 pound dog would get two to three tablets every three hours. Do not use aspirin indiscriminately. Just as in humans fever is only an indication of illness. Fever while dangerous, is not itself the problem, but the result of the body trying to cope with the infection. Your vet should be consulted as soon as possible.

Because virtually all Old English Sheepdogs sold in the United States are carefully inoculated against the major infectious diseases, distemper, hepatitis, and leptospirosis, there is little point in describing the nature and danger of these diseases. It is extremely important that your dog be properly inoculated while young, and thereafter receive yearly booster shots to assure continued immunization. Should your dog exhibit any indications of illness combined with a temperature, get in touch with the veterinarian immediately. The variety of powerful antibiotics on the market today is amazing. These drugs have been used with impressive results on even the sickest dogs. The best hope for a quick and complete recovery from any illness is early diagnosis and treatment.

Most Old English Sheepdog puppies will require worming. This is usually done before the pups leave the breeders. However, all pups under a year should be checked regularly for reinfection. Adults that travel to strange areas or are shown should also be checked regularly. A loose stool that does not correct itself in two days may be an indication of worms. A veterinarian can examine the feces under his microscope, determine what the type of worm is and prescribe the deworming agent. Instructions for using these poisons should be followed *exactly*. In virtually every section of the United States it is a good idea to have your dog checked twice a year or so for heartworms. The treatment for heartworms is particularly grueling, and the best chances of success are in cases discovered early.

Caring for a sick dog is largely a matter of following the instructions of the vet. Quiet, warmth, and comfort are essential. Perhaps the only point that need be discussed here is administering medicine to a dog. Tablets or capsules are literally put down the dog's throat forcing him to take it. Many people accustom their dogs to this procedure by giving vitamins this way to their pups. In an adult it is usually recommended that the animal be in a corner on the grooming table so that he cannot back away. Because Old English Sheepdogs are very gentle, and seldom snarl or threaten anyone or thing by growling, they are particularly easy to give medicine to.

First Aid

Accidents are endless. You may have to deal with anything from cuts and bruises to a major broken bone and heavy bleeding. You should use reasonable caution. Any dog, even your trusted household companion, that has had a major accident may react violently. Shock is almost certain to accompany a serious accident. If the problem is serious, get or have someone contact the vet immediately. Speed can be the difference between life and death. In any accident where the dog has obviously been injured, whether from a fall, a fight, being struck by an automobile or what have you, you must do certain basic things. They are all predicated on your remaining calm and taking the necessary action. First of all, evaluate the situation. If you did not see the incident, determine, *without moving the dog,* the nature and extent of the accident. Contact a veterinarian. If the dog is conscious, put on a temporary muzzle made from a gauze or ace bandage. Unless the dog appears to be about to vomit (which dogs will routinely do to void their stomachs), or bleeding is so profuse it must be attended in order to prevent the animal from bleeding to death, the first positive action you should take is muzzling the victim.

Dog accidents seem to come in two varieties, fatal and not so bad. A dog that has been injured even slightly should be muzzled as a routine precaution. Accidents are usually followed by excited crowds, and even the mildest dog may be confused or scared. Automobile accidents are far and away the most common accidents involving Old English Sheepdogs. Most of these are either instantaneously fatal or are very quickly so. Often a running dog will be struck a glancing blow, resulting in minor cuts and abrasions or a broken leg or foot.

Bleeding in dogs is controlled exactly as in humans. A bandage or a pressure pack will usually stop most minor cuts. Major wounds are likely to prove fatal, irrespective of what action you take. Dogs bleed to death very rapidly, but do not suffer as many major wounds as one might think.

The typical household will have on hand most of the items you might need for dealing with an accident, poisoning, or other unex-

232

pected problems that might arise, *until the veterinarian can be reached.* Some of the things to have set aside, or know the exact location of in case they are needed, are:

An agent such as syrup of icapec, 3% solution of hydrogen peroxide or dry mustard for inducing vomiting.

Peroxide is also a good all purpose antiseptic for washing minor cuts and bruises.

Gauze bandages in several widths up to three or four inches and a supply of sterile cotton. The bandage rolls of gauze can be used as a muzzle, to dress a wound or make a tourniquet if necessary. The cotton is excellent for cleaning the ears and applying ointments.

Kaopectate in liquid or powder, mineral oil and milk of magnesia are good for controlling diarrhea (kaopectate) and as laxatives (the other two). Mineral oil is a good cleaning and lubricating agent as well.

Vaseline is also a good lubricant.

Baking soda and a universal antidote are good for poisoning. In addition, many other household items such as mild baby shampoo for washing the face, eye drops, an antibacterial soap, alcohol, witch hazel, and innumerable other things may be useful. First aid kits for dogs, children, and yourself should have many of these same items. It is foolish not to have such an emergency kit available, even if all it does is collect dust.

Care of the Older Dog

Unfortunately your Old English Sheepdog is going to grow old and die. As a breed Old English Sheepdogs are relatively long-lived and virtually free of health problems. Still, as in humans, passing years will take their toll. The average Sheepdog lives about 12 years. A properly cared for Old English can ease gracefully into old age with almost no change from his early days. Older dogs are much more creatures of habit. This is true of Sheepdogs. It is unfair to an old dog to subject it to sudden or abrupt changes in routine or diet. The problems of the old dog are much like those of humans. A little thought will make his last years easier.

Food, exercise, grooming, and the various infirmities of age must be considered. No dog should be allowed to become overweight. Excess weight will probably prevent your Sheepdog from living to his old age in the first place. As the dog gets older his metabolism and amount of daily exercise required will decrease. He needs less food. The food he receives, unless especially prescribed by the veterinarian for a specific condition, should be as it has always been. Old dogs may suffer from constipation, which can be reduced by two or three small feedings daily instead of one large one. Dogs suffer from chronic kidney malfunction as they age. Some studies indicate that 80% of all dogs past eight suffer from kidney malfunction of one degree or another. There are specially prepared dog foods which your vet can prescribe to help control this condition.

The old dog's regular grooming procedures should be carefully attended to. His skin will no longer have the resiliency of the youngster. In addition to being more susceptible to external parasite and skin conditions, these problems will cause the old dog greater discomfort and trouble than the youngster. The teeth can go, as well as hearing and sight. There is not much that can be done in any of these conditions. The mouth should of course be regularly checked and cleaned, but a tooth or several teeth may still have to be removed. Failure to remove infected teeth can be fatal. Diminished hearing and eyesight are common in dogs past ten. There is almost nothing that can be done about these conditions except to make the dog more comfortable. Care should be taken not to startle the dog or to allow him to get into situations that might force him to rely on senses that are no longer useful. A dog cannot comprehend that it is losing its sight or hearing. It will assume the world is growing quieter or darker. If automobiles make noises, then they still should. It is unfair to let a dog that has always known how to avoid the road and cars wander when his senses are no longer reliable. Older dogs are also subject to tumors and other aging disorders.

As glum as this may sound Old English Sheepdogs age remarkably well. Stud dogs have been used regularly until 12 and beyond. Hearing and sight remains good in most Sheepdogs through 12 years or longer. Older Sheepdogs slow down, and seem to have their share of arthritic conditions to contend with. Clean, dry, quarters help mitigate the effects of arthritis.

Death comes to dogs most frequently at night, when the animal sleeps and life is at its low ebb. If your dog is afflicted with a crippling or painful disease that he cannot recover from, it is frequently the best course to put the dog away. Dogs have no concept of the future or tomorrow and death. They do feel pain and the inability to be the companion they have always been. Putting a dog to sleep is exactly that; it is humane and painless. The usual method is a massive overdose of barbiturates injected directly into the bloodstream. The dog goes easily to sleep.

There is an inherent depressing quality to any chapter that deals with health problems. Rather than ending this section on the depressing note of the old and faithful companion that must inevitably die, a brief account of an incomplete but indicative study of

176 Old English Sheepdogs over nearly two years might prove interesting. Included in the total of 176 are 47 puppies (under a year of age), 80 youngsters between one year and 30 months, 32 adults between the ages of 30 months and eight years, and 17 dogs older than eight. The average cost of veterinary bills for all 176 dogs was slightly more than $20. This includes the cost of booster shots against rabies and distemper, hepatitis, and leptrosporisi, which all dogs should have yearly. The average puppy cost $55 for his first year. This figure includes only the cost after the pup left his breeder.

Of the 47 puppies, 33 of them required additional wormings after having left their breeders. The 14 puppies that did not need additional worming were at least five months old before they left their breeders. Two of this group of 47 died before a year of age. One was struck by an automobile, the other from a "pneumonia-like infection." Three pups had to be treated for illnesses, one for an ear infection, and one for breaking a leg when he jumped off a table.

Of the 80 dogs between the age of one year and 30 months, 37 had to be treated for intestinal parasites, and two (both owned by the same person) for heartworms. One of the 80 dogs in this group was struck by an automobile and killed. Of the 25 that were known to have been X-rayed for hip dysplasia, ten were found to be dysplastic. None of the dysplastic dogs required treatment by a veterinarian, although two did seem to have a hitch in a hind leg.

The dogs between 30 months and 8 years in this group were amazingly healthy. Two of them died, one from bloat, the other from heart failure. Three had to be treated for worms (one case of whip worms and two cases of roundworms). There were three cases of vaginal infections in the bitches, one of which was serious enough to require the bitch to be spayed. Four other bitches were routinely spayed by their owners to avoid possible trouble as they got older. One male had a low grade urinary tract infection that required medication. Other than these problems, none of the 32 dogs between the ages of 30 months and eight years required any veterinarian attention.

Of the 17 dogs older than eight, three died at the ages of 11 years and 10 months, 13 years 4 months, and 12 years 1 month. Six bitches were spayed because of age, although only one spaying was called for by an infection. Three dogs required treatment for kidney difficulty.

The point of this compilation, which is neither complete nor statistically significant in terms of what you might expect for your own dog, is that Old English Sheepdogs do have problems that require veterinary attention, but for the most part the problems are not serious. With proper attention you can expect your Old English Sheepdog to live a long healthy life.

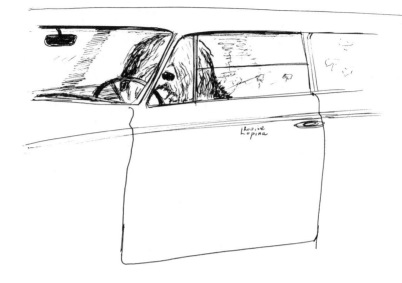

Traveling With or Shipping Your Sheepdog

It is surprising how few people give proper attention to their dog's comfort when traveling. In the case of Old English Sheepdogs this is understandable, as they will all insist, if given the opportunity, on riding in the front seat of any car where they can comment on the merits of the driver's ability. Old English Sheepdogs are remarkably good travelers. They almost never have motion sickness. The mature dog accustomed to his crate will tolerate hours of rather cramped confinement gladly.

In this day and age most Old English that must be transported from one place to another will go by automobile, or when speed is necessary or great distances must be covered—by plane. No matter how much you may like your dog, no matter how well behaved he is, you are better off putting him in a crate when you are going any distance. The dog is safer. Crates come in several styles. There are wooden and metal ones that are extremely heavy duty and do not collapse. There are also wire crates that collapse. Ventilation, an important consideration when you ship a dog, is usually better in wire crates. Dogs that are being shipped by plane have to have a tray in the bottom of the crate to prevent accidents. Most of the good quality wire crates made especially for transporting dogs, conform to airline shipping specifications.

A dog that is being transported across state lines, whether by car or plane, should have a health certificate and a rabies immunization certificate. These health records, usually no more than 90 days old, are required to ship a dog by plane, and are required when entering certain states or crossing into Mexico or Canada.

If you intend to ship a dog, some common sense precautions should be taken. Your crate should be sturdy and locked shut. It is possible to ship a dog between virtually any two points in the United States in less than ten hours. It is better to securely lock the dog in its crate and have it thirsty but safe on arrival. If it is at all possible, it is best to arrange to ship the dog on a nonstop flight. When you take your dog to be shipped by plane, remain at the airport until the animal has been loaded and the flight departed. Unless you are accompanying your dog on the flight there is the possibility your dog will be delayed in the event a number of passengers on the flight are transporting dogs. When you must ship a dog that will have to change planes allow ample time to make connections. If a shipping agent tells you your dog is going to arrive at a given airport at 10:00, and the connecting flight to the ultimate destination will leave that airport at 10:30, you had better make other arrangements. A dog will not be unloaded and transferred in less than forty minutes to an hour at the best. When you have the possibility of using more than one airline to get your dog to its destination, check with other dog owners to see what their experiences have been. For the most part airline employees go out of their way to provide fast, comfortable service for dogs they handle. However, there are always stories circulating about this or that airline, or shipping point and so forth. Some checking in advance might make you feel more secure. No one should hesitate, with proper care and attention to the details, to ship a dog by plane today.

Large dog owners seem to also be large car owners. The percentage of Old English Sheepdog owners that drive either station wagons or vans is probably amazingly high. A Sheepdog can easily travel in the back seat of a conventional sedan. However, a station wagon or van with their ability to accomodate a crate or to have an effective dog barrier put in place, are both easier and safer means of traveling with your Old English.

Perhaps the most common problem Sheepdog owners who vacation with their dogs report, is a tendency to loose stools or diarrhea. This is usually because of a change in the dog's water. One method for stopping this problem, used with considerable success by many Old English owners, is to take along two or three five gallon containers of the dog's usual drinking water. This is mixed half and half with safe drinking water found along the way. This method seems to eliminate, to a large degree, the problem of loose bowels. It is a good idea when on vacation with your dog to bring a supply of food from home adequate for the entire trip.

Basic Training

More dog owners become ex-dog owners because of their inability to make their dogs behave than for any other reason. Innumerable Old English Sheepdog owners have animals that they would like to have better behaved, but they cannot do it. In 99% of all cases, this is the owner's and not the dog's fault. Few Old English Sheepdogs are given up because they are behavior problems. As a breed, Old English Sheepdogs are co-operative and interested in getting along with and pleasing their human companions. Old English are adaptable and quick to adjust to almost any situation.

On the other hand few Old English Sheepdogs are as well behaved as their owners would like. A basic understanding of the principles of dog training can go a long way toward making the tolerated pet a much more pleasant companion. There are many books readily available devoted to dog training. You should own and use one, if you own a dog as large and powerful as an Old English Sheepdog. Almost every community in the United States has one or more dog training classes. Adult education programs, local recreation departments, and special dog obedience clubs all provide regular courses for training your dog. These classes, which seldom cost more than thirty dollars, for a ten to fifteen week course meeting once a week for a couple of hours, are one of the great bargains available to all dog owners. There are almost no Old English Sheepdogs and owners that would not benefit from some simple obedience training. The basic training your Old English Sheepdog needs is housebreaking, and the willing response to the commands *no, come, sit, stay,* and *heel.*

Housebreaking

Old English Sheepdogs are remarkably easy to housebreak. However, without some attention to this problem it can take many more weeks or even months than is necessary. An Old English Sheepdog at two months of age can be housebroken in a few weeks with no difficulty. This is much younger than is generally thought possible in some breeds. Housebreaking, as is all training, is based on lavish praise when the animal does as he is supposed to, and effectively harsh correction when the animal misbehaves.

The time of year and age when you get your puppy are two important considerations in deciding whether to paper train as an intermediate stop in housebreaking, or to simply go directly outdoors. During wet and cold weather, common in most of the United States from late fall to mid-spring, you may not want to go out with a young

238

puppy as often as necessary to properly train the dog. A puppy should not be taken outside to relieve itself until the veterinarian assures you there is no danger of it picking up distemper.

If you decide to paper train first, the process is relatively simple. The dog is confined in an area, usually the kitchen or part of it, completely covered with paper. Gradually the amount of paper covering is decreased until the dog has a single sheet. From the single sheet to the outdoors is a simple task.

There is no point in paper-training a dog if possible and then having to recondition the dog to relieve itself outside. One paper-trained four months old Sheepdog was being taken to his new home, an overnight drive away from his breeder's. At the motel, the dog was left while his new owners went to eat. Paper was provided on the bathroom floor. The new owners had also left the evening paper on the bed. The paper-conditioned but inexperienced pup used the evening paper on the bed rather than the intended paper in the bathroom. The point is that a paper-trained dog will usually be conditioned to any paper when none is available that has his message from the last time he relieved himself.

Nonetheless, a paper-trained pup is better than a completely untrained one. Once the animals are three months or older, be certain to have a small piece with the odor of the dog's last urination on the paper you intend for the dog's use.

Old English Sheepdog breeders recommend very highly the crate method of housebreaking. This should be easy inasmuch as getting a crate for the dog at the time you acquire him is a good idea. The dog is, in a sense, conditioned to think of the crate as his home. A puppy will naturally prefer a protected, out of the way, quiet spot. The crate provides this. Later the dog that is accustomed to the crate will be easy to travel with, should you ever want to take him on a plane. It is much safer for humans and dogs to travel in a car in which the dog is in his familiar crate. Confining a puppy or adult in a crate is neither cruel nor harmful provided the animal is accustomed to the crate and the crate is safe.

The idea behind housebreaking a dog by using a crate is that the puppy will be sleeping and living for the most part in the crate, and will therefore be reluctant to soil his living quarters. The process is simple. The animal is confined in the crate, and taken out to relieve itself. When it goes, it is lavishly praised. Gradually the amount of time in the crate is reduced, and the periods out of the crate for exercise, play and going are extended. Accidents are going to happen. By using the crate system you will not be taking the dog out unless someone is around to watch. When the accident happens you will be able to correct on the spot, taking the dog to the paper or out of doors immediately. If you are not on the spot when an accident happens there is no point in correcting the dog, as he will not understand you.

Many experienced Old English Sheepdog housebreakers suggest *not* having water readily available at all times when housebreaking. Water can be provided at meal times, and for a while prior to your going to bed. Between the regular meals and watering at intervals the pup will get more than enough. There is no reason to give the puppy free access to water all night. Other breeders provide water at all times for their pups, whether they are being housebroken or not.

An Old English Sheepdog at 18 weeks of age should be close to 100% housebroken. If your dog is more than five months old and you are still having problems, you are not being sufficiently demanding of the dog.

Companion Training

Beyond a thoroughly reliable, housebroken dog you want your Old English Sheepdog to be a reasonably responsive, cooperative companion. An Old English that is not properly conditioned to behave himself, on or off lead, is too much dog to be a very enjoyable pet. Old English are big, fast, and strong. If your dog will not come when you call it, you are never going to catch him. This is not only foolish, it can be fatal to the dog. A dog that cannot be trusted off lead is a good candidate for getting run down by an auto. The best way to train your dog is simply to keep after him from the time he is young. The pup should learn "come" at an early age and be expected to come the *first* time you call him. If he does not he should be severely corrected, and then lavishly praised.

Most formal training of a dog begins with accustoming him to a lead. The usual way to do this is by putting a collar and lead on the dog and letting him drag it around. Eight weeks is not too young to begin this type of training. Gradually the time on the lead should be increased and you should begin walking the dog in the direction you want to go. A choke collar and gentle correction on even a young Old English Sheepdog are very good ideas. Once the animal is accustomed to the lead, the commands sit, stay, and come should be drilled into him.

There are endless systems for teaching these simple commands. Some people recommend using special food rewards, others are absolutely against them. One system widely used has the dog's name used on any command that entails motion, while any stationary command is given without the dog's name. It is more than worthwhile to

Eng. Ch. Beckington Lady of Welbyhouse, one of the all-time great winning bitches of the breed. Shown c. 1960, Lady was owned by Mrs. M. Keith Gibson of Denbighshire, North Wales.

Eng. Ch. Lameda Perfect Pal, winner of Best in Show all-breeds at 1974 Ladies Kennel Association show in England, judged by the American Judge, Mrs. Augustus Riggs, IV. Owned by the Lameda Kennels of John P. Smith and Stuart J. Mallard, London.

talk with an experienced dog trainer, and look into the various books available on how to train a dog. It is almost never too late to train a dog that is not properly behaved. Naturally an older dog, accustomed to doing as he pleases when he pleases, will be a bigger problem. He will probably require expert guidance to become well trained.

Any dog that has been brought up with proper human attention from puppyhood should learn the basic commands that will make him a better companion. There are two points of view on obedience training and showing dogs. Some people feel that a rigorously trained obedience dog lacks the spunk and vitality to be a good conformation show dog. Others feel that this is not particularly true with an Old English Sheepdog. A lot depends on the individual dog. Some Sheepdogs show in obedience with a choke collar. When the choke collar is removed for conformation they adapt perfectly to the different requirements. If precise obedience training detracts from a dog's showmanship in the conformation ring, there is no question that all Old English benefit from modified obedience training for conformation shows. A misbehaved dog can make you feel ridiculous anywhere, anytime. This is doubly true when you want and expect the dog to behave, whether it is at a dog show or at a shopping center. The easiest and best way to have a well-behaved dog is to demand proper behavior from early puppyhood. The youngster that never learns to misbehave is the best type of dog to own.

Discipline Problems

There are several discipline problems that almost all dogs have. This is especially true of youngsters. Included here are biting and chewing, jumping on people, excessive barking, stealing food, digging, getting on furniture and beds, chasing cars, kids, kids on bikes or cats, as well as getting into assorted other types of mischief. The best way to deal with any of these problems is to not let them develop. A dog that develops bad habits is particularly difficult to train to acceptable behavior. Generally speaking all discipline problems are corrected by catching the dog in the act and *severely* correcting him on the spot. Specific types of correction can be used on specific problems. All corrections require a firm, harsh, "NO!!" Women frequently have difficulty making a correction in a sufficiently deep, firm voice. If at all possible you should not lose your temper or become distraught by your dog's misbehavior, as the dog will sense your emotions.

Some trainers and experienced Sheepdog people have found an especially effective training tool can be made by tying several tin

242

cans together with a piece of cord. This device is then thrown at the dog when it is caught in the act of misbehaving. The clatter and noise of the cans serve as an effective warning to the dog. This can be very useful in correcting excessive barking, attempts to steal food, getting on furniture or beds, digging, and chasing things, as well as biting and chewing.

A dog that continues to misbehave, when admonished by voice, and then by the cans, will require more severe measures. Old English Sheepdogs will tolerate reasonable correction by hand across the muzzle without becoming hand shy. A rolled newspaper and a sharp blow, designed to sting, *not hurt,* can also be effective. Needless to say you should not take out your own frustrations on the dog. It cannot be stressed too much that a properly behaved dog is the owner's responsibility. A dog, even one as seemingly intelligent as your Old English Sheepdog, has no way of knowing what is right and what is wrong, *unless he is conditioned.*

Suggestions for Further Reading

Jeannette W. Cross and Blanche Saunders, *The New Standard Book of Dog Care and Training* (1952); Edward H. Greene, *The Law and Your Dog,* Olwen Gwynne-Jones; *Modern Kennel Management,* (1953), James R. Kinney; *How to Raise a Dog in the City and in the Suburbs* (1969); W. R. Koehler, *The Koehler Method of Dog Training;* Charles Leedham, *Care of the Dog* (1961); Arthur Liebers, *How to Housebreak and Train Your Dog* (1958); C. M. McCay, *Nutrition of the Dog* (1949); Clarence Pfaffenberger, *The New Knowledge of Dog Behavior;* Maxwell Riddle, *Complete Book of Puppy Training and Care;* Phyllis Robson, *Popular Dogs, The Breeds, Their Care and Management* (1951); Blanche Saunders, *Training You to Train Your Dog* (1965); R. F. Wall, *Keeping a Dog* (1957); Leon F. Whitney, *The Complete Book of Dog Care* (1953); L. F. Whitney, *Dog Psychology, the Basis of Dog Training* (1964); L. F. Whitney, *How to Select, Train, and Breed Your Dog* (1969); L. F. Whitney, *Natural Method of Training Your Dog* (1963), and Richard A. Wolters, *Family Dog* (1963).

–Photo by Sam Haberman

244

Grooming the Old English Sheepdog

IN a sense the essence of the Old English Sheepdog, and in all likelihood whether or not you will be able to live with one, depends on maintaining his unique appearance. With or without coat a Sheepdog is a great companion and clown. However, few people seem satisfied to live with their Old English shaved down. Yet the most frequently heard reason for reselling is the inability to cope with the coat. A Sheepdog's coat should be his pride and joy. The most fastidiously maintained show dog and the pet who never leaves the house can both look impressive. There is no excuse for any Sheepdog not being neat and presentable most of the time.

This chapter cannot teach you *how* to groom. Learning how to groom a Bobtail is like learning how to ride a bicycle or how to swim; *you have to do it.* Grooming a Sheepdog is hard work. It is time consuming and often a messy, dirty business. You should be forewarned that owning and in turn grooming an Old English is not a snap.

The problems of grooming Old English Sheepdogs are monumental and endless. More than one professional groomer feels there is nothing in dogdom that compares with maintaining an adult Sheepdog in full coat.

That precise meticulous grooming is the rule today is indisputable, but in fairness to the breed, beneath the beauty parlor exterior of show conditioned dogs is basically the same dog of forty or fifty years ago. Although the coat is beautifully kept on today's show animals it remains, in most specimens, the harsh, shaggy, protective covering it was meant to be.

In contrast to the Poodle, it is almost always possible to salvage

245

coat on a neglected Old English. If the Poodle's grooming and conditioning is neglected for any length of time, the coat will invariably suffer major damage. Even today Old English have spent summers in fields and oceans, survived days at a time in the brush and mud, been put on a grooming table, carefully worked on, and put back in the ring and won Groups and Bests in Show. The amount, quality, and type of grooming done on today's show Old English Sheepdogs is one of the two biggest differences between the breed today and the breed in the era before the Second World War (the other being the general increase in size).

Given the fact that showing is by its very nature and purpose an artificial attempt to present dogs at their very best, it is not necessary to bemoan today's practices. On the other hand the increased perfectionism of grooming and presentation places an increased burden on any who judge the breed. It is possible to hide almost any fault under an Old English's expanse of coat. Even the basic quality and texture of the coat can be improved by sprays and lotions for the relatively short time a dog must be in a show ring.

Virtually every major authority on the Old English Sheepdog until the last fifteen years has warned against excessive scissoring and grooming. Henry Arthur Tilley of the most prominent English kennel of all time warned bluntly in the late 1920s, "in no circumstances should the coat on the hindquarters be cut with scissors." This same warning was repeated by Mrs. Wilbur Kirby Hitchcock, P. Hamilton Goodsell, and a host of others including Mrs. Edward P. Renner of the Merriedip Kennels. Needless to say, scissoring rather than being minimal, has today become and is practised extensively in grooming today's show Bobtails.

P. Hamilton Goodsell complained bitterly about the tendency toward excessive grooming in the early thirties when he overheard an exhibitor complaining because there was a wait at ringside for a judge, and it was "such work to get every hair in place." He wrote in answer to this complaint, routine at today's shows, "I submit no Bobtail coat could ever have every hair in place. Were that possible, would the coat be shaggy? Don't let us have drawing-room dogs but real Bobs with shaggy coats as the standard calls for."

It may not be possible to have every hair in place on an Old English, but some of today's specimens enter the ring as close to this state of perfection as it is possible to imagine. One of the funnier, and frequently seen sights at today's shows, is someone struggling to carry his full grown male Old English Sheepdog to ringside, in order to prevent the coat from being mussed. This is seen at indoor shows as well as outdoor ones, where it could possibly be claimed the grass was wet or the ground muddy.

There are few sights in all of purebred dogdom that compare with a large class of mature, full coated and properly conditioned and presented Old English Sheepdogs. Excellence in grooming, presentation, and showmanship should be encouraged, provided the basic qualities called for in standard are not overlooked because they are hidden.

It should be recognized that grooming as opposed to conditioning is a separate but related part of caring for an Old English. Conditioning, of course, applies to the dog's coat, but it also means the animal is properly exercised, in good muscle, and in overall good shape. A dog in top condition has tough pads, no cuts or bruises, clear skin, and a coat that is well-kept and clean. Insofar as the coat goes, good condition is vital for the show animal. Basically this means putting coat on the animal. The best way to assure that a Sheepdog has ample coat of proper quality and texture is to see to it that the dog receives good food, regular exercise, and spends as much time as possible outdoors.

A number of things can be done to prevent a dog from breaking off or ruining coat as it grows in. An exercise yard with a heavy layer of gravel or some other clean surfacing that easily sheds water is a great help. A dog that is allowed to run freely in a field full of burrs or other underbrush will get his coat thoroughly tangled with twigs and branches that will not only break and tear holes in the coat, but require an incredible amount of time to remove without further damaging the coat. A large run will permit the dog to get sufficient exercise without making the dog feel confined. It will make keeping a dog in top condition much simpler. Some Old English like to rub their coats, especially face coat, on fences, walls, or any available abrasive surface. Concrete steps and walks are especially popular for this pastime. If observed the dog can be corrected, just as you would correct for any form of misbehavior. A Sheepdog that rolls on his back or sides and appears to be using the ground or other hard surface to scratch may be trying to rub dead coat off.

Bathing

Bathing is a care or conditioning problem, not a distinct grooming worry. All dogs, young and old, full-coated and shaved down, require regular bathing of one sort or another. The consensus of opinion among experienced Sheepdog people seems to be that any Old English should be bathed *only* as often as necessary to keep the dog clean. How often this is or should be varies greatly. There are dogs that have gone four years and more without having a full bath. These animals are groomed regularly, have their paws and faces washed when needed, but have never been in the tub for a thorough soaking. This is possible with care. The coat is cleaned by brushing with corn starch or some other "dry cleaning" agent. There are a variety of spray cleaning powders made for women that are useful in keeping a dog clean without wet bathing. A dog that is not bathed requires special attention when he has been out to exercise in the rain or mud.

Most Old English Sheepdogs get bathed at irregular intervals varying from one to three or four times a year. There is seldom any reason to bathe a puppy before it is six months old. No puppy should be bathed in the winter. Many breeders recommend bathing a Sheepdog in the spring when the weather is warm enough to do the job outside, then again in the fall before the weather becomes too cool to do it outside. Some extra care should be taken to keep an older dog clean so that bathing will be needed infrequently, if at all. A few experienced Sheepdog people recommend regular bathing frequently, perhaps once a month or more. The reasons against frequent baths are the possibility of illness in cold weather and that bathing softens the coat, making it more prone to matting.

The white areas of the Old English coat are a separate problem when considering whether to bathe or not. The color of Old English white can vary to a surprisingly large degree. Some dogs have a distinct, clear, sparkling white. Others never seem to sparkle. Still others are decidedly off-white. Whatever the exact shade, the white easily discolors, and worse over a period of time can stain so badly as to be impossible to get clean. This is especially true of the face coat. Whenever the white coat looks off-color the animal needs to have this area washed. The white on the legs, chest, neck, and face can be washed in a variety of ways without completely dousing the dog. One method is to put the dog on a grooming table, soaking the areas by hand with a soapy spray of water. The soapsuds are worked into the coat and then flushed clean with a clear spray. Given a couple of hours time it is possible to do this to a dog at a show, if it is necessary. A somewhat more thorough way to get the white clean without bathing is to dunk the dog's legs into buckets of soapy water, then rinse with a hose. This method gets the dog wet, but does not soak the main areas of the body with the resulting loss of texture and worry about matting. When the white areas have been thoroughly rinsed, the animal should be pat-dried as much as possible with clean toweling. Then some cleansing agent, cornstarch is almost universally used, rubbed into the coat and the hair allowed to dry. When the coat is completely dried the cornstarch should be brushed out.

Bathing is not much of a problem, requiring care and much elbow grease. Old English take to water for the most part. Few object strenuously to getting bathed. But no Old English Sheepdog should be bathed until it has been groomed completely free of mats. Depending on how you are maintaining your dog, this can be done with a comb or by careful picking and brushing. Mats on the dog before a bath will become almost-impossible-to-separate clots after bathing. Moreover, the basic reason for bathing is defeated if the dog is matted. You cannot get a matted dog clean no matter how much you soak him, no matter how much soap you use, no matter how powerful the hose is you use to rinse him.

Once the dog has been thoroughly freed of mats, you should put a couple of pieces of cotton in his ears. Some breeders also recommend that eye drops be put in each eye to prevent irritation. Then carefully lift him into the tub. The bathing tub should be filled with four to eight inches of warm water. Soak the dog to the skin from head to toe before soaping him. Getting a Sheepdog thoroughly wet is not as easy as it might appear. The coat, particularly in an adult, is very dense and water resistant. Unless you have a special setup for bathing there are two choices, the family tub or outdoors. Weather permitting, outdoors is a better choice. A children's wading pool or some other tub big enough to accomodate the dog and deep enough to at least get to his elbows is needed. Indoors or outdoors you should be prepared to get soaked yourself. Initially the bath water should be warm, but not too hot. Some experienced Old English bathers recommend having hot water running into the bath water with the drain open as the dog is put in. Hot water makes cleaning easier. A spray head attachment and a hose are essential for getting the dog soaked.

Once the dog is completely soaked, a mild soap should be worked into the coat by hand. There are many special products on the market for bathing dogs. A mild children's shampoo is satisfactory. The best method is to work the soap in along the animal's body lines, down the neck and front legs, down the back and down the hind legs. Once the soap has been thoroughly worked in, it should be rinsed out and the entire process repeated. Two or three such soapings and rinses usually get the dog clean. Completely rinse out the soap and grime after each new soaping. No matter what you try to do when the dog is taken out of the tub he is going to shake himself. This will spread water and lots of it in every direction. You might try to towel the dog down as much as possible after draining all water from the tub, but before letting the dog out.

Once the dog is out, he should be towel dried as best as possible, and then put in his crate or some other warm, draft free place to dry. When the coat is nearly dry the animal should be brushed out. A commercial dog dryer makes drying time much faster. While the dog is drying he should be confined. A wet dog easily gets filthy. Grass stains seem to be much worse on a wet animal.

Grooming Equipment

There are several common factors to be considered in grooming any Old English, young or old, matted or shaved. Good equipment, working space and conditions as well as a reasonably co-operative dog are all prerequisites for accomplishing anything. A dog should be trained to tolerate grooming, even very lengthy periods, which will be necessary at one time or another on even the most meticulously maintained dog, belonging to the most fastidious owner. Since the overwhelming majority of people acquire their Old English Sheepdogs as puppies, there should be no problem in accustoming the youngster to being groomed. Grooming should be as much a part of the Sheepdog's life as walking on lead or any other regularly performed exercise.

In order to work on an Old English anywhere near effectively the animal must be willing to stand, sit, and lie on either side on an elevated grooming table of comfortable working height for the groomer. Next to a well-behaved dog the most important thing needed for grooming is a grooming table or platform. Many people groom young puppies on the floor. This is fine for teaching the pup to like and expect grooming. It is also reasonably tolerable to the groomer, as puppies do not require much time to be thoroughly groomed. However as the puppy goes from infancy to adolescence, and the first adult coat comes in requiring more time, continued working on the floor will result in severe backaches for whoever is doing the grooming. When you acquire an Old English Sheepdog you should either buy or convert something into a grooming table. Most of the heavy duty crates are also specially constructed to double as grooming tables. Wooden and metal crates can be purchased with special tops for grooming. Wire crates can have special grooming tops put on them. These can be bought or made with a suitable sized piece of three-quarter inch plywood and a rubber or heavy plastic or rubberized surface.

Crate tops are particularly useful for grooming a dog at a show. The animal can be transported to the show in his crate, groomed on its top, and safely kept in it when not being groomed, shown or exercised. Around the house some other grooming table is usually a little more comfortable than a crate top. It is difficult or impossible to work at a crate and sit at the same time, as you cannot put your

250

legs under the crate as you can with some sort of table. Also crates tend to be only 28 inches or perhaps slightly higher, and many people find this too low for real comfort when working on a dog that is lying on its side. Extended grooming sessions are much easier if you are comfortable.

It is pointless to begin grooming an Old English when you are tired. If you become excessively fatigued while working you are better off stopping and resting or even waiting until another day. Grooming when tired is, as often as not, a waste of time. It is very important to find out where and how you are most comfortable while grooming. Some people prefer to groom standing, and consequently like to work at a table that is 36 inches or even higher. Others prefer to sit at ordinary table height. Still other prefer a bar stool for sitting and the higher grooming table height. You will be surprised at the difference attention to these details can make in how easy, and more importantly how effective, your grooming sessions are.

The only considerations in deciding what to use for a grooming table are that it be comfortable for the groomer and sturdy enough to support the dog. A wobbly table is useless. There are several specially made grooming tables on the market. These are usually heavy duty, folding pieces of equipment. It is possible to purchase special grooming arms that attach to these tables so that the dog can be comfortably made to keep his head and neck up for finishing touches. Some models come equipped with wheels, so that when the table is folded it serves as a hand wagon; a crate or other equipment can be put on the table and wheeled about easily. Grooming tables in sizes big enough for Old English Sheepdogs cost from $25 up. Many old tables have been converted to Sheepdog grooming tables. An old double pedestal wooden or metal desk makes a large sturdy grooming table.

Around the house it is important to think twice about where you are going to groom. Aside from an abundance of hair that is bound to be flying about during a grooming session, Sheepdogs require ample quantities of dry cleaning substances, such as cornstarch, brushed in and then out of their coats. This is a dirty, dusty business at best. When the weather permits, the best place to groom is outdoors. If that is not possible, it should be in a garage, a basement, or any out of the way comfortable place.

Finally, in addition to a sturdy grooming table and a place to groom, you should remember that Old English Sheepdog grooming is strictly an old clothes operation. Sweat shirts and other work clothes are fine. At a show, aprons and smocks or lab coats are helpful in keeping clean, but they are not 100% effective.

Grooming equipment is important. You should buy the best quality brushes and combs. No matter how good the brush, it is not going to last indefinitely. A high quality stainless steel comb *will* last indefinitely, while a cheaper tin or low quality comb will break teeth and have to be replaced relatively often. The basic grooming tool is called a pin brush. It is a set of metal pins set in a rubber base, which is in turn set in a brush handle. These brushes are frequently referred to as Poodle brushes. They can be surprisingly difficult to get hold of, but good supply outlets usually have them. Do not buy anything you are not reasonably certain will do the job.

Before you get your Old English you should check into the various grooming equipment you will need. If the person you intend to buy your dog from cannot show you what is needed and how to use it, you might have reason to reconsider whether or not to purchase a dog from these people. Pin brushes come in at least three sizes. The very small sizes are useful for the mouth and other areas where you want to be particularly careful not to break off coat. The medium sized brush is often easier for a woman to use without becoming wrist sore. It is also useful for areas of the coat where you want to be careful not to break off guard hair. The large size pin brush is the basic grooming tool. The pin brush has been specially designed not to break off and damage coat. The large size costs four to five dollars, while the smaller ones cost between a dollar and a half and three dollars.

There are many types of combs on the market. You will need a comb to clean the face coat, work out the feet, and anus, and to strip out the coat on the shoulders and neck. If you do not intend to show your dog, but want him to have a basic Sheepdog appearance the best way to keep him mat free and impressive looking is by grooming with a comb. Any comb worth buying should be one piece, all metal. Combs that have wooden or plastic handles will not last. There are two basic types of comb. One is a large toothed, heavy duty comb, usually between six and nine inches long with five to eight teeth to the inch. The teeth are between an inch and a half and two or more inches long. These large, heavy duty combs are the best grooming tools for keeping a pet and household companion's coat stripped out of undercoat, free of mats, and still looking very much the shaggy clown. The second basic type of comb has teeth that are an inch or less in length. They have a handle and are useful for doing the careful work around the mouth and feet that are necessary to keep an Old English looking its best. These combs are available with three teeth spacings. It is useful to have one of each.

In addition to the basic combs and brushes, there is a wide variety of other grooming equipment and aids you may need or want to have.

The best course is to acquire what you need as use for it arises. In addition to the usual pin brushes there are several styles of slicker brush. Slicker brushes are used for stripping out the undercoat. They are like a cushion of sharp slightly bent wires, that dig in and tear out coat. A slicker brush is an excellent grooming aid and very useful on a dog that is not being prepared for show. With care and experience a slicker brush can be effectively used on a show animal. However, the novice is more likely to shred or tear the coat and should use extreme care before using one on his first show dog. There are also several style heavy duty rake-like combs that can be used to strip out coat and break up mats.

For the neglected dog there are a number of special mat splitters available. These are usually a handle and holder for a single edge razor blade. Mat splitters are sharp and dangerous. They should be used on a dog with care, and when not in use they should be put in a safe place.

A container and spray nozzle can be very useful. A fine mist sprayed on the coat while grooming aids in keeping the dog clean and in preventing the coat from being broken off.

The most controversial, but necessary, grooming aids are the scissors and thinning shears. Only buy the best quality steel, easily sharpened cutting tools. Good scissors or thinning shears cost from four to fifteen dollars. Some groomers prefer the longest bladed, heaviest duty scissors they can obtain. A heavy duty nine inch scissors can hack a great mass of coat with one careless swipe. Because of this, many groomers recommend a lighter weight four inch scissors. Thinning shears can be double or singled edge. Here again the heavier duty, double edged models will remove more coat. The basic trick to using a thinning shears is to never use it across the hair. This will have the same effect, although not as disastrously, as a scissors. Use a thinning shears like a dagger pointing into the coat. There are any number of other special grooming aids that you will add as you go along.

Grooming the Puppy

Without the dog's cooperation you are never going to get much grooming accomplished. Puppies, sometimes until a dog is nearly a year, do not require much grooming. Because little grooming is needed many people miss the best opportunity to accustom their dogs to grooming procedure. The minute or two it takes to brush over a puppy of two months should be done every day. Not so much because the dog needs daily grooming, but to begin adjusting the dog to being worked on.

Ideally the Old English Sheepdog should want to be groomed. The natural temperament of the breed makes it want to be the center of attention. Getting groomed is one time when the dog is the absolute center of attention. A properly raised Old English will bound on to the grooming table in anticipation. Puppies should be worked on and made to feel at ease on the grooming table from the time they are brought into your home. Once the puppy will stay still and calm while you brush him gently, he can be taught to lie on his side for regular grooming. Many experts recommend giving the dog a special treat during and/or after each grooming session. The dog is rewarded for his good behavior. Any misbehaving should be dealt with quickly and harshly by voice, followed by lavish praise.

Particular care should be taken with any puppy to be certain it does not accidently jump or fall from the grooming table. Grooming is an art. Some people are fast workers, others require more time. A Sheepdog can be worked on every day for hours. They can be groomed once a week or less. Some people prefer to work a little bit every day, others hours on end once a week. The amount of time it takes to keep an Old English Sheepdog looking presentable is invariably underestimated. Be prepared to devote three to five hours a week or more to grooming, until you know what to do and how to do it. Remember until a puppy's coat starts to change it requires relatively little attention. Once adult coat begins coming in you will have your hands full.

Puppy grooming is simple. The animal is brushed over the entire body with a pin brush. The hair immediately surrounding the mouth, on the feet, and anus should be carefully separated with a fine tooth comb, and the trouble spots checked for any minor mats that might form. Young pups do not mat badly, although they can develop them if totally neglected. This is particularly true of the so-called danger spots. These are the places where a Sheepdog is more prone to matting. Trouble spots are at any point on the body where there is a joint and movement. The bases of the ears are sure spots for mats to develop on any Sheepdog that is not frequently checked. So too are the elbows, the place where the front legs join the body, and the corresponding places on the rear legs where the thighs join the body. The withers or points of the shoulders on the top of the dog's body are also a trouble spot. The coat at the outer rim of the ear flaps seems particularly prone to matting. All of these spots and the rest of the body should be checked at every grooming session on any dog, young or old. A puppy should be groomed often enough to train it to tolerate grooming. This will be far more frequently than the animal needs to be worked on to keep in perfect shape.

The first major problem with grooming most novice Old English

Sheepdog owners encounter is when the puppy coat begins to be replaced by the adult coat. This is the worst time in an Old English Sheepdog's life insofar as the coat goes. Puppy coat at this time is a fairly dense, soft pile, particularly prone to matting. At this stage, it sometimes appears as though a mat-free pup turns into one big mat overnight. This is almost possible in some cases. At this time in the dog's life it is a good idea to try and prevent him from getting wet. A pup that sits happily out in the warm spring shower or romps under the sprinkler with the kids may turn into one big mat before the next time he gets up on the grooming table.

Unfortunately, it is almost impossible to give a precise age when you should be especially on the lookout for the puppy coat to go. In some dogs it can begin as early as three or four months, while others seem to be nothing but puppy coat at a year or 15 months or more. Basically the puppy coat begins to lighten, and the new, first adult coat can be seen as lighter hairs growing through the puppy coat. When you notice your puppy has definitely begun to change color you should be extremely careful to groom the dog regularly. This means at least once a week for an hour or more. Between complete groomings it is a good idea to put the dog on the table and brush out a trouble spot whenever there is time. When a Sheepdog changes from puppy coat to adult coat he may look terrible, even with the best of conditioning and grooming. The coat itself may go through a series of colors, all horrible. Dogs that are not excessively exposed to the sun even turn off-brown. Dogs who spend a lot of time in the open may turn almost chocolate. When the puppy coat has been cast the youngster may be very light gray. Frequently this light color will darken in the fully mature coat that develops after two years of age. The best indication of the approximate type of coat you can expect your puppy to have is from his parents.

At times you may feel your puppy is never going to have a respectable coat. If you have purchased your dog from a reliable source, it is virtually a certainty that your dog will eventually have a halfway decent coat with proper care and grooming.

There are two points of view on how to cope with the Old English coat as it changes from puppy to adult. The first is that there is no reason to try and save coat on a youngster. Those who feel this way think it is best to help the process of the adult coat coming by grooming the dog often with a heavy comb or slicker brush, thus stripping out puppy coat as it is ready to be cast. The other point of view is to groom the dog in the normal manner for an adult Old English. This is recommended for anyone who wants to show while the coat is at this awkward stage.

It should be noted that many experienced Old English exhibitors have been disappointed in judges' decisions whereby dogs with obviously soft, flat in-between coats that have been carefully groomed and sprayed are put up over somewhat more mature dogs of merit that have not as yet grown sufficient adult coat. It is possible for a puppy of 15 months or thereabouts to have more coat of less quality than a dog of 22 months or so. Because of the importance of coat in the breed it is difficult to justify awarding any dog that is not yet old enough to have an adult coat any important win. It should be noted that this problem is almost entirely one that has arisen in the last five years or so, during the period that the breed has skyrocketed to popularity. Many Old English Sheepdogs have made championships from the puppy classes in the last several years. Prior to 1960 it is virtually impossible to find any Sheepdog that made a win from the puppy classes, and few championships were completed before dogs were two and three years of age. It was common for dogs as old as five and six to just be entering the show rings before World War II. The tendency toward showing and completing championships on very young Old English cannot be regarded as an advantage for the breed. No one denies the breed is extremely slow to mature, but too few seem willing to wait and show their mature dogs. It is disappointing to note how many dogs in the last few years have made championships while still in puppy coat and then have never been heard from again.

Grooming the Adult

There is no secret to grooming an adult Old English Sheepdog. The only trick is hard work, ample time, and thoroughness. The basic procedure, whether you are working with a small pin brush to save as much under coat and do as little damage to the guard coat as possible, or with the heaviest comb or slicker brush, is the same. *You want to work systematically.* Wherever you groom on the dog you want to be able to *work all the way down to the skin.* One of the commonest reasons people end up with completely matted Sheepdogs, although they have been spending a surprisingly large amount of time working on them, is the failure to brush down to the skin. Brushing over the surface of the coat may make it fluffy and better appearing at the moment, but in the long run everything underneath will turn to mats.

The only effective way to work on a full grown Old English Sheepdog is with the animal laying on its side. Not only can you groom the side of the dog that is up, but you can at the same time get at the inside of the front and rear legs of the side of the dog that is resting on the table. Some groomers advise starting at the bottoms

Beneath all that coat—a clipped Old English Sheepdog.

of the feet and working up. After the front legs have been done, the hind legs are done. The animal is then turned over and the opposite side legs done in the same way. The reason for doing the legs first is that they can be more trouble and should be attacked when you are fresh. Also leg coat is most important in the dog's overall appearance. Finally Sheepdogs can be very fussy about having their legs groomed. This is especially true of the paw areas. Many if not most Old English will try and pull a paw that you want to work on in and tuck it under their bodies. You have only to groom a Sheepdog for a while to find out how annoying this can be when you are tired.

After the legs have been groomed out, the mouth, head, throat, neck, chest and shoulders should be done. The mouth can be the most time consuming part of the Old English to keep adequately groomed. The drier the beard is, the easier it is to work on. After the head and shoulder areas have been done, the body of the coat is attended to, again first one side and then the other with the animal on its side.

The basic goal in grooming is to separate every hair. For the show animal you want to also try to keep as much undercoat on the animal as possible. Whether it is on the leg or body the best way to separate every hair and keep as much undamaged coat on the dog as possible is by hand. This is time-consuming and next to impossible to do on a mature adult. A full grown Sheepdog is too big to be groomed by hand. A few people determined to put as much coat as fast as possible on their mature dogs have thrown away all brushes and combs and separated every hair by hand for months on end. This technique which has long been used by terrier people to promote coat growth and texture, is amazingly successful in putting coat on. No novice and only a rare veteran would want to go to the trouble of grooming an Old English by hand. However, the technique for separating mats and saving coat is the same as grooming entirely by hand. A mat or clot of hair is gripped between the thumb and forefinger of the left and right hands and pulled apart. On smaller clumps of clogged hair you can feel the coat separating. On large mats you can hear the tearing sound as the coat is separated. When a mat has been as thoroughly as possible pulled apart by hand a brush can be taken to it and the dead coat and clots swept out. A comb can be used as well. It is faster and also takes out more coat. Even a dog with mats as large as your hand can be handpicked apart and a surprisingly large amount of coat saved.

Salvaging a coat that has been allowed to form enormous mats is a major proposition. Unless you have a specific need or desire to keep as much coat as possible on the dog, it is better to shave the animal down and then take care of the coat as it grows back. If you are set on saving a badly neglected coat you must be prepared to put in the necessary time to get the dog virtually completely free of mats in a short period of time. The reason for this is that once a dog has mats on it they tend to grow faster and faster. An experienced and determined groomer can take a full grown Sheepdog that is mostly mats and in 35 hours time turn it into a relatively well-groomed representative of the breed. The same job can be done in a much shorter period of time with extensive use of the mat splitter and heavy duty comb. Of course, the more mechanical aids to dematting are used, the less the coat will be salvaged. Professional grooming services more than earn their fees when they work on Sheepdogs. Many professional services will not even touch an Old English, unless it is to shave the dog down. Thirty to fifty dollars is the usual fee for shaving an Old English down. Grooming for other work is usually figured at a flat per hour rate or by the job, depending on the particular dog's state.

When you groom, whether it is on a leg or the body, the best technique is to work in a series of parts. The coat is groomed down to the skin, all mats and clots separated and removed, then another part is made an inch or so further up the leg or body and the process repeated. Most groomers recommend using a fine mist to keep the coat just barely damp as you groom. A variety of fluids can be used for this, some of which help to keep the dog clean, others of which can temporarily improve the texture of the coat, and still others which make the dog smell sweet. The simplest spray solution is tap water. Many groomers use tap water and a disinfectant cleaning agent such as Listerine. Others use pure witch hazel or a combination of witch hazel and water. Beer is also a good spray. Beer has been used by various Old English groomers for the past forty years, at least. The virtue of beer is that it dries almost instantly, and has a slightly more masculine odor to it than most of the commercial dog spray products, which many Old English Sheepdog fanciers feel are not suitable to the supposed robust, hardiness of a working dog.

When your dog has been thoroughly picked clean of mats and brushed out, there are a few finishing touches that must be attended to. In the show dog the finishing touches can take as long or longer than the entire grooming job. When the animal is completely brushed out a whitening agent can be put on the coat, brushed in, and then *completely out* of the coat. Cornstarch has long been the favorite whitening and dry cleaning agent of the majority of Old English Sheepdog fanciers. There are several commercial dog powders made for this job. The special products tend to be somewhat finer than cornstarch, which is a decided advantage. They also tend to have a pleasant odor. However, they are expensive in terms of the quantities that are required on an Old English Sheepdog. Some groomers report they use cornstarch, and then finish off bad spots with a commercial powder. It is important to brush the cornstarch thoroughly into the coat and then completely out. A dog in the show ring that still has cornstarch in the coat should be excused from judging, but few judges are as strict on this point as American Kennel Club rules require.

Scissoring

The most significant final touch in grooming an Old English Sheepdog is scissoring. As has been pointed out, the practice of scissoring was at one time highly frowned on. Today it is acceptable as part and parcel of preparing an Old English to its best advantage for the show ring. It is always the intention to make the dog better looking when a scissors is used, remember the best trim job is one that is not particularly noticeable. An expert can work a Sheepdog over and scarcely have it noticeable, yet the before and after product are like two different dogs. The basic tools for trimming are a sharp high quality pair of hair cutters and a thinning shear. The thinning shears is perhaps the most useful tool in preparing a Sheepdog for the show ring. Used correctly it can produce startling changes in the appearance of a dog without giving the animal the hacked or freshly shorn look that too frequently results from using a scissors.

The basic spots to use the scissors are the feet and rear end. The removal of all hair between the pads is less a grooming necessity than

259

it is proper care and conditioning. Hair between the pads can become matted and cause the dog to be down on its pasterns. In a neglected animal the matted hair can pick up and hold irritating pebbles, twigs, or other dangerous objects. A cut can quickly become a major infection. The hair surrounding the paw is trimmed to give the foot a neat, clean-cut appearance. You want to trim in an even circle, with the front leg as the center of the imaginary circle of hair you are trying to cut. The best technique is to trim all around the foot, carefully brushing away the hair as you trim. Once you have made one trim line you can step back and see if there should be additional hair removed. You should trim reasonably close to the paw, but not so much as to expose the nails. Also bear in mind that the dog has two feet and you want the trim job on each leg to be approximately the same. Any time you use a scissors or do anything to take coat off your Sheepdog the best policy is to go slowly. You can always take off more coat, but you have to wait for it to grow back once you have hacked off too much. Some dogs get dancing feet when you attempt to trim around the paws. Needless to say a dog that jumps just as you are about to make a cut can end up with a pretty messy trim job. The best way to keep an edgy foot in place is to have an assistant hold it down. If the dog does not like this, an almost fail proof way is to pick up the opposite foot from the one that is being groomed. A dog that is having its right front leg groomed, and has its left front held off the table is effectively hobbled and will usually stay still long enough to get the trimming done. The rear legs are trimmed like the front. Some groomers thin the hair on the hocks, especially on the insides. Excessive coat can make even a wide rear appear close.

Rear end trimming is required to a greater or lesser degree on all Old English Sheepdogs. All Sheepdogs need to have the hair in a circle of about two inches around the anus removed for sanitary reasons. The rear can also be scissored and shaped to make the dog neater and more importantly appear shorter in back. Both the scissors and thinning shears are used in doing this type of work. A single-edged thinning shear does not remove as much coat as a double-edged one. With it, there is less chance of taking off too much.

A good rear trim is the product of careful work combined with the ability to visualize the appearance you are trying to achieve. Remember to consider the way the rear will appear when the animal is gaited. Frequently a rear will be trimmed and look perfect on the grooming table. When the animal is put on the ground and gaited the coat will flop over and trail behind. As you trim the rear, periodically put the dog down and move him to see how he looks.

The thinning shears should be used pointing in toward the body rather than across the hair. The anus or a point slightly above it can serve as the center of an imaginary circle you are attempting to trim. Remember that you want the trim to be symmetrical. If you take off too much coat on one side, there is almost no alternative to taking off a similar amount on the other. The bushy coat growing on the backs of the thighs should be in balance with the amount of coat on the rear itself. Frequently a dog will be seen that has had its rear carefully trimmed, but the bushy thigh coat has not been touched. This makes the dog look unbalanced. The best way to thin the coat on the thighs is with a thinning shears.

When an Old English Sheepdog is groomed for show, the coat on the rear is swept forward. This is to accentuate the desired squareness called for in the standard. It also helps to emphasize the desired top-line, which slopes from the withers *upward* to the rump. A rear that is higher at the rump than at the shoulder is rare among purebred dogs. The characteristic method of grooming the coat on the hindquarters is unique in purebred dogs. Many groomers feel the best way to scissors the rear is to brush all the coat on the hindquarters backward over the rear. That is, in the exact opposite direction from what is required for presenting the dog in the show ring. With the coat swept back it is possible to see how much excess there is and to more effectively trim levelly and evenly the mass of hair. It is important to remember that any time you are doing a major trim job on the rear great care must be exercised. In general you are less likely to make a major mistake if you scissor a light amount, groom the dog in the normal way, gait him, and then continue trimming.

Other groomers feel that trimming with the hair swept back over the hindquarters results in a hacked appearance, no matter how carefully the job is done. Those who hold this point of view trim with the dog's coat in the usual position. Most people who prefer to trim in this way say they use a thinning shear for most of the trimming, using a scissors only for the very last touches.

There are many people who do extensive scissoring on other parts of their Sheepdogs. You can attempt to make your dog look better by thinning the neck, shaping the head, and front legs.

Any trimming done on the animal in these areas should be done with the utmost care. Most experienced exhibitor-breeders of Old English Sheepdogs are against using a scissors or thinning shears excessively. The feeling most often expressed is that the natural lines of the dog should be emphasized as best as possible by stripping out coat where excessive. This is the traditional way of making the neck appear ample and prevent the shoulders from being loaded. Today exhibitors will use a scissors and thinning shear to accentuate the square appearance of the head or the muzzle.

Old English Sheepdog ring at 1969 Westminister Kennel Club show at Madison Square Garden.

Showing and Obedience

ONE of the great pleasures in owning an Old English Sheepdog that you have taken the time and effort to properly condition and groom is in showing it. Dog shows are one of America's booming leisure time activities. It is probably the only sport where the rankest amateur can compete against and even defeat the most accomplished professional. The following discussion pertains only to the conformation dog show.

Conformation shows are those in which dogs compete against each other and against the ideal dog for the breed described in the standard officially approved and recorded with the American Kennel Club. For practical purposes all dog shows held in the United States are governed by the rules of the AKC.

There are several types of conformation shows. There are licensed and sanctioned shows. A licensed show is one at which points toward an American Kennel Club championship of record can be earned. A sanctioned show (usually called a match instead of show) operates virtually the same as a licensed show, but no points toward a championship are awarded. Licensed or sanctioned shows can be for all breeds, for a particular Group, or for a specific breed.

At an all-breed show there are classes for all breeds recognized by the American Kennel Club. Every breed is assigned to one of the Groups. There are six variety groups: Sporting, Hound, Working, Terrier, Toy, and Non-Sporting. Obviously the Old English Sheepdog is a Working dog. A show for a specific breed, known as a specialty show, has only dogs of a single breed competing. Specialty shows are sponsored by the breed clubs of the various breeds. The Old

English Sheepdog Club of America has several specialty and supported shows in different regions of the country each year.

Far and away the majority of dogs are shown in the classes in an effort to win enough points for an official AKC championship. Once a dog has qualified for a championship it no longer has to compete in the regular classes. A champion is eligible for competition in the Best of Breed class. All champions compete for the glory of Best of Breed, Group, and Best in Show wins. Most dogs are shown to a championship and then retired from the ring. Competing for glory wins of Best of Breed and beyond requires an exceptional dog, highly competent handling, and a dog with a flair for showing. Some dogs of good or great merit do not do as well as others that are no better representatives of the breed, but have that difficult-to-define quality of showmanship.

In order to become a champion a dog must win 15 points at AKC licensed shows. Points at a show are determined by the number of dogs in the ring and competing. There is a scale of points for dogs and a scale for bitches. It may be that in order to win the same number of points there would have to be more dogs than bitches or vice versa. The United States is divided into several geographical areas for determining points. The number of competitors required to win a given number of points usually varies from region to region. In Old English Sheepdogs it is necessary to have nearly three times as many dogs or bitches shown in the East or California as it is in the Great Plains to win the same number of points. One to five points can be won at a show. Of course, if the number of dogs or bitches needed to win one point is four and there are only three competing, no points are awarded. Wins of three, four, and five points are called majors. Included in the 15 point total to make a championship must be two major wins under different judges. The AKC readjusts the required number of dogs competing to win a specific number of points each spring. Twenty to twenty-five percent of all shows in a region are intended to be majors. If a breed is increasing in popularity and more are being shown each year, then the number of dogs for a given number of points will increase in effort to keep the percentage of major shows the same. In this way the relative difficulty for making a championship in any breed is kept approximately even. The required number of Old English Sheepdogs competing for points has jumped by leaps and bounds in all regions of the country in the last five years.

A conformation dog show is a process of elimination. At an all-breed show this process of elimination culminates with the selection of the winner, second, third, and fourth places for each of the six variety Groups. The six Group winners are the finalists. Whether a show has 300 or 3,000 entries the final decision comes down to the six

Group finalists, one of whom wins Best in Show.

The process of elimination that ends with the Best in Show judging begins in each breed. An all-breed show is like a multi-ringed circus. Shows usually begin at nine in the morning. The first order of business is to select a Best of Breed winner for all the various breeds.

The process of selecting the Best of Breed is exactly the same in every breed. First the class dogs are judged. These are the animals that are attempting to win points for a championship. Except at certain shows, such as Westminster, the vast majority of all dogs competing in a show are class dogs. There are six classes for dogs (males) and six classes for bitches. From all the class dogs and all the class bitches competing at a show, one of each sex will win the points. *Only one dog and one bitch can win points at any given show.* The six classes, which are exactly the same for dogs and bitches, are: Puppies, six to nine months; Puppies, nine to 12 months; Novice; Bred-by Exhibitor; American-bred; and Open. Frequently, there will be only one puppy class for all dogs or bitches under a year of age. In order to compete, a dog must be at least six months of age and properly registered with the American Kennel Club. A dog that has not been bred in the United States or Canada can only be shown in the Open class, regardless of how old it is, whether the breeder is exhibiting it, or—as occasionally happens—it was whelped in the United States, but only registered with a foreign stud book at the time of breeding.

The increased professionalization of dog shows in the last 20 years has changed the nature of entries. Prior to World War II it was common for all classes, Novice, American-bred, Bred-by-Exhibitor, as well as Puppies and Open to have nearly equal entries. If anything the American-bred class was the most popular in Sheepdogs. Today the Novice, American-bred, and Bred-by-Exhibitor classes seldom have more than a couple of entries except at shows sponsored by the Old English Sheepdog Club of America or a local club. Most entries in the Old English Sheepdog classes today are either Puppies or Open dogs or bitches. In 110 sample shows between 1966 and 1970, the point winner came from the Open classes 166 times, from the Puppy classes 40 times, and from the other classes 14 times. There is a definite trend to show dogs in the Puppy classes until they are a year old, after which they are put in the Open class. Too many are clearly not mature enough to compete equally with older, more mature dogs. The Novice class can be entered by any American or Canadian bred dog that has not won a first prize in another class (except a puppy class). The American-bred class is for dogs bred in the United States, while the Bred-by-Exhibitor class is for a dog that is being shown by the breeder or a member of his immediate family. The Open class is for any dog that is properly registered with the AKC. The toughest competition, apart from the specials, is in the Open class.

At a show the judge will do the six dog classes first, starting with the puppies and working through to the Open dogs. In each class, if there are enough entered he will award four places. A judge does not have to award a first place and three runners up, if he does not feel the dogs competing merit the awards. First, second, any or all places can be withheld. After the winner in the Open class has been selected the winners of each of the other classes is brought back into the ring. If all classes have had entries there will now be six dogs in the ring. These six dogs make up the winners class. The judge selects one of them as Winners Dog. The Winners Dog receives the points for the dogs competing that day. He is the *only* male to receive points. When the Winners Dog has been selected, the second place dog from the class the winner comes from is brought into the ring. He and the other class winners are judged for Reserve Winners Dog. The Reserve Dog receives the points in case the Winners Dog is disqualified when the official records are tabulated by the AKC. After the Reserve Winners Dog has been chosen, the judge repeats the exact same process from puppies to Open bitches. A Winners Bitch and Reserve Winners Bitch are chosen exactly as in dogs. At this point the Winners Dog and Winners Bitch are the only two class dogs left in competition for best of breed. All the other dogs and bitches have been defeated and eliminated from judging. Now the Specials along with the Winners Dog and Bitch are brought into the ring. The Specials class is for dogs that are champions of record. It is not divided by sex as are regular classes. Three awards must still be made: Best of Breed, Best of Opposite Sex to Best of Breed, and Best of Winners. The Best of Breed dog can be one of the Special dogs or bitches, or the Winners Dog or Bitch. The animal chosen Best of Breed remains in competition for Group awards. All other animals in the breed are finished for the day. If a male is elected Best of Breed, then the Best of Opposite Sex award goes to a bitch, vice versa if a bitch is chosen Best of Breed. The Best of Winners award goes to whichever of the Winners Dog or Bitch the judge finds better. Best of Winners can be an important win. For example, if there are enough dogs (males) competing to make the show worth three championship points, but only enough bitches competing to make the show worth one point, the Winners Bitch can win three points by being named Best of Winners over the dog. If this happens, the dog still wins three points, as does the bitch, even though there were only enough bitches competing on that day to earn one point in her sex.

At the end of the day at an all-breed show the Best of Breed winners from the six variety Groups are judged against each other, and a winner and three placings awarded in each Group. The six Group

Ch. Langley Snowmaiden, foremost Best in Show winning Old English Sheepdog of all time with 19 BIS scored during 1972–73. A daughter of Ch. Fezziwig Vice Versa, Snowmaiden was bred by Joan and Roy Butler, and is owned by Major and Mrs. Ben Bedford. She was handled to her record by Don Bradley.

Ch. Happy Hay Crumpet, another Best in Show daughter of Vice Versa. Pictured winning at Naugutuck Valley KC 1975 under judge John Honig. Crumpet is co-owned by Mr. and Mrs. Joseph Manning and Wendy K. Perry, and handled by Bob Forsyth.

winners compete for Best in Show. At a specialty show there may be several special classes offered that are not ordinarily offered at a regular all-breed show. These include Veterans (over seven usually), Brace (two dogs), Team (four dogs), Stud dog and Brood bitch, and several others.

The world of dog shows is a booming cult that is surprisingly unknown to the general public. Many people, including a good number of Old English Sheepdog owners, never get involved in showing their dogs because they do not know how to go about it. There are dog shows within easy driving distance in every part of the country. The Northeast was long the center of dog show activity in the United States, but today there are many shows in every metropolitan area and at least one or two annually in most rural regions. The largest shows in the country are in California, where entries of 1,500 and more are routine.

The process of putting on a dog show is complicated and rigidly governed by the American Kennel Club. Judges must be arranged for, entries distributed, etc. months in advance. The American Kennel Club can provide anyone with a list of dog shows in their area. Listings are published in the major dog periodicals, including the AKC official magazine as well as *Dog World and Kennel Review.*

Because putting on a dog show is complicated, involving much paper work and at the show site a host of equipment, the AKC licenses several organizations around the country to put on dog shows. These organizations are known as superintendents. Entry forms for shows they are superintending can be obtained from them. A list of the superintendents is included each month in *Pure-Bred Dogs— AKC Gazette,* the official American Kennel Club magazine.

Entry forms are included in a packet of information called a premium list. This tells you the precise date and location of the show, what prizes are being offered, who will judge, what the entry fee is and when entries close, as well as such things as if the number of dogs able to compete in the show will be limited, and other special information. Dog show entry fees vary from seven dollars up.

If you think you might be interested in showing your dog in conformation classes or in Obedience find out when a show will be held near you. Go see it. Obedience trials are frequently held in conjunction with all-breed conformation shows. The listing of Obedience trials and obtaining premium lists for them is the same as for conformation shows. If you decide to enter a show, write for the premium list and entry form far in advance of the show date. Entries for most shows close two to three weeks before the show itself.

Going to a dog show is simple. Common sense will help in making

Ch. Loyalblu Hendihap, top winning Bobtail of 1975 with 4 BIS, 3 Specialties, and 17 Groups won in less than a year. Pictured in win under judge Heywood Hartley. Bred by Dr. and Mrs. Hugh Jordan, and co-owned by them with Dick and Lorry Boerner. Handled by Mrs. Jordan.

Ch. Barrelroll Blues In The Night, outstanding winner from the last litter sired by Dan Tatters. Co-owned by Lt. Col. William B. Garvey (breeder) and Sherman J. Katz, and handled by Colonel Garvey. Pictured winning Group under judge Joseph Faigel.

your first dog show as a participant much more pleasant. You will receive your official show entry the week before the show. Almost all dog shows are held on Saturday and Sunday. The entry will admit the dog and one person to the show. It will include a judging program. The program tells what ring and what time Old English Sheepdogs will be judged. It will also include your official number for the show. At the show your dog will be identified by this number, which is worn as an armband on the upper left arm. The armband can be picked up at ringside from the steward shortly before judging begins. Plan your time in the days before the show so that you can have your dog completely groomed out and ready for the ring. If a bath is in order, try to give it three days or so before the show, to allow the natural texture of the coat to return. Decide what you need to take to the show, and get it together and packed the evening before.

Dog shows can be great family ventures. They can also be torture to the child or teenager that is not interested. Young children ordinarily do not have the attention span to survive a long day at a dog show. You should be prepared to provide them with sufficient diversions to keep them happy and out of trouble. A dog show can be a dangerous place for a curious child. Because your son or daughter is completely safe with your dog does not mean any other dog can be trusted. Children frequently do not appreciate this fact. Invariably the most responsible person when a child is bitten at a show is a negligent parent. Teenagers often have interests of their own. They should not be forced to go to a dog show. Having been warned, it is only fair to add that the majority of children of all ages love dog shows. There are junior showmanship classes for children of varying ages and skills, which many youngsters enjoy. In junior showmanship the ability of the youngsters to handle, rather than the quality of the dogs they have, is being evaluated. The high point of a junior showmanship career is qualifying with five open class wins, for the special junior showmanship competition held in conjunction with Westminster every February. Any Old English junior showman has a worthy goal to shoot for—Mona Saphir Berkowitz with her Ch. Crest of the Wave won the junior showmanship class of Westminster in 1939, and placed second in 1940.

Old English families frequently make dog show weekends family outings. The children help in the grooming and exercising and take the dog in junior showmanship. Children often enjoy training a dog for Obedience. In some families the parents provide the transportation and the children are the avid dog fanciers.

Having decided what to do with the kids, you should decide what other equipment to take. A grooming kit of brushes, a comb or two, a spray bottle, cornstarch or some other whitener, and something to groom on is essential. You will want to groom the dog out prior to taking it into the ring, no matter how well groomed it may be the day before. A crate cannot be recommended too strongly for anyone going to a dog show. The animal can be kept in it safely while traveling. At the show, he can be groomed on top of it. Some tidbits for the dog, and a supply of the dog's usual drinking water are a good idea. You might want to consider bringing food or a snack and something to drink for yourself.

Be sure your car is in good working condition. Check the gas and oil and tires. If possible get precise directions to the show. Allow ample time to travel to the show, to get unloaded and to exercise and groom the dog out. Dog shows are usually on the outskirts of town. It may take an hour to get to the town where the show is held. Once there it may take another 20 minutes or more to locate the show grounds.

Whatever you do, you want to remain calm. Your dog will pick up your natural excitement from going to the show in any event. Any additional excitement or confusion may mean the difference between a well-behaved dog and a chance to win.

Once you arrive at the show, unload, park and get settled. Then find the ring where Sheepdogs are being shown. If the judge doing Old English is judging another breed watch how he goes about it. Most judges will work the same way throughout the day. Note how the dogs are gaited. You will almost certainly be asked to gait your dog in the same pattern. When you first exhibit your dog, no matter how beautiful he may appear to you, you should do so solely with the intention of having a good time and gaining some experience. The dog show world is filled with bad losers. There is no point in beginning your interest with a bad attitude. A judge is expected to judge slightly more than twenty dogs in an hour. Some judges work much faster, others slower. Some classes will go very fast, others will require more time. If there is a large entry and you are showing a bitch you can figure to go on in the length of time all entries before your class, multiplied by two to three. If there are 15 dogs ahead of your class you can expect to be on 30 to 45 minutes after the judging of the breeds begins. Judging may run late, but it can never begin before the time published in the official program you receive with your entry.

For exhibiting your dog you should wear clothes that are neat and comfortable. Shirts and ties are usual for men. Cullottes are increasingly popular for women.

Exercise your dog thoroughly a half hour before you expect to go on. Then put the dog back on the grooming table and finish up. Keep informed, or have someone check, on the progress the judge

Am. & Can. Ch. Morrow's Christopher Beowulf, multi-BIS winner of 1973–74. Owned by Kathleen Rafferty of Detroit and handled by Barbara Dempsey Alderman.

Am. & Can. Ch. Tamara's Shaggy Shoes MacDuff, one of the Top Ten winners of 1969. A son of Ch. Tempest of Dalcroy, "Duffy" is owned by Don and Jean McColl of Birmingham, Mich.

Am. Can. & Mex. Ch. Ragbears Lady of Agincourt, wh. 1970. Lady finished to American title in ten days at age of only 9½ months, to Canadian championship in four shows at 10 months, and to Mexican championship at 15 months with three Group wins including a First. Bred by Gail H. Fletcher, and co-owned by her with Alex and Lillian Gross.

272

is making so you will be able to get in the ring on time. If you are showing a puppy dog, you will be the first class judged. Unless you are showing an older, calmer dog it is a good idea to get the dog off the grooming table and let him stretch ahead of the judging. This is especially true of a puppy.

Showing Your Sheepdog

Good grooming and conditioning can go for naught if the dog is not presented to its best advantage. Seeing how other people, particularly accomplished amateurs and professionals, show their Old English is the best way to pick up hints on what you should do.

A well-behaved dog is the basis of good showmanship. There are two basic types of show leads. One popular style is a three foot length of nylon or fiber material with an adjustable noose on the end. The noose is slipped over the dog's head and adjusted. This type of lead is inflexible once it is adjusted. The other style lead is a choke or modified choke. Many exhibitors prefer a nylon choke and attachable lead. This is probably the most effective means of controlling a dog without resorting to chain chokes. There is a specially designed one piece choke collar and lead known as an English show lead. The exact lead arrangement used for showing the dog is less important than how easy the dog is to control. Some dogs do better with one type than another. In general you should try to use the least noticeable lead. This makes a more impressive exhibit. Whatever lead you use, it should be positioned high on the dog's neck, immediately in back of the ears. This is the best place for getting quick response from the dog and for correctly positioning him in the ring.

Getting into the ring first is not as important as many believe. First or last most judges will spot and place excellence. Some handlers prefer to be first so they can set the pace when the judge wants the entire class gaited around the ring. The most easily understood reason for this is that they can then move their dog slowly, thus forcing everyone else to a slow pace. Poor moving dogs are easier to spot at a slow pace. If you should be in back of someone moving too slowly hang back. Then move the dog at the pace you prefer. Never pass anyone. Always follow the direction of the judge; if he asks you to move faster, do so; if he asks you to slow down, do so.

The best way to show your Sheepdog is on a *loose lead*. This is not natural for many dogs, especially at a show where there are innumerable interesting smells on the ground. A little work beforehand will help. A dog that is deprived of food for a day or fed very lightly is more responsive to training by using a tasty piece of bait. A wedge of cooked beef or chicken liver is useful for this purpose. Take the dog out on the lead you intend to show him on and set him up in show pose. Then bait him with the liver. A good way to do this is on a choke collar and lead held in your left hand. Snap the dog's head to attention, while standing in front of him and offer the liver beyond the reach of his extended neck. With correct response give him a tiny bit. Then walk backwards slowly having the dog move after the bait. From slowly backing and baiting, switch to baiting the dog with your right hand extended in front of him while walking him on your left side with the lead in your left hand. With increased practice the bait can be removed and a quick tap under the dog's chin substituted for bait when you want the dog to gait. This is not difficult to train a dog to do. It improves the appearance. A dog lunging, determined to keep his nose to the ground with a frustrated handler in tow equally determined to keep the dog's head up, is an awkward sight at best.

This is all the training a dog needs to be exhibited in a conformation class. Few people bother to work with their dogs at all. Showmanship can be greatly improved with a minimal amount of effort. When you practice showing it is a good idea to have a knowledgeable observer. He can tell you how your dog looks, what can be done to improve his presentation, and what speed the dog should be gaited at to look its best. Too many Sheepdogs are gaited at a uniform speed suited to few dogs. Some dogs look better gaited slowly, others when moved very fast. Most professional handlers move all their Sheepdogs at the same pace. This is one area where a knowledgeable amateur can best the professional, who will seldom have time to adequately study the best speed at which to gait all his various dogs. Even so a judge should examine all dogs at different speeds to adequately evaluate a breed with a supposed unique rolling or ambling gait.

More points are lost by a poor first impression than by any other cause. Most judges will check the class into the ring. After you have been checked in, you will walk down a side of the ring and set the dog up. How the dog looks at this time is extremely important. When a judge has checked every dog into the class he will usually look over the dogs before him. If your dog looks impressive at this time, you are at a decided advantage. By the same token if your dog is misbehaving or hung up in some gawky or awkward position, you are at a decided disadvantage.

It is most important when showing, both in positioning him and gaiting, not to overhandle. Too many novices overhandle their dogs. The dog is upstaged by assorted hand motions, exaggerated steps, or other obviously contrived but amateurish "professionalisms."

274

Ch. Seefur Tackle, son of Ch. Fezziwig Vice Versa ex Ch. Sunflower Fancy Lady. Bred by J. and C. Fenton and owned by Dr. and Mrs. Robert Lamb.

Ch. Bobtail Acres Rough 'N Ready, Midwest Group winner of the early '70s. Co-owned by Arnold Kamens and Jim McTernan.

Am. & Can. Ch. Misty Isles Elite Barrister, wh. 1973, Group-winning son of Ch. Bobtail Acres Rough 'N Ready. Bred by Gary and Lindan Coram, and owned by James and Karen Murdock and Jim McTernan.

Ch. Bahlamb's Brazen Bandit, Specialty and Best in Show winner, top winning Bobtail of 1974. Bred by Caj Haakansson and co-owned by him with Mrs. Robert Wetzler. Shown in win under judge Glen Sommers with Bob Forsyth handling.

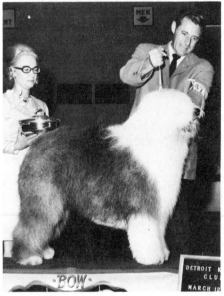

Ch. Brooks Blue Boy, multi-BIS winner, pictured winning the Group at Detroit 1972 under judge J. J. Duncan. Handled at Detroit by Bob Forsyth, Blue Boy was also handled by George Carlton.

Am. & Can. Ch. Cheerio Ragged Pacesetter winning 1974 OESCA Specialty in California. Pacesetter, a bitch, was bred by Ken and Paula Leach, and is owned by Bruce and Donna Samuelson.

276

The best showmanship for handler and dog is seemingly effortless natural actions. A good handler works extremely hard for the few minutes judging requires. The trick is to look completely natural.

As far as positioning the dog goes, if you have done a little work on baiting him it may not be necessary to do any positioning at all. You want the dog to look square and balanced. This means the legs should be firmly and squarely placed at each corner of the body. You want the legs to be straight and evenly placed. When you get the dog where you want him check to see that the front legs are properly positioned. If they are out of line, one of them will usually have to be corrected, not both of them. Always keep a firm grip on the lead with the dog's neck up in approximately the position you want him to maintain. To reposition a leg use the same hand as the dog's leg, left for left, right for right. Grab the leg just below the elbow, lift it and place it in the proper position. Whenever you move a leg keep a firm grip on the lead at the neck. Some handlers grab the collar and coat in back of the ears when they do this. For positioning the hindlegs try to keep the dog's neck up by holding on to the end of the lead and pulling up as you lean over to position the leg. A number of handlers have complete confidence in their dog's training and will "showboat" in positioning the dog by casually tossing the lead on the dog's back and walking around the dog to check that each leg is in the right position. This is all right, but can be overdone. It is better to leave the dog alone than to spend too much time fussing over his positioning.

Always keep one eye on the judge. When he looks in your direction you want the dog at its best. Many judges will carefully watch a dog they are having gaited as it moves away from them and then cast a quick glance over the other dogs in the ring as the animal turns to come back. One useful skill to develop is the ability to palm the lead you are showing the dog on. When the dog is standing still you will probably only need six inches to a foot of lead, but when the dog is moving you will want a full three feet. If you can quickly fold the lead over itself and hold it in your palm, the excess will be concealed and not distract from the dog by flapping about. Another good hint for quickly positioning a dog is to grasp it firmly at the scruff of the neck in your left hand and under the jaw in your right and simply lift the front end off the ground and let it fall into place. This same technique can be used on the rear, by placing a hand between the legs and lifting the dog's rear three to six inches off the ground and letting them fall into place.

One of the most common concerns in presenting Old English Sheepdogs is what to do with all the hair. This is beyond getting the dog groomed to take in the ring. Many professional handlers do not position the hair on Sheepdogs particularly well. When you groom the dog out for the final time and take him off the table he will usually shake himself once or twice. It is at this moment the dog should look its best. You have groomed the coat to the best of your ability and the dog has shaken himself so that your grooming is a more natural part of his appearance. Too many handlers get in the ring and sweep the hair from the rear forward using a hand as a plow. This is all right, but only to a certain extent. The hair on the neck must also be swept down and meet the hair coming forward from the rear in the characteristic crested wave. The place the wave of hair crests is very important. It is common to see hair from the rear swept too far forward so that it crests where the shawl of white begins. This will make the dog appear dumpy, lacking in neck, and with a level topline. Carefully work with the dog before you show him to determine where the crest looks best on him.

Because virtually all Old English Sheepdogs are pets, and show dogs in particular are carefully conditioned, there is a tendency to think the more coat the better. This is a mistake. Some dogs look better with more coat than others. Many Sheepdogs look their best with surprisingly little coat. Although, of the two extremes of excessive coat and poor coat and conditioning, the latter is more frequently seen. No Old English looks its best for show purposes when it is dripping with coat. No matter how good the natural texture of a dog's coat may be, the animal can be over-conditioned to the point where the guard coat is so long it becomes flat and lacks texture. Some expert conditioners and exhibitors think the best way to get a Sheepdog is top show shape is to condition it to the point where it is excessively coated and then with judicious use of thinning shears, comb, and scissors trim the dog to its best appearance. Excessive coat usually means the guard coat has been conditioned to be too long, and that when the animal moves the guard hairs flap in the breeze. This can be seen most readily on the rear where the coat will flop over and trail behind as the dog moves sideways. When the dog is coming at you the excess coat will be flying out the sides at the shoulder line. An excessively coated dog will have skirts on the sides that hang like a Yorkie when standing still and fly in the breeze when the animal moves. The chest on an excessively coated dog will have hair that may almost sweep the ground. Should your dog have too much guard coat on its rear, sides or chest thin it down. Do this job well in advance of a show. Do it carefully; you do not want the dog to appear hacked.

Old English Sheepdogs can also have excessive undercoat. This can make the animal appear overfat and dumpy. The usual place for excessive undercoat to develop and detract from a dog's appear-

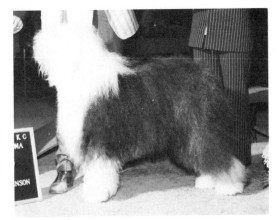

Ch. Echo Valley Tidley Wink winning 1975 Best in Show under judge Virgil Johnson. Owned by Dr. and Mrs. Oren Bush, and handled by Jack Potts.

Ch. Dustmop's St. Nicholas, multi-BIS winner, Group placement winner at Westminster 1973. St. Nicholas, killed in a tragic hunting accident at height of his career, was bred by Claire March and owned by Terry and Kathy Crow of South Dakota.

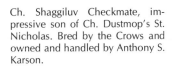

Ch. Shaggiluv Checkmate, impressive son of Ch. Dustmop's St. Nicholas. Bred by the Crows and owned and handled by Anthony S. Karson.

Ch. Mitepa's Burhead Kid, 1974
Best in Show winner, co-owned by
Gail Wallis and Dr. Oren Bush.

Ch. Dandalion's Lord Tanker, consistent mid-70s winner. Bred, owned and handled by Janice McClary.

ance is over the shoulders and neck. This makes the shoulders look loaded and the neck appear short. Excessive undercoat can be stripped out with a comb or slicker brush. Many expert groomers routinely groom the shoulders and neck with a comb.

When the judge comes to examine your dog you want to stay out of his way and do what he tells you. It goes without saying that if your dog will not stand for inspection by the judge you are not going to win. An Old English that has a controlled out-going friendliness when the judge approaches has an advantage. The judge will want to examine the dog's bite, eyes, and the rest of the animal. Many judges will not actually open a dog's mouth to check the bite, as there is always the possibility of carrying infection from one dog to the next. Most judges approach a dog, check its head and head features first. When the judge is examining your dog's head you should stay out of his way. Some handlers hold the dog's lead firmly in the left hand and the underjaw in the right. Others keep away from the head with their hands and allow the judge to go about his examination as he pleases. When the judge is finished examining the head he will want to check the rest of the body. As he moves down the neck to check shoulder layback, and then the body and around to the hindquarters, many handlers take the lead in their left hand bring it around and under the dog's muzzle and hold the head in position with both hands while standing in front of the dog. This allows the judge to examine the dog on all sides without your being in his way.

When the judge asks you to gait your dog you should follow his instructions exactly. He will want you to move in a certain pattern and perhaps at a certain speed. The usual patterns are down and back, that is directly away from the judge and straight back to him, or down and across and back to him. This is a triangular pattern or a modification of it, which permit the judge to see the dog coming and going and sideways. Correct showmanship when moving means you keep the dog between yourself and the judge. It is also a good idea to keep the dog on the inside of the ring, separated from the ring barrier by your body. In this way the dog is less easily distracted by spectators at ringside. The dog will be in correct position if he is kept on your left side at all times, except when a judge asks you to gait across a ring and then back across the ring before returning to him.

Even the most accomplished professional will occasionally get between the dog and the judge. It is better to do this than make a clumsy or confused turn in attempting to keep the dog between yourself and the judge. Many amateurs botch their showmanship when making turns by switching the hands they are holding the lead with and going in confused little circles attempting to get turned around.

Ch. Merryrogue Modest William winning Group at Faith City (Texas) 1975 show under Gerhardt Plaga. Owned and handled by Marilyn Klinger, New Mexico.

Ch. Shannonbo's Jumpin' Jack Flash, CD, current Midwest star. Owned and handled by Rob and Cindy Bowe.

Ch. Blindbluff Heatherenmist winning Group at Tri-State KC 1974 under judge Roy Ayers. Owned by Laura Linck and Cheryl H. Stueggen (handling) of Pittsburgh.

Unless you can switch the lead smoothly and efficiently from one hand to another you are better off not doing it. In any gaiting pattern it is necessary to change lead hands only once. If you do it more than once you are unnecessarily overshowing the dog and in all probability detracting from his appearance.

If a judge asks you to move your dog on a loose lead, you should try to do so, even if you are certain you have a better chance of getting your dog to fly than look well on a loose lead. A judge has an express reason for wanting to see a dog moved in a certain way and at a certain speed. Even if your dog is not going to move in the way the judge asks you, you should try to comply with his directions. Nothing is more annoying than having to watch some hapless soul trying to gait his dog on a loose lead three or four times, each time the judge being forced to ask to have the dog moved again, "This time on a loose lead, please." One manuever that may help get the head off the ground is to sweep the fall away from the eyes as you step off to begin moving.

Obedience

Obedience work is a form of showing. It is much different from conformation. To a large degree the subjective, arbitrary nature of conformation judging does not exist in Obedience judging. In an Obedience trial a dog is trying to defeat all the other dogs in his class by scoring the highest. Every dog is also trying to earn a qualifying score toward an official American Kennel Club Obedience title. Every dog or none in an Obedience class can be a winner in the sense that all can earn credit toward their Obedience degrees. There are also prizes for the highest scoring dogs in each class, so Obedience dogs can be double winners—they can qualify toward an obedience title and they can win prizes by being a high scoring dog.

There are three levels of Obedience work: Novice, Open and Utility. There is a fourth type of work that relates to Obedience and for which an American Kennel Club title is awarded: Tracking.

In the three principal types of Obedience work there are a variety of exercises each worth a certain number of points. All the exercises together are worth 200 points, a perfect score. At each level of Obedience work a dog must score 170 points or higher and get at least 50% of the points possible on each of the different exercises three times to earn the Obedience degree. For Novice work, the Obedience title is called Companion Dog; for Open it is called Companion Dog Excellent; and for Utility, Utility Dog. A dog that

Driftwood's Bo-Peep, UD, first Old English Sheepdog bitch (and just second of the breed) to earn the Utility degree. Owned and trained by Anne Raker.

Ch. Amiable Archibald, CD with his owner-trainer, Roberta Solomon Lott.

284

wins an Obedience title is issued an official AKC certificate, just as a dog who wins a conformation championship. The dog's obedience title is listed after his name, C.D., C.D.X, and U.D. In order to compete at the next higher level of Obedience work a dog must first have completed the requirements for the lower obedience title(s). The Novice level of obedience work is little more than what a properly trained household companion should be capable of: heeling on and off lead, come, sit and down, stand for inspection by another person, set in test conditions. The Open and Utility work becomes increasingly difficult and interesting.

In the almost forty years that the American Kennel Club has awarded official Obedience titles only six Old English Sheepdogs have ever won a U.D. title: Ch. John Marksman, who is credited with having earned a Tracking title, Driftwood's Little Bo-Peep, Ch. Greyfriar's Sir Fang, Fezziwig Lord Plushbottom, Shepton Arabella and Sheplin Raggedy Shag. Surprisingly few Old English Sheepdogs have ever competed in Obedience work. This is perhaps because Old English, while willing workers, lack the self restraint and preciseness necessary in advanced work. The natural clownishness of the breed was as evident 30 years ago as today. The first Old English Sheepdog to earn a C.D. and C.D.X. title was Edith Buckingham's owner-breeder-handled Ch. Cleoftagel Grimbald. Margaret Holmes reporting on Grimbald's performance at the 1941 Eastern Dog Show in Boston related, "Grimbald has one glorious failing, however; he just cannot help clowning and after doing his job properly, the moment he hears applause he starts his antics and puts on a show, sending the audience into gales of laughter. He endears himself to all, and according to Mrs. Lewis at Boston he 'stole the show.'"

Obedience work is an important part of the world of purebred dogs. It is one of the few ways that the ability of dogs to work and serve man as more than companions can be effectively demonstrated. This is particularly important for supposed working breeds. One of the best ways to dispel the notion of the Old English as a pampered drawing room sissy is to have more in the Obedience rings.

Effectively training a dog for Obedience work requires taking part in a training class. At a training class there will be other dogs. It is important for any dog that is expected to work to perform when there are distractions and other dogs around. At a training class there will be expert instructors who can spot weaknesses in your training and, of course, teach you how to teach your dog. The more advanced work in Open and Utility competition is always interesting to watch.

Ch. Jendower's Queen Victoria and Ch. Sunnybrae Jack Frost.

T O THOSE of you who have worked your way to the end a final few words about the Old English Sheepdog. This book is meant to introduce you to the Old English Sheepdog and the world of purebred dogs in many of its endless facets. Material has been included to be of interest to the most experienced, as well as the rankest amateur. If you have thumbed through to this final paragraph and find it all too imposing do not be discouraged. You should be warned that any dog, *and the Old English Sheepdog in particular,* requires work and worry. The Old English Sheepdog in the opinion of its admirers comes as close as any breed to being the ideal companion for city or farm, young and old. But owning an Old English Sheepdog is not a casual proposition. It is certainly hoped if you have considered buying an Old English you will now take the time and care to get the right dog for you, and begin your own fascination with these delightful shaggy beasts.

BIBLIOGRAPHY

ALL OWNERS of pure-bred dogs will benefit themselves and their dogs by enriching their knowledge of breeds and of canine care, training, breeding, psychology and other important aspects of dog management. The following list of books covers further reading recommended by judges, veterinarians, breeders, trainers and other authorities. Books may be obtained at the finer book stores and pet shops, or through Howell Book House Inc., publishers, New York.

Breed Books

AFGHAN HOUND, Complete	Miller & Gilbert
AIREDALE, New Complete	Edwards
ALASKAN MALAMUTE, Complete	Riddle & Seeley
BASSET HOUND, Complete	Braun
BEAGLE, Complete	Noted Authorities
BLOODHOUND, Complete	Brey & Reed
BORZOI, Complete	Groshans
BOXER, Complete	Denlinger
BRITTANY SPANIEL, Complete	Riddle
BULLDOG, New Complete	Hanes
BULL TERRIER, New Complete	Eberhard
CAIRN TERRIER, Complete	Marvin
CHESAPEAKE BAY RETRIEVER, Complete	Cherry
CHIHUAHUA, Complete	Noted Authorities
COCKER SPANIEL, New	Kraeuchi
COLLIE, Complete	Official Publication of the Collie Club of America
DACHSHUND, The New	Meistrell
DALMATIAN, The	Treen
DOBERMAN PINSCHER, New	Walker
ENGLISH SETTER, New Complete	Tuck, Howell & Graef
ENGLISH SPRINGER SPANIEL, New	Goodall & Gasow
FOX TERRIER, New Complete	Silvernail
GERMAN SHEPHERD DOG, Complete	Bennett
GERMAN SHORTHAIRED POINTER, New	Maxwell
GOLDEN RETRIEVER, Complete	Fischer
GREAT DANE, New Complete	Noted Authorities
GREAT DANE, The—Dogdom's Apollo	Draper
GREAT PYRENEES, Complete	Strang & Giffin
IRISH SETTER, New	Thompson
IRISH WOLFHOUND, Complete	Starbuck
KEESHOND, Complete	Peterson
LABRADOR RETRIEVER, Complete	Warwick
LHASA APSO, Complete	Herbel
MINIATURE SCHNAUZER, Complete	Eskrigge
NEWFOUNDLAND, New Complete	Chern
NORWEGIAN ELKHOUND, New Complete	Wallo
OLD ENGLISH SHEEPDOG, Complete	Mandeville
PEKINGESE, Quigley Book of	Quigley
PEMBROKE WELSH CORGI, Complete	Sargent & Harper
POMERANIAN, New Complete	Ricketts
POODLE, New Complete	Hopkins & Irick
POODLE CLIPPING AND GROOMING BOOK, Complete	Kalstone
PULI, Complete	Owen
SAMOYED, Complete	Ward
SCHIPPERKE, Official Book of	Root, Martin, Kent
SCOTTISH TERRIER, New Complete	Marvin
SHETLAND SHEEPDOG, The New	Riddle
SHIH TZU, The (English)	Dadds
SIBERIAN HUSKY, Complete	Demidoff
TERRIERS, The Book of All	Marvin
WEST HIGHLAND WHITE TERRIER, Complete	Marvin
WHIPPET, Complete	Pegram
YORKSHIRE TERRIER, Complete	Gordon & Bennett

Breeding

ART OF BREEDING BETTER DOGS, New	Onstott
BREEDING YOUR SHOW DOG, Joy of	Seranne
HOW TO BREED DOGS	Whitney
HOW PUPPIES ARE BORN	Prine
INHERITANCE OF COAT COLOR IN DOGS	Little

Care and Training

DOG OBEDIENCE, Complete Book of	Saunders
NOVICE, OPEN AND UTILITY COURSES	Saunders
DOG CARE AND TRAINING FOR BOYS AND GIRLS	Saunders
DOG NUTRITION, Collins Guide to	Collins
DOG TRAINING FOR KIDS	Benjamin
DOG TRAINING, Koehler Method of	Koehler
GO FIND! Training Your Dog to Track	Davis
GUARD DOG TRAINING, Koehler Method of	Koehler
OPEN OBEDIENCE FOR RING, HOME AND FIELD, Koehler Method of	Koehler
SPANIELS FOR SPORT (English)	Radcliffe
STONE GUIDE TO DOG GROOMING FOR ALL BREEDS	Stone
SUCCESSFUL DOG TRAINING, The Pearsall Guide to	Pearsall
TOY DOGS, Kalstone Guide to Grooming All	Kalstone
TRAINING THE RETRIEVER	Kersley
TRAINING YOUR DOG TO WIN OBEDIENCE TITLES,	Morsell
TRAIN YOUR OWN GUN DOG, How to	Goodall
UTILITY DOG TRAINING, Koehler Method of	Koehler
VETERINARY HANDBOOK, Dog Owner's Home	Carlson & Giffin

General

COMPLETE DOG BOOK, The	Official Publication of American Kennel Club
DISNEY ANIMALS, World of	Koehler
DOG IN ACTION, The	Lyon
DOG BEHAVIOR, New Knowledge of	Pfaffenberger
DOG JUDGE'S HANDBOOK	Tietjen
DOG JUDGING, Nicholas Guide to	Nicholas
DOG PEOPLE ARE CRAZY	Riddle
DOG PSYCHOLOGY	Whitney
DOG STANDARDS ILLUSTRATED	
DOGSTEPS, Illustrated Gait at a Glance	Elliott
ENCYCLOPEDIA OF DOGS, International	Dangerfield, Howell & Riddle
JUNIOR SHOWMANSHIP HANDBOOK	Brown & Mason
MY TIMES WITH DOGS	Fletcher
OUR PUPPY'S BABY BOOK (blue or pink)	
RICHES TO BITCHES	Shattuck
SUCCESSFUL DOG SHOWING, Forsyth Guide to	Forsyth
TRIM, GROOM AND SHOW YOUR DOG, How to	Saunders
WHY DOES YOUR DOG DO THAT?	Bergman
WILD DOGS in Life and Legend	Riddle
WORLD OF SLED DOGS, From Siberia to Sport Racing	Coppinger